RESTORATION AND REVOLUTION: POLITICAL,
SOCIAL AND RELIGIOUS WRITINGS 1660-1700

WORLD AND WORD SERIES
Edited by Professor Isobel Armstrong,
University of Southampton

Literature and the Social Order in Eighteenth Century England

Stephen Copley

English Humanism: Wyatt to Cowley

Joanna Martindale

RESTORATION
AND
REVOLUTION

EDITED BY WILLIAM MYERS

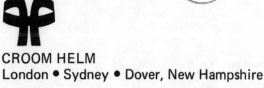

CROOM HELM
London • Sydney • Dover, New Hampshire

Selection © 1986 W.F. Myers
Croom Helm Ltd, Provident House, Burrell Row,
Beckenham, Kent BR3 1AT

Croom Helm Australia Pty Ltd, Suite 4, 6th Floor,
64-76 Kippax Street, Surry Hills, NSW 2010, Australia

British Library Cataloguing in Publication Data

Restoration and revolution. – (World and
    Word series)
    1. England – Social conditions – 17th
    century – Sources
    I. Myers, William   II. Series
    942.066   HN385

    ISBN 0-7099-3502-1
    ISBN 0-7099-3558-7 Pbk

Croom Helm Ltd, Washington Street,
Dover, New Hampshire 03820, USA

Library of Congress Cataloging in Publication Data

Main entry under title:
Restoration and Revolution.

    Bibliography: p.
    Includes index.
    1. England–Intellectual Life–17th Century–Sources.
I. Myers, William, 1939-
DA440.R47   1985   942.06   85-24272
ISBN 0-7099-3502-1
ISBN 0-7099-3558-7 (Pbk.)

Printed and bound in Great Britain
by Billing & Sons Limited, Worcester.

Contents

Series Editors' Preface

The *World and Word* series, as its title implies, is based on the assumption that literary texts cannot be studied in isolation. The series presents to students, mainly of English literature, documents and materials which will enable them to have first-hand experience of some of the writing which forms the context of the literature they read. The aim is to put students in possession of material to which they cannot normally gain access so that they may arrive at an independent understanding of the inter-relationships of literary texts with other writing.

There are to be twelve volumes, covering topics from the Middle Ages to the twentieth century. Each volume concentrates on a specific area of thought in a particular period, selecting from religious, philosophical or scientific works, literary theory or political or social material, according to its chosen topic. The extracts included are substantial in order to enable students themselves to arrive at an understanding of the significance of the material they read and to make responsible historical connections with some precision and independence. The task of compilation itself, of course, predetermines to a great extent the kind of connections and relationships which can be made in a particular period. We all bring our own categories to the work of interpretation. However, each compiler makes clear the grounds on which the choice of material is made, and thus the series encourages the valuable understanding that there can be no single, authoritative account of the relationships between world and word.

Each volume is annotated and indexed and includes a short bibliography and suggestions for further reading. The *World and Word series* can be used in different teaching contexts, in the student's independent work, in seminar discussion, and on lecture courses.

Isobel Armstrong
University of Southampton

Introduction

The purpose of this collection of late seventeenth-century writings is a provocative one. Students of 'English' are rarely required to attend to the constitutional order operating in English life in the way that students of American or French culture are expected to become familiar with French or American political thought and political institutions. This vagueness regarding the political context in English literary studies is a reflection of a more widespread tendency in English society generally. The English tradition has consistently devalued or excluded what other societies particularly prize, a tendency most evident in the pejorative senses which English usage imposes on the words 'academic', 'theoretical', and 'dogmatic'. One consequence of this has been to make especially opaque the cultural assumptions of the last period in English history when literature, politics and dogma had very different, and far more intimate, relations with one another than they have had since. It is my hope that students working with this volume will rediscover those relationships, and not only begin to read the great neglected texts of the period — the plays and later poems of Dryden, some lesser-known works of Bunyan and the plays of Otway — but will also begin to question many orthodoxies — about restoration literature and its social and political contexts, about the scope of literature in general and, perhaps most importantly of all, about the implications, particularly the political implications, of recent literary and critical theorising.

I have deliberately chosen not to organise the texts selected for this volume on thematic lines in the manner of some other titles in this series, but to offer instead substantial extracts, different parts of which may be taken from widely separated passages in the original but which, read together, constitute a single coherent argument. Such a procedure produces fundamental changes of emphasis from those in the complete texts, and the reader therefore should not judge, for example, either Thomas Sprat or his *History* from this volume. Its abridgements and the arrangement of its parts make it, not just as a whole but in its constituent elements, my work in a limiting sense, and not the work of its original authors. It should not be regarded, therefore, as providing access to the 'background' of restoration literature. The texts I reprint, after all, are themselves part of that literature. Their meaning in this volume is rather to be found in the relations revealed by their selection and arrangement within it. Together they constitute an essay in inter-textuality which is intended to reveal, through unstated and shifting connections, not the 'presence' of a particular period of English history, but traces of its passage.

Absolutism and the English Constitution

As we shall see, of all the themes highlighted by the writings in this volume, the one that was to prove the most decisive was that of abso-lutism. The accepability of this idea in seventeenth-century political thought is particularly difficult for the modern reader to grasp, not least because its logic, when baldly stated, has a disconcerting force. The argument (as summarised by Peter Laslett) runs as follows. The 'exercise of will' is 'the only form of authority . . . [;] only one mind [can] will effectively and continuously . . . [;] therefore authority . . . Divine, Natural, Political, Constitutional, Social or Domestic' can and should be exercised by one person only (Laslett, 1949, 18). John Locke, for example, justified the subjection of women with this argu-ment (see p. 197). Some theorists, notably Thomas Hobbes, believed that government might be vested in a Council, but only if state power remained unified and absolute. Any practical resistance to the will of the sovereign authority, Hobbes argued, reintroduced 'the sword' into society, and in consequence the state in principle and in practice ceased to exist (Peters, 1962, 319). Reinforcing such views was a widespread conviction that all authority, domestic, ecclesiastical and political, derived directly from God. Such beliefs could be quite literal. Richard Baxter, for example, argued that Christ was actually reigning through the agency of protestant princes in whom the prophecy in the Book of Revelation of a millennial reign was currently being fulfilled (Lamont, 1979, 263). In the City of London even late in the century there were powerful interests favouring 'authoritative and patriarchal concepts of society' (Plumb, 1969, 31). In Europe absolutist ideas everywhere pre-vailed, being as protestant and Scandinavian as they were catholic and French. In such a climate there was nothing obviously absurd in claim-ing, as Samuel Parker did, '*That it is absolutely necessary to the Peace and Government of the World, that the Supream Magistrate . . . should be vested with a Power to govern and conduct the Consciences of subjects in affairs of Religion*' (see p. 75).

In England, however, absolutist arguments were heavily qualified by another idea, that of an ancient, unwritten constitution, the 'Ark' of Dryden's *Absalom and Achitophel* (1681, *l*.804). This constitution had both written and unwritten elements. Common law was deemed to be part of the unwritten constitution, even though precedents in law were, of course, recorded (see p. 60), but there were aspects of the constitution that were genuinely unwritten. The question of whether the King was above common law, for example, 'had never been settled, largely because it had so very rarely been raised' (Kenyon, 1966, 7), while the right of Parliament to grant supply, John Pym argued in 1628, 'was not introduced by any statute, or by any charter or sanction of princes, but . . . [issued] from the first frame and constitution of the kingdom' (ibid., 16-17). On the other hand, English society was literally founded upon a mass of semi-constitutional documentation — the charters of colleges, companies and boroughs, the patents of monopolists and the titles to freeholders. Church livings, judgeships, army commissions were all 'proprieties' — often purchasable — and expected to yield substantial profits. They were frequently linked to 'franchises' — exemptions from ordinary duties to the Crown — so that every manor became, as it were, 'a kingdom in little' (Ogg, 1969, 65), in a limited way a law unto itself: in the words of the Earl of Strafford in 1641, prerogative and propriety were 'fellows and companions that have been and ever must be inseparable in a well-governed kingdom' (Kenyon, 1966, 212). The function of the monarchy was 'to protect law, order, and property against Parliament's arbitrary claims backed up by popular violence' (Hill, 1969, 128). Hence the crucial importance for all property-holders of succession, for if succession in the state were not clearly defined in principle and effected in practice, the inheritance of all subordinate proprieties — whether by birth, election, purchase or appointment — would also become insecure.

This principle acted as an implicit restraint on the absolute exercise of royal power. 'The Estate of England is indeed the King's,' Dryden wrote in 1683; ' . . . but it follows not, that the people are his goods and chattels on it; for then he might sell, alienate, or destroy them as he pleased; from all which he has tied himself by the liberties and privileges he has granted us by laws' (Scott, Saintsbury, 1882-92, VII, 215). The 'royal' possession of a propriety, in other words, was inconsistent with the notion that ownership implied absolute power over what one owned. Proprietorial absolutism was confined to goods and chattels, the sort of ownership that a trader in commodities, but not a prince or a gentleman, enjoyed. The King could thus be represented as the supreme exemplar in the nation of power that was at once stable, restrained and in an important sense disinterested.

On the other hand, the King's power to recall 'the liberties and privileges . . . he granted . . . by laws', that is to dismiss justices and lords lieutenant, to revoke charters and to extend the liberties and proprieties of local government to dissenters (as both Charles II and James II tried to do), was an ever-present threat to the security of established, anglican proprietors. Hence the urge to set up law as 'the boundary, the measure', as Pym put it, 'between the King's prerogative and the people's liberty' (Kenyon, 1966, 214). To surrender a charter to the Crown, Charles Blount wrote in 1691, was 'to betray, nay, to rob the people of their Inheritances' (Blount, 1695, *The Oracles of Reason*, 176). The resulting ambivalence in the Crown's relations with landed proprietors is most effectively caught in Dryden's *The Hind and the Panther* (1687), where James II as a 'Plain good man' (III, *l.*906) represents one of the nation's landed gentlemen, even though the greedy discontented doves on his farm symbolise those same gentlemen jealously guarding their exclusive possession of highly profitable 'liberties' (Myers, 1973, 116-27).

'Prudence' and the Restoration of 1660

The situation in *The Hind and the Panther* was the consequence of an unresolved tension in English society which no talk of an ancient constitution could conceal, and which one highly original thinker, James Harrington, subjected to a particularly striking analysis. In classical antiquity, Harrington believed, social stability had been maintained by the power of 'the Many' (the lesser landowners) balancing that of 'the Few' (the King and the nobility). In medieval times, however, a 'modern prudence' had favoured 'the Few' until the fifteenth century, when 'a great part of the lands [passed] unto the hold and possession of the yeomanry' (Pocock, 1977, 197). Later the dissolution of the monasteries 'brought . . . so vast a prey unto the industry of the people, that the balance of the commonwealth was . . . apparently in the popular party' (ibid., 198). Like most of his contemporaries, Harrington used the word 'people' to refer not to the populace at large, but to 'those who own property' (Hill, 1984, 194). It is not my purpose here to discuss the republican theories he built on these insights, only to emphasise their secular and pragmatic character. Whatever 'civil laws' or an ancient constitution might say, he argued, 'government . . . of necessity must be new modelled' whenever law ceased to reflect the actual balance of interests in society (Pocock, 1977, 187). Harrington is thus a useful reminder of how seventeenth-century political theory was constantly (if often silently) modified by a quasi-machiavellian recognition of the importance of actual power relations.

Such prudential factors undoubtedly came into play at the restoration. On the one hand, former proprietors, bishops prominent among them, were eager to enjoy their own again. Edward Hyde, Earl of Clarendon's vivid account of their actions (see pp. 29ff) can easily be misunderstood; we need to remember that restoration England was a society which identified 'rights' not with the morally elevated abstractions of later constitutional declarations, but with rents, fees and fines. The problem was that quite literally parts of the fabric of the written constitution had been destroyed during the civil war (see p. 40). The Declaration of Breda, issued before Charles II's return, had recognised the problem (Kenyon, 1966, 358). This and the *ad hoc* manner of Parliament's resolution of it (see pp. 39ff) are clear indications of men's willingness at this time to operate within an existing *de facto* distribution of power at the expense, if necessary, of strict constitutional principle.

Tensions between principle and practical politics were even more seriously reflected in the struggle over the revised Prayer Book of 1662. The Declaration of Breda had announced the King's wish for laws 'for the full granting [of] . . . indulgence' (ibid., 358), but these proved unacceptable to Parliament (see p. 35), which wished to use ceremonial allegiance to the established church as a means of keeping political institutions under the control of anglican landowners at the expense of rising commercial and other interests identified with non-episcopalian protestantism. The Corporation and Uniformity Acts accordingly declared the Solemn League and Covenant of 1643 of no effect and required clergymen to affirm their 'unfeigned assent and consent to all and every thing' in the Book of Common Prayer (ibid., 380-1). Thus the *'power to govern and conduct the Consciences of Subjects'* was claimed not by the King but by Parliament. The law was used in effect to define what a man meant by his own words. Clarendon accordingly refused to acknowledge a difference between the words 'assent' and 'consent' (see p. 35). The consequence of taking these oaths for some, notably presbyterians who lapsed into latitudinarianism (Hill, 1984, 268), was to change the political status of the language of belief; it was no longer comfortable to regard professions of principle as having exact, practically serious consequences. On the other hand, those who stood out for meaning and refused to take the oath on St

Bartholemew's day 1662, placed themselves in internal political exile. In both cases, the language of religion was politically disabled, a development of considerable importance for a society in which religion and politics were inseparably united.

Anti-Catholicism and the Bible

A crucial component of this interlinking was the prevailing hatred of catholicism in England. Based on memories of the Marian persecution and fears of Spain and France, it was fed by rumours that following the rising of the native Irish against protestant settlers in 1641, a 'plot' had been hatched by catholics and royalists to suppress English liberties with catholic troops from Ireland. Even intelligent men saw catholic conspiracy everywhere. Many who believed in the 'plot' of 1641, for example, were also inclined to hold catholics responsible for the execution of Charles I. Richard Baxter (himself accused of being an 'Anabaptized Jesuit' — Lamont, 1979, 147) was convinced that many dissenters more radical than himself were also disguised jesuits. Anti-catholic hysteria reached its climax during the years of the exclusion crisis (1678-81), but even in quieter times toleration of the catholic minority — subject as they had been to heavy (if often neglected) penal laws, and intermittently massive confiscations and fines — was out of the question. Henry Neville, a republican, and a rare tolerationist, attributed this to 'the craziness of our polity' (Robbins, 1969, 158), but there was more to it than that. English society was defined by its anti-catholicism. The confiscation of abbey lands in the sixteenth century — which Harrington rightly saw as fundamental to the 'balance' of the modern nation — was still a live issue during the exclusion crisis (Blount, 1695, *An Appeal*, 36-7) — it is mentioned also in the Declaration of Indulgence of 1687 (Kenyon, 1966, 413). Besides, since the Henrician reformation the nation's independence had been based on the claim of its kings to derive their power directly and exclusively from God, rather than from pope or emperor. Protestantism, under a protestant sovereign, or at any rate under a sovereign lawfully reigning, was as fundamental to the nation's sense of itself as its mythical constitution.

One consequence of the intense hatred of catholicism associated with this national identification with protestantism was a preoccupation among men as learned and sensitive as Henry More and Sir Isaac Newton with the apocalyptic books of the Bible which were believed to show that the church of Rome was the antichrist. Thus Henry More believed that the papacy was the 'little Horn' on the head of the fourth beast in the Book of Daniel (Budick, 1970, 207), and was very upset when Baxter denied this in 1684 (Lamont, 1979, 22). (It was because his new church was so frequently identified with the beasts of biblical prophecy that Dryden represented catholicism as a harmless hind in *The Hind and the Panther*.)

The literal pedantry of such biblical scholarship is an indication of the Bible's immense power of legitimation in the seventeenth century, but it was an ambivalent power. The argument in Sir Robert Filmer's *Patriarcha* (written about 1640 but only published in 1680 as part of the court's anti-exclusionist campaign) that kingly power derived from the divinely sanctioned patriarchal rule of Adam and Noah, acquired incalculable force from its apparently scriptural basis, making it particularly difficult for his latter-day whig opponents — sceptics and deists like Blount and Anthony Ashley-Cooper, Earl of Shaftesbury — openly to challenge some of his arguments. On the other hand, in religious controversy, as over the Prayer Book of 1662, the Bible could divide the nation. It filled the minds of people like the younger Beaumonts — often prosperous but without formal education — with so profound a sense of self that they were ready to defy paternal or state authority in its name (see pp. 87ff). The Bible could thus become the focus of serious personal, domestic and social unrest, which opponents of the regime might exploit, whatever their own private opinions of biblical truth might be. Hence the conservative impulse to weaken the impact of scripture. In *Religio Laici* (1682), Dryden bitterly regretted that 'Men would still be itching to *expound*' (*l*.410). Recent scholarship, he suggested, had revealed complicated inaccuracies in the transmission of the biblical text, which made it relatively unreliable as a guide except to the main doctrines of Christianity, about which there was no serious disagreement anyway. The argument was in some ways the same as Clarendon's, but unlike many middle-of-the-road anglicans Dryden believed that in the end some meaning mattered. His fiercest denunciations of dissent in *The Medall* (1682), for example, arose from a conviction that the plain sense of scripture was threatened by religious enthusiasm.

The State of Nature

Scripture, however, was by no means the only ground on which religious and political controversies were fought out. Three others of particular relevance to the writings in this collection were the state of nature, history and natural law. Notoriously, according to Hobbes, 'the estate of men in . . . natural liberty, is the estate of war . . . as we know . . . by the experience of savage nations that live at this day' (Peters, 1962, 279-80). In making this claim he was effectively taking possession of instinct, which was supposed to operate most freely among men in the pre-social state, for his peculiar brand of determinist absolutism, a position far from popular with more conservative monarchists. Accordingly, in *The Conquest of Granada* (1672) we find Dryden making a countermove. The play's hero, Almanzor, comes by chance to maturity in the equivalent of the state of nature, without known family and social ties; he is

> as free as nature first made man,
> Ere the base laws of servitude began,
> When wild in woods the noble savage ran
> > (Scott, Saintsbury 1882-92, IV, 43)

Almanzor is undoubtedly attracted by violence but he is in no simple Hobbesian sense a brutal predator, and he finally submits to paternal and royal authority. 'Natural' man, as Dryden presented him, was thus instinctively capable of family and social integration. This was also the view of Sir William Temple, whose account of the origins of patriarchal monarchy (see pp. 139ff) was firmly based on nature as Filmer's had been on the Bible, though the latter also cited evidence concerning primitive man from Aristotle (Laslett, 1949, 79). Because of its basis in nature and custom, Dryden and Temple's patriarchalism was more flexible than Filmer's and correspondingly less popular in court circles in the 1680s. Nevertheless, all three had the polemical advantage over Hobbes of defending an already highly popular idea. 'In assuming that the family always had been and always would be patriarchal,' Laslett writes, 'Filmer could be justifiably confident that he would never be challenged' (ibid., 24). As Agnes Beaumont discovered, paternal authority could prove stronger than the word of God itself. Any attempt to detach the family and the primeval natural human order, therefore, was bound to fail. The more daring speculative writings of men like Henry Stubbe, whose *An Account of the Rise and Progress of Mohametanism* implicitly condoned polygamy, or Sir William Petty, who discussed setting up an experimental colony based on complex rules of polygamy and polyandry (Lansdowne, 1927, II, 49-58), could make no headway against the 'obviousness' of this protestant patriarchalism. Not surprisingly their work circulated only in private. Even the more publicised libertine tradition associated with the plays of Wycherley and Etherege and gentlemen-poets like John Wilmot, Earl of Rochester, ultimately capitulated to the stern and (in the eighteenth century) the sentimental norms of male-dominated domesticity. When Rochester told Gilbert Burnet 'that all pleasure, when it did not interfere, with these [the well-being of oneself and others], was to be indulged as the gratification of our natural Appetites' Burnet's reply, unedifying though it might be, was at the time unanswerable: 'the Injury is . . . great,' he said, 'if a Mans Wife is defiled, or his Daughter corrupted' (Burnet, 1680, 38-9). That is the voice of the true man of mode.

The territory of natural man could in fact only be won for those opposed to patriarchal theories of kingship by forces defensive of the patriarchal family. This John Locke achieved by distinguishing between the origins of the family and those of the state, while grounding both on the principle of contract (see pp. 196ff). The problem with this argument was that it presupposed equality between all persons. Locke got round this difficulty, however, by proposing an ingenious theory of property (see pp. 190ff) which reinstated family and social subordination, but not the primeval claims of kingship. Locke's arguments in effect looked forward to Defoe's natural man, Robinson Crusoe, just as Dryden's natural man, Almanzor, had looked back to Filmer's *Patriarcha*. Almanzor discovers the naturalness of social and domestic authority; Crusoe, on the other hand, cast away among a savage people, who like Locke's 'Americans', though 'rich in Land', are 'poor in all the Comforts of Life . . . *for want of improving it*' (see p. 191), discovers the advantages of solitary labour by which, like a good colonist, he justifies turning his island into a propriety and ruling it as a sovereign. These polemical victories of economic over natural criteria, and of individual effort over social collaboration as the ultimate ground of political and even family relationships, had immense significance in the evolution of modern English culture.

History and Providence

Whatever man's primeval state might have been, however, his subsequent history also demanded interpretation. Thus Anne T. Barbeau has argued that Dryden's plays represent history as 'the temporal expression' of divine justice (Barbeau, 1970, 10), and Alan Roper that Dryden used historical parallels 'as a species of proof' in a naively uncritical fashion (Roper, 1965, 31). But 'right' does not always succeed in the serious literature of the period, as Barbeau's analysis suggests that it should, certainly not in Otway's *Venice Preserv'd* (1683), or Dryden's *Don Sebastian* (1690), and even when it does so, notably in *Absalsom and Achitophel*, the results are often deliberately unsettling (Myers, 1973, 83-95). Dryden's analogies were also stronger than Roper implies. In the Preface to *Religio Laici* for example, and the Postscript to *The History of the League* (see pp. 151ff), he represented history as exposing hidden structural affinities between apparently different situations and beliefs, such as the Catholic League in sixteenth-century France and the Protestant Association in seventeenth-century England. (This was a much-contested territory: Andrew Marvell and Slingsby Bethel used the same historical parallel to support the whig cause (see pp. 83 and 136ff).) For Dryden history was not the consequence of random special providences — the equivalent in life of coincidences producing 'poetic justice' in a play — but the logical unfolding of psychological and political processes in ways which, though ultimately compatible with human freedom and divine justice, were often opaque to temporal human scrutiny. Dryden's writings, especially the plays and translations produced after 1688, and above all his masterwork, *Fables Ancient and Modern* (1700), brilliantly exploit the uncertainties and the insights made visible in historical parallels, witnessing at once to his sense of the troubling uncertainty of all readings of history and the urgent need, nonetheless, to interpret it (Myers, 1973, 129-91).

Some periods, of course, had greater significance than others. The French wars of religion was one, the reign of the first Christian emperor, Constantine, another. In 1664, Nathaniel Bacon described this notoriously corrupt and erratic emperor as 'greater than the greatest *Cæsars*' on the grounds that his conversion made him the first prince to reign 'by a divine right that no power on earth can take away' (Bacon, 1664, 2). Hence the common protestant view that the conversion of Constantine marked the start of Christ's thousand-year reign on earth. Constantine raised other issues besides divine right, however. He had endowed the clergy with wealth and power, and had promulgated the Athanasian doctrine of the Trinity in opposition to Arius's denial of the Son's equality with the Father, yet he had also maintained good relations with arian bishops. Thus, like Charles II he had subordinated church to state, enforced doctrinal uniformity, established a clerical elite, and played one church party against another. To write about Constantine's reign, therefore, was to write about Charles II's. Dryden's

Religio Laici, for example, refers patronisingly to Athanasius, and the Preface compares his creed to the Test Acts of 1673 and 1678, which had been forced on the King following the withdrawal of the first Declaration of Indulgence, granting toleration to dissenters. In thus downplaying the creed Dryden was evidently challenging anglican hardliners just as he challenged dissenting extremists in downplaying scripture. As has already been noted, however, he remained committed to a minimal doctrinal base, and his position was becoming increasingly uncomfortable in the 1680s. Among royalists an assertively dogmatic Filmerian defence of monarchy had replaced Clarendon's view that doctrinal differences were trivial. Meanwhile some freethinking radicals were moving in the opposite direction, though the main body of protestant opinion remained as committed as ever to resisting any romanising tendencies in the church. Dryden sooner or later was bound to join either the freethinkers or the dogmatists. As is well known, he chose the latter, opting, however, for Roman rather than Stuart claims on his ultimate allegiance.

On one matter, however, Dryden's position was the popular one. He was firmly anticlerical. This was not unusual among intelligent conservatives, as plays like Otway's *Venice Preserv'd* and Dryden's own *The Spanish Fryar* (1681) make clear. Naturally they distrusted dissenting ministers, but the position of anglican clergymen was almost equally suspect. Despite the close connections between church and king, the clergy were distrusted by conservatives for their worldliness and careerism on the one hand, and their claim to independent spiritual authority on the other. This the radicals also disliked — hence their tendency to support strongly Erastian notions of church-state relations, so long, at least, as this did not put other freedoms at risk. But another ground of radical anticlericalism (and nonconformist anger) was the power which the local clergy exercised 'over the daily lives and opinions of the flock . . . blasphemy, atheism, and immorality' being subject to rigorous investigation and punishment (Ogg, 1967, 213). They thus reinforced the power of local proprietors to whom they often owed their livings — hence the fierce anticlericalism of Andrew Marvell (see pp. 80ff) and Bethel (see pp. 131ff). The Declaration of Indulgence, therefore, was an anticlerical move, allowing a landlord's tenants and dependants to evade parsonical control. Accordingly radicals like Marvell and Stubbe were able briefly to align themselves with the King — Locke even supplied Shaftesbury with arguments in favour of royal supremacy at this time (Jacob, 1983, 117). With the Test Acts, however, and the strict enforcement of penal legislation after the defeat of the exclusionists in 1681, 'the Ecclesiastical Itch to Dominion' (see p. 131) became increasingly intolerable, and even Baxter (usually a supporter of royal authority) was driven to ridicule the theory that the thousand-year reign of Christ could be dated from the reign of Constantine (Lamont, 1979, 247-8). But Baxter also believed passionately in the role of the pastor as the guardian of true Christian consciousness in the populace. He longed for the establishment of an inclusive 'National Church' protected by a protestant prince under whom ministers like himself would care for their flocks without interference from remote diocesan bishops or rack-renting landlords, and so he soon reverted to the view that Constantine's reign had after all initiated the millennium, and that it therefore made sense to look to a protestant prince, as the instrument of divine rule, to establish the 'National Church' of his dreams (see pp. 217ff).

One consequence of this change was to force Baxter to reconsider his view about the antichrist, who could no longer be identified with the pope. His alternative candidate was Mohamet, a figure very differently regarded by more radical opponents of anglican hegemony, such as Stubbe and Blount. Originally a protégé of Sir Henry Vane (executed in 1662), Stubbe had adapted cleverly to the restoration and (until the recent researches of J.R. Jacob) was generally held to be a turncoat, notorious for his opposition to the Royal Society. His interpretation of Mohametanism, however, shows that he remained a radical thinker. The manuscript of this work circulated privately and two extracts from it were published in Blount's *Miscellaneous Works* under the guise of letters to Hobbes and Rochester (see pp. 101ff). Stubbe detested Constantine for supporting the clergy and enforcing high trinitarian notions of orthodoxy. He saw Mohamet as preserving a purer and simpler monotheistic tradition, and establishing a religion which came as near as possible to the inclusive, undoctrinaire deism favoured by Blount and his circle. In seeking to demystify religion in this way, and so break down clerical authoritarianism, however, Stubbe also introduced a radically determinist principle into his analysis of history. He saw millenarianism simply as a form of mass hysteria which provided the necessary conditions for the early success of Christianity (see p. 105). In effect, the later radicals not only saw economic rather than instinctual relations as initiating history, they also saw its continuance as less a matter of will, divine or human, and more one of process.

Reason and Natural Law

The development of such deterministic views was one aspect of a larger dispute over reason, natural law and materialism which had important ideological implications in the restoration period. Stubbe, for example, made great play of the low level of intellectual achievement among the orthodox bishops during the reign of Constantine (see pp. 108ff), not only to establish the sound philosophical credentials of arian or deist traditions, but also to expose the crude superstitions on which clerical power was allegedly based. In this he was following in the footsteps of Hobbes (Jacob, 1983, 13). For both, as for many radicals, the issue was whether it was ever reasonable to believe in the miraculous — direct and marvellous interventions by God in present times or in the past. Deists like Blount had great fun attacking conservative attachment to miracle stories (see pp. 118ff). However, their dissenting allies were also vulnerable to charges of this kind — Baxter and Bunyan were both prone to believe such stories (Lamont, 1979, 31) — and even liberal anglicans like Burnet found it difficult to abandon altogether the notion of the miraculous. Ultimately more effective, therefore, than arguments against the miraculous on rational grounds was a fundamental questioning of the notion of free will (see pp. 122ff). Polemic such as Blount's on this issue considerably strengthened the frequently urged opinion that, as Rochester put it to Burnet, man is 'not master of his own Belief' (Burnet, 1680, 77), a view shared, incidentally, by Marvell (see p. 85) in spite of its incompatibility with his friend Milton's opinion that individuals were responsible for their convictions. The result was a further weakening of the idea that religious and political beliefs were intrinsically important. Hence, perhaps, the speculative daring of the rationalists. Rochester entertained the idea of reincarnation (ibid., 65-6), and Shaftesbury was said to have believed in astrology and an afterlife in the stars (Hamilton, 1972, 208). More seriously, Blount's *Miscellaneous Works* brought together various eastern and classical religious ideas. This pioneering work in comparative religion and biblical criticism was, however, premature. Deism was capable of diluting anglican and some dissenting teaching, but the cultural strength of the Bible and of orthodox dogma was too considerable for Blount's Catholic Articles (see pp. 121ff) to gain many disciples for pure deism.

Sprat's strategy for dealing with the challenge of rationalism to faith was far more politic. Formally *The History of the Royal Society* privileged Christianity and the Church of England (see p. 48). Belief in the afterlife had to be kept up if only for the sake of social order (see p. 51), but 'Natural Knowledge' now prevailed, so God could dispense with modern miracles. Having thus elevated Christianity above discourse, Sprat used religion to thrust philosophy below it. Religion, he declared, 'ought not to be the subject of Disputation. The *Peripatetic* [or aristotelian] Philosophy [had] long triumphed', but he could not 'imagine on what right. The spiritual and supernatural part of *Christianity* no *Philosophy* [could] reach: And in the plain things there [was] no need of any at all' (see pp. 55ff) . Ostensibly attacking only aristotelianism and the traditional university syllabus, Sprat effectively excluded everything but 'natural philosophy' from serious intellectual attention. Action arising out of argument in the fields of religion, conduct or politics was thereby deemed 'irrational'. His whole position was inherent in his account of how the Society began with a few gentlemen conversing quietly together 'without being ingag'd in the passions and madness' of commonwealth controversy (see p. 46). Casually deciding to entertain themselves with natural philosophy, they are represented as having quickly and spontaneously evolved a 'Philosophy for Mankind' in which religion and philosophy as they had been understood hitherto were decisively marginalised.

Writing and Power

This marginalisation has fundamental importance to an understanding of the Royal Society's ideological function within the system of power relations established after 1660. To emphasise this ideological function is in no way to impugn the scientific credentials of its membership or the integrity of men such as Joseph Glanvill and Robert Boyle in their defence of moderate anglicanism. Nevertheless, Sprat evidently intended to secure a place for the Society in the world of power and influence. He, therefore, adroitly aligned the Society not only with the Crown but also with commercial interests (see p. 49), and above all with the gentry (see p. 50). By the same token, as Sprat's proposed *History of the Civil War* (see pp. 45ff) and even more strikingly Chamberlayne's account of *The Present State of England* indicate, the Society could be deployed to advance views of English society which were entirely subservient to the interests of the governing class. Chamberlayne's claims concerning Christianity in Britain are particularly significant: the first Christian church, the first Christian king, and the first national bench of bishops were all, he claimed, British (see pp. 61ff). He thereby linked royal with episcopal government, and asserted the independence of both from the papal and imperial systems. The established church, he claimed, was 'the most exact and perfect Patern of all the Reformed Churches in the World' (see p. 63), being 'Transcendent' in two respects in particular — its toleration of other Christians and its total loyalty to the Crown (see pp. 63ff). Chamberlayne subsequently exemplified this spirit of toleration by describing his dissenting fellow-countrymen as 'the *Pudenda* of the Nation' (see p. 66), a remark of which Bethel was justifiably deeply resentful (see p. 134). He saw the early years of the reign of Charles I in an idealised haze (see pp. 64ff). and the revolution as a disease infecting mainly the lower classes, and still disturbingly rife in the land (see pp. 66ff). Thus,. while the '*Nobility* and chief *Gentry* of *England*' were 'the *finest Flowre*, . . . the lower sort of common People . . . [were] the *coursest bran*' best kept obedient and deferential to their betters by heavier taxation (see pp. 67ff). The lack of system and consistency in Chamberlayne's survey is particularly significant, expressing at once a sense of social disorder which he could not confront, and a desire to govern coercively in ways that he was not certain could be logically defended. His disgruntled account of the vices of the poor and the detailed description of legal sanctions that follows it are chilling reminders of the barbarities of seventeenth-century social controls.

Much of the writing of the period is conditioned by these oppressive relations. It is no accident that so many of the texts in this volume were published anonymously or posthumously or circulated in manuscript. Opinions cost lives in the reign of Charles II. In 1662, Sir Henry Vane's assertion of parliamentary sovereignty at his trial almost certainly led to his execution (Ogg, 1967, 179). Catholics were killed for their faith during the exclusionist crisis. In 1683 Algernon Sidney was executed, in part for opinions about resistance to royal authority expressed in private papers (ibid., 649). Both whig and tory were eager to inflict the vilest punishments on their opponents. Vane was hanged, drawn and quartered, and Bethel did his best to ensure that the same punishment was inflicted on the aged Lord Stafford, an innocent catholic impeached on the perjured evidence of Titus Oates. Clarendon only escaped a charge of high treason by going into exile; Bunyan and Baxter were among hundreds of dissenters imprisoned for their beliefs; Burnet and Locke had to take refuge abroad in the years before 1688. This explains why Milton (Hill, 1984, 312), Stubbe (Jacob, 1983, 41ff) and, in the later years of the century, Dryden (Myers, 1973, 128ff) had to resort to indirect and coded expressions of their political convictions. Writing in the years from 1660 to 1700 could stridently assimilate the oppressive authority of the state — Chamberlayne is an example of this — or else it could try to outmanoeuvre state power by appealing cynically to the hysteria of the mob, or, more interestingly, by adopting the tactics of camouflage and indirection. The adoption of such tactics, however, necessarily produced changes in the substance of oppositon writing during the period, a process we must now consider because of its long-term implications for English culture.

Milton and Marvell

We can begin with Milton, not because his position was typical but because it was so sharply defined. Where he stood on political issues was invariably consistent with the theological views secretly recorded in *De Doctrina Christiana*. His arianism and his anticlericalism, for example, were aspects of each other. As a providentialist and a millenarian, he was still expecting the imminent return (literal or metaphorical) of Christ in 1660, and this burning hope, though moderated thereafter, was never abandoned; nor was the political hope inherent in such expectations, that the saints would finally establish a Christian commonwealth, if necessary by force (Hill, 1984, 315-9). Intrinsic to this conception of historical change was a belief in free will: *Samson Agonistes* (1671) asserted that people must choose liberty whenever Providence gave them the opportunity of doing so. This political arminianism was reflected in the classically aristotelian representation of choice in *Paradise Lost* (1667) and *Paradise Regain'd* (1671); we know therefore how Milton must have regarded both the downgrading of Aristotle by the Royal Society, and the view that men are not masters of their beliefs. 'Reason also is choice' declares the God of *Paradise Lost* (III, *l*.108). Milton's theological politics penetrate even the most 'human' passages in his verse. The great marriage-bed scene in *Paradise Lost*, for example (IV, *ll*.736-73), shows Adam and Eve turning straight from prayer to lovemaking. They pray as equals: so much for liturgy and the clergy. Their pleasure is 'Founded in Reason, Loyal, Just and Pure': in Eden instinct is not Hobbesian, yet Eros reigns there and revels; the Fountain of Domestic Sweets flows perpetually as it did for saints and patriarchs, who enjoyed themselves far more vigorously than the starved lovers of libertine courts. Evidently the sweetness of life was known during the English Revolution, not before or after it. Even the allusion to patriarchs is a coded vindication of polygamy, which is defended in *De Doctrina Christiana* in part with anticlerical arguments. Finally Milton declares wedded love to be the 'sole proprietie' in Eden, thus disposing of Filmerian arguments that God has made Adam proprietor over all the earth.

Exact though it was, Milton's position was, nonetheless, weak polemically simply because he had to disguise it so heavily. The situation was hardly easier for his friend Marvell, who remained in the public eye after 1660, but could only satirise his fellow M.P.s anonymously. When Charles II allied himself with France against the Dutch, however, and issued the first Declaration of Indulgence in 1672, Marvell, in common with other radicals, found himself unexpectedly allied to the King and in consequence able to write more freely. He could represent the issue of toleration as involving loyalty to the Crown, and this gave him scope to ridicule the clergy (see pp. 82ff), to enlist the support of powerful commercial interests (see p. 79), and even to derogate from Charles II's dignity by jokingly dressing him in prelatical lawn (see pp. 77ff). But the heart of the argument was deeply serious. He was challenging the devaluation of language inherent in the confusion between 'assent' and 'consent' (see pp. 80ff) required by the Act of Uniformity, and thus sounding an early warning about the authoritarian as well as the anarchic implications of devaluing signifiers (see pp. 81ff). This is one reason why Marvell remained close to a dogmatist like Milton, but it is also why *The Reheasal Transpos'd* is a backward-looking text. Marvell's skirmish with Parker resulted in the rout of the latter, but in strategic terms it was not significant. The Prayer Book was not terrain on which important victories could be won.

Free-thinking Radicals and the Exclusion Crisis

A more promising front was that held by the free-thinking radicals of the 1650s, associates and circumspect disciples of Hobbes and Harrington, of whom Stubbe is representative. They had a lot in common with Milton but they were also fundamentally undogmatic and so more responsive to shifting political circumstances. Stubbe's predilection for Mohametanism, for example, is compatible with Milton's arian, anticlerical and polygamist convictions, but his rejection of the doctrine of the atonement and his overt contempt for millenaries neuter Milton's conception of Christianity as an historically revolutionary force. Similarly Blount's 'deconstruction' of religious discourse in *Religio Laici*, his remorseless questioning of 'presence' in 'inspired' texts (see p. 118), linked to his implicit determinism (see pp. 122ff), would have appeared to Milton as a scandalously pessimistic surrender of intellectual and political responsibility, though he would have relished Blount's stylish anticlericalism. He would have hated also the unabashed libertinism of the whig nobility.

A more coarsely grained radicalism was in the ascendant, however, and paradoxically it was the political realignments following the withdrawal of the Declaration of Indulgence in March 1673 which gave it its chance. The Earl of Danby, as new chief minister, set about establishing a party of loyalists or tories in Parliament. Former ministers among the nobility — notably Buckingham and Shaftesbury — were now in opposition, but they had an issue with which to break Danby and prise the King and Commons apart, the possibility of the catholic Duke of York's succeeding to the throne. As early as 1674, Shaftesbury was attempting to destabilise the nation by announcing that 16,000 papists were about to attack London. Rumours of plots were rife thereafter, reaching their climax with Oates's 'revelations' in 1678. The crisis did not subside until 1681 when the Oxford Parliament was dissolved, Shaftesbury arrested, and the perjurers who had hounded catholics to death in the previous three years were unleashed by the authorities on their former allies and on each other.

Constitutionally this may have all been no more than 'a crisis of detail' (Plumb, 1969, 61), but it transformed radical discourse. Bethel was still arguing for religious toleration in 1680, but on practical grounds of commercial self-interest (see pp. 136ff), for him the only possible motive in political life (see p. 129). Ultimately he, too, was a determinist: belief is the work of God (see p. 130). He favoured a neo-Harringtonian 'prudence'; 'diffusive wealth', he argued ' . . . makes a Country rich' (see p. 132). Thus, while Marvell had called on the support of the City in opposition to clerical domination, Bethel appealed to anticlerical feeling in the interests of the City.

An equally significant development was the beginning of a *rapprochement* between elements in the church and the emerging whigs. A key figure here is Burnet, who represents the more radical wing of the early Royal Society membership and who appears so prominently alongside Hobbes, Stubbe and Rochester in Blount's *Miscellaneous Works*. In a letter to Boyle in 1682, however, an old enemy of Stubbe's 'lumped together "Hobbians and Stubbians, atheists, scoffers, blasphemers" ' (Jacob, 1983, 143-4). Burnet's willingness to be yoked unequally with such unbelievers was significant. It counterbalanced the conservative tendencies of the Royal Society at its foundation. Like the Clarendonian constitutionalists but for different reasons, latitudinarian radicals were unwilling to press the meaning of words too far. Burnet's easy way with meaning was evident in the bland elision of 'Principles' and 'Persons' in his account to Rochester of the doctrine of the Trinity: 'in one Essence', he wrote, 'there are three different Principles of Operation, which, for want of terms fit to express them by, we call *Persons'* (Burnet, 1680, 104). This is a far cry from Milton's painful, if not always coherent, efforts to define his categories in discussing the doctrine of the Trinity, the exact political implications of which he understood so precisely. The whigs had found their discursive mode but only at the expense of much of what earlier radicals had contended for.

This unabashed intellectual opportunism was probably an inevitable response to the threat of absolutism. Nevertheless, men died as a result of exclusionist propaganda in the 1670s. The infamous pamphlet, *An Appeal from the Country to the City*, for example, incited the London mob to kill all catholics on sight if they heard even rumours of 'the King's untimely End . . . for that there is no such thing as an *English* Papist, who is not in the Plot, at least in his good Wishes' (Blount, 1695, *An Appeal*, 5). Especially troubling is the eagerness of Blount's friends to reprint such propaganda among his *Miscellaneous Works* in 1695, particularly in a context which confirmed the religious scepticism of their party. A volume which intelligently questioned the whole notion of biblical inspiration was not the place to frighten simple protestants with visions of catholics tearing 'the Ministers of God's Holy Word . . . in pieces before your Eyes' (ibid., 3). Shaftesbury, according to Burnet, was 'a deist at best' (Hamilton, 1972, 208). His enthusiasm, and that of his allies, for the purity of the protestant religion was entirely feigned. Indeed, what the whigs really believed in at this time is impossible to elucidate.

Dryden, Filmer and Locke

Tory writing, on the other hand, moved in the opposite direction, towards discursive specificity. Dryden, it is true, remained faithful to a royalist reading of the ancient constitution. Any traditionally established political order seemed to him to enjoy divine approval — like Otway, he disliked republican constitutions such as those of ancient Rome and Venice, but he acknowledged their legitimacy. Like Temple, he was content to defend the English constitution as the will of God for

Englishmen, but he avoided positing a uniform and universally applicable political theory of the kind favoured by Filmer and Locke. The English monarchy was 'Hereditary [and] . . . naturally poiz'd by our municipal Laws', just as 'explicit Laws' were balanced by prerogative (see p. 152). Thus, behind the fierce expressions in *The Medall* and The Postscript to *The History of the League* one may detect the moderate Clarendonian constitutionalism of *Religio Laici* and *The Hind and the Panther* (Myers, 1973, 102-11, 116-27). Such caution was rare, however. According to Laslett, in the early 1680s 'the thought of Sir Robert Filmer formed the *ipsissima verba* of the established order' (Laslett, 1949, 34). Filmer, like Temple later (see pp. 140ff), had seen the weaknesses in contract theory, but after 1681 his appeal lay chiefly in his dogmatic, scripture-based assertion of royal supremacy over all forms of government. At the same time the Church of England was reasserting the principle of non-resistance to the Crown with considerable enthusiasm.

The apparently irresistible power of the state, in the closing years of Charles II's reign, gave these views immense authority, but they were also dangerously inflexible, as George Savile, Marquis of Halifax, evidently realised (see p. 165). This becomes very obvious when one compares the arguments of Filmer and Locke. (The latter would have found Temple a more difficult opponent.) Locke was an intellectual opportunist, advancing patriarchalist and non-resistance arguments when they were convenient (Laslett, 1970, 29). He apparently developed his theory of property simply to meet Filmer's argument that primitive communism was entailed in any rejection of patriarchalism, and he never directly addressed the argument that there was 'no stopping place between the ground he . . . occupied and logical individualism, final democracy [and] the sharing of political power with women, children and servants' (ibid., 69). He is often inconsistent on important issues, arguing in one place, for example, that the law of nature is 'as intelligible and plain . . . as the positive Laws of Commonwealths; nay possibly plainer' (see p. 188), and in another that 'human reason . . . never from unquestionable principles, by clear deductions, made out an entire body of the "law of nature" ' (Laslett, 1970, 88). The elusiveness of Locke's real position, if he had one, is particularly noticeable in his arguments about the death penalty, a key element in the seventeenth-century conception of sovereignty. Locke held that a thief might be lawfully killed at the moment of his crime because the threat to property implied a threat to life (see p. 189), and that a commanding officer might order a soldier's execution for failing to show 'blind obedience' in battle, but he might not sieze one 'jot of his Goods' (see p. 202). This privileging of property over life compares unfavourably with Dryden's view that unless state authority is of divine institution, no human contract could justify any man's taking the life that God had given to another (see p. 151). Locke's arguments were generally more humane than those of his opponents, but there was a commitment to possession, authority and coercion in his work, as ruthless as anything in Chamberlayne and possibly more dangerous because not so plainly stated.

Locke and Halifax

The problem, of course, is not that Locke was wrong *vis-à-vis* Filmer and Dryden but that, at least before 1688, he could only be right by stealth. (Laslett argues that he came very close to revolution and treason in the early 1860s — Laslett, 1970, 31). Such an explanation is not available, however, in the case of a man of power like Halifax whose use of such tactics significantly alters the status of this kind of discursive elusiveness. Halifax was the leading 'Trimmer' during and after the exclusion crisis. He wished to restrict the powers of a catholic king and he disagreed with government without Parliament, but from 1679 to 1681 he defended the succession and was largely responsible for Shaftesbury's defeat in the House of Lords in 1680. He twice withdrew from public affairs in 1679 and 1681, but he seems to have written *The Character of a Trimmer* for Charles II (Ogg, 1967, 655), and was regaining influence when the King died in 1685. He opposed Charles's policy of ignoring the law requiring Parliament to meet at least every three years, and the calling in of charters which were subsequently reissued on terms strengthening royalist and anglican control over the boroughs and parliamentary elections. Against these abuses he protested with modest good sense. He argued for a union of king and 'people' (proprietors), in effect for consensus, for the rule of law, for parliaments, for an upright judiciary and for freedom of the press (see pp. 163ff).

The correlative of such public decency in private life is most reassuringly evident in Locke's writings on education. In an age when the most celebrated schoolmaster, Richard Busby, was renowned for the brilliance of his scholarship and the brutality of his floggings, Locke's oppositions to flogging (see pp. 204ff), his advanced views on language-teaching (see pp. 207ff), on the development of practical skills (see pp. 213ff), on travel and marriage (see pp. 214ff), lighten the heart. His ideal of a gentleman as one who manages 'his Business abley, and with fore-sight in this World' (see p. 203) evokes the assured decency of Congreve's Mirabel or Jane Austen's Mr Knightley, equally remote from the heroic or hedonistic literary posturing of the years between 1660 and 1680. It is in no way to undervalue the importance of this great shift in sensibility, however, to scrutinise with some caution the discursive practices associated with its emergence.

There were undoubtedly losses as well as gains. Breeding, for Locke, took precedence over learning (see p. 204); boys should aspire to be 'fine Gentlemen' (see p. 206), but not painters (see p. 207), poets (see p. 209) or musicians (see p. 212). Dryden — like Locke a fierce opponent of flogging — provides an interesting contrast. His description of the education of Plutarch is no less liberal and humane than Locke's, but it is also uninhibitedly intellectual. Study for his young scholars 'so far from being a burden . . . [becomes] a habit, and philosophical questions and criticism of humanity [are] their usual recreations at their meals' (Scott, Saintsbury, 1882-92, XVII, 25). Locke's students also learn about 'the Systems of *Natural Philosophy*', but only to familiarise themselves with the 'Terms and Ways of Talking of the several Sects', and not to gain 'a comprehensive scientifical and satisfactory Knowledge of the Works of Nature' (see p. 211). It would seem, then, that the low valuation of meaning which would have been a necessary tactic in the *Two Treatises of Government*, if Laslett is right in assigning the main work of their composition 'to the years 1679-80' (Laslett, 1970, 35), was transformed in *Some Thoughts Concerning Education* into a way of life.

This is perhaps the most important link between Locke and Halifax. Both perceive the limiting of coherence, consistency and depth as a principle of conduct. This is especially obvious in Halifax's *The Lady's New-Years-Gift*, which addressed the situation of upper-class young women as Locke addressed that of upper-class young men. Halifax wrote with great frankness. He knew sexual double standards were an *'Injustice'*, though necessary, he thought, for 'the *Preservation* of Families' (see pp. 176ff). But his list of unfaithful, drunken, covetous, spendthrift and foolish husbands chillingly anticipated male protagonists in the works of Vanbrugh, Farquhar, Fielding, Richardson and Jane Austen — Malcolm Kelsall has already drawn attention to the connections between Halifax's view of the situation of women and Congreve's (Kelsall, 1981, 40-1) — and when he offered a theoretical justification of this injustice, he lapsed into half-hearted reliance on unexamined notions of the natural rationality of men (see p. 175), and shadowy narratives of wives controlling their husbands by their beauty, tact, tears and childbearing (see pp. 177ff), all of which not only lacked intellectual conviction but also set limits on the level of intimacy he was likely to enjoy with an obviously much-loved daughter. A comparison of Halifax's *Advice to a Daughter* with the passionate anger and devotion in Agnes Beaumont's relations with her father and brother is not entirely to the advantage of the Savile family.

Inconsistency was also the hallmark of Halifax's political writings. He could assert that the source of law was 'innocent and uncorrupted Nature . . . which disposes Men to chuse Vertue, without its being prescribed' (see p. 163), and yet argue a little later 'that without Laws the World would become a Wilderness, and Men little less than Beasts', and that religion was 'the Foundation of Government' because 'without it man . . . is one of the worst Beasts Nature hath produc'd'. Out of 'the Veneration due to the Laws' (see p. 170), he opposed declarations of indulgence, but he also favoured 'a prudential Latitude' in enforcing penal laws against dissenters, thus silently transferring the prerogative from the explicit, written decrees of a sovereign to an unwritten discretion lodged in the collective wisdom of an administrative class. Even obsolete laws should be enforced, and yet by what he chose to call 'Connivance', that is methods of enforcement that would 'look rather like a kind Omission to enquire more strictly than an allowed Toleration', they would in fact be conveniently circumvented (see pp. 172ff).

In all this Halifax was a much more 'modern' writer than Locke. Locke had had to appeal to the authority of reason, nature, law and scripture if only because the ground-rules of the contest with Filmer had been laid down by the ascendant court party; Halifax, on the other hand, as a man possessed of power throughout his life and free to choose the 'middle ground' on his own terms, was never under any pressure to prove anything at all. When, for example, he told his daughter that '*Nature* is so far from being unjust to you that she is partial on our side' (i.e. against men – see p. 175), the casual resort to personification signalled a bland refusal on his part to contend for the territory of 'Nature' as Filmer, Hobbes, Temple and Locke had contended for it. Again, in *The Character of a Trimmer* he argued that government required 'a kind of Omnipotence' which could best be secured by that 'virtual Consent of the whole' which only a representative assembly of the people could provide; the advantage of such consent was that it made every act of government seem 'to be an effect of their Choice', and the people would therefore be more willing to put the laws into effect (see p. 167). What was unclear in this argument was whether the choice was real or only a matter of appearance. Did Parliament enact the people's real wishes, or did it seduce them into co-operating with the government by making it appear so? Halifax's elegant comparisons of political and organic processes obscured this issue. He loved such analogies because they invited agreement without implying the sort of conviction from which retreat was difficult. For Dryden analogy revealed consistent and generative processes in human history; for Halifax it was a device of art by which pragmatism accrued to itself the legitimacy of seeming natural. His language in effect enabled and transcended what Edward Said has called in another context 'the transfer of legitimacy from filiation to affiliation' (Said, 1984, 24). *The Character of a Trimmer* marks the moment when style, practicality, affinity, 'tone' became the touchstones of good sense in argument, and the generative notions of logical consistency and legitimate intellectual authority begetting real assent and so deliberate action were decisively — that is to say socially — disregarded. It is no accident that patriarchalism lost its power to convince in political, if not in any other, discursive practice at this time, nor that this was also the moment when the Church of England dramatically abandoned what it had regarded up till then as its defining characteristic *vis-à-vis* other Christian churches, its doctrine of non-resistance.

1688 and the Principle of Exclusion

Political events reflected and enforced these changes. Historians are agreed, that, wilful, oppressive and inept as he may have been, James II generally acted within the law but that 'this was irrelevant since . . . [he] was flying in the face of the opinion of those who mattered in the country' (Hill, 1969, 208). The most effective plank in William of Orange's platform was his promise to maintain religious discrimination, a commitment carefully calculated to reassure those same interests. James never appreciated that the Test and Uniformity Acts were designed to exclude from the political order only those with positive beliefs of their own, not the sceptical, the cynical or the self-interested. When the political pickings are rich enough, as Dryden noted with alarm, 'Ev'n Atheists out of Envy own a God' (*The Hind and the Panther* III, *l.* 1212). The political nation would never have bound itself by the oaths and affirmations with which it restrained others. James, however, naively continued to believe that his subjects really meant what they wrote and said. The framers of the Declaration of Right, on the other hand, were under no illusions about the gulf between signs and any actual state of affairs to which they might be thought to refer. They certainly knew that only six of its thirteen articles affirmed old law, that one other article was in conflict with a recent statute, and that a second amended existing law. They were also concerned to secure and conceal important ambiguities in the ceremony of its acceptance, so that a wholly false impression might be created that William of Orange's accession was conditional on his agreeing to the Declaration (Schwoerer, 1981, 283). In effect, by violating the principle of succession, the Convention Parliament of 1689 abolished the ancient constitution while purporting to affirm it, and substituted for it, without saying so, an absolutist assembly with powers comparable with those of Peter the Great of Russia or Charles X of Sweden. Hobbes, not Locke, was the political victor of 1688, though at the level of discourse Locke's sanctioning of common sense and inconsistency also triumphed. Genuine radicals were quick to see what was happening, as the whigs chose the House of Lords for their power-base, replaced triennial with septennial elections to Parliament and reduced the democratic franchise of the City of London. '*We can never be thoroughly ruin'd but by a Parliament*', Blount wrote in 1691, quoting Burleigh, 'They may cut the Throats of us and our Posterity by a Law' (Blount, 1695, *Oracles of Reason*, 177).

Culturally the principle of exclusion lies at the heart of what was achieved in 1688. The revolution deconstructed the political language of the English people and thereby excluded 'from a mere scruple of conscience' both jacobites and 'a great part of the Protestant freemen of England' from the political nation (Ogg, 1969, 232). In effect, the settlement established (again to quote Said) a fundamentally new 'system of exclusions legislated from above but enacted throughout [the]|polity, by which such things as anarchy, disorder, irrationality, inferiority, bad taste and immorality' were redefined and 'then deposited outside the culture and kept there by the power of the State and its institutions' (Said, 1984, 11). These were processes to which Baxter was subjected in a particularly significant way.

Baxter was typical of that great body of intelligent men who scrupulously 'searched the Scriptures' for religious and therefore human truth, 'a process in which he became earnest but uncompromising' (Ogg, 1967, 214). With Edmund Calamy he led negotiations on behalf of the dissenters at the ill-fated Savoy House Conference of 1660-1 which failed to produce an agreed settlement with the episcopal establishment. He refused an offer of a bishopric at this time, but doctrinally his position was the opposite of subversive. Admittedly, in 1683, at the height of the reaction against exclusionism, the University of Oxford officially condemned and burnt his book, *The Holy Commonwealth* (1659), along with 'most of the great treatises on political theory which seventeenth-century England had produced' (Hill, 1969, 207); but whereas the writings of Milton and Hobbes were in very different ways truly revolutionary, *The Holy Commonwealth* was not. It purported 'to be an attack on Harrington's *Oceana*', but according to Lamont it was rather 'a millenial document, embodying [Baxter's] hopes in Richard Cromwell [to whom it was dedicated] as a . . . Christian Emperor' (Lamont, 1979, 24). Baxter was in fact 'prepared to commit to the magistrate formidable discretionary powers; . . . he had a deep historic sense of the injustices which an overambitious clergy had perpetrated in taking power from the civil magistrate' (ibid., 133), and a genuine hope of seeing the establishment of a National Church in England which would encompass and unite the entire nation, a church, therefore, at once 'holy' and 'catholic', under the overall protection of a Christian prince, with the Christian minister free from political and prelatical interference in his care of the souls in his local community. Packed off to prison under James II, he had every reason in principle to welcome the accession of William III. In fact, however, the consequence of 1688 was effectively to redefine rationality, discursive propriety and good sense in such a way as to exclude precisely such men as Baxter from what Matthew Arnold was to call the main stream of national life.

In *The Poor Husbandman's Advocate*, Baxter revealed his radical awareness of the relationship between such exclusions and actual oppression. 'We are no Levellers', he protested (see p. 229). Nor was he; but he was, and remained to the end, a man who believed in believing, and who, therefore, could not accept the notion of '*Absolute Propriety*' in a christian nation, any more than Dryden could do so. He tried to overwhelm his readers with scriptural evidence, yet at the same time he knew his little book would not be read by the landlords who alone had the power to do something about the husbandman's lot: 'the very Title of it will provoke them to cast it by with scorn' (see p. 223). The power of the word was blocked, on the one hand by the 'system of exclusions' according to which the landowning class defined the 'readable', and on the other by the sheer difficulty of enlarging the consciousness of those he sought most to help. They lacked books, and they came 'in weary from their labours, so that they [were] fitter to sleep than to read or pray' (see p. 225). Oppression of the spirit and oppression of the body met in the discarded book. Baxter was in the hopeless position of knowing that his husbandmen depended for the relief of both needs on those very landowners whom he could see dismissing his own scriptural citations as canting enthusiasm or hypocritical dissent, the Allworthys, the Squire Westerns and the Tom Joneses of the coming century.

The texts contained in this volume, therefore, illustrate a struggle and its outcome. It would be incorrect to suggest that this struggle was primarily for control over discursive practice in itself, but it is the case that English writings at the close of the seventeenth century registered and confirmed a deep-seated change in social and political relationships; they are marked with the anxieties of struggle, the assurance of victory and the experience of defeat. The result of these changes was the establishment of parliamentary sovereignty (as Hobbes would have understood it) and the exclusion of dissenters and catholics from the political nation. Culturally this meant the recognition of the educational practices and *mores* of a particular class as normative; knowledge was admired, common sense respected and scepticism condoned. Conviction, and the cultural means of acquiring it on the other hand − in scripture or in argument − lost their legitimacy. The result was to change fundamentally the way English people wrote and the way they read each other's writings. Anyone operating within established norms could anticipate certain kinds of recognition and acceptance, while anyone operating outside such norms, anyone, that is, who searched earnestly for truth or manifested what their opponents termed enthusiasm and they themselves devotion, could anticipate corresponding forms of rejection. 'There is no reason to doubt', writes Said, 'that all cultures operate in this way' (Said, 1984, 14), and he goes on to discuss how 'an isolated voice out of place but very much *of* that place' can stand 'against the prevailing orthodoxy and very much for a professedly universal or humane set of values' (ibid., 15). English cultural orthodoxy has had to confront and assimilate many such voices since Baxter's day, from Defoe, Wesley and Richardson to Blake, Hale White and Lawrence. And there has been another, less prominent but no less insistent 'jacobite' tradition, including figures such as Newman and Waugh, which has derived its orientation (and social placement) from the milieu that supported Dryden in the 1690s. Both these traditions have repeatedly challenged what one may justifiably describe as the ethos of Halifax in English culture and they have both been repeatedly withstood. That is a measure of the importance and the power of the changes in English discourse which this volume has attempted to illustrate, changes which have made all literature written before 1688 so strange to us and all literature written thereafter the site on which a distinctively 'English' and familiar form of urbanity has contended with the no less 'English' and yet alien manners of dissent.

1

From: *The Life of Edward, Earl of Clarendon, in which is Contained a Continuation of the Grand Rebellion*

The Earl of Clarendon

During the Interval of Parliament, the King had made Choice of many very eminent and learned Men, who were consecrated to some of the Sees of Bishops which were void; that the Preservation of the Succession[1] might not depend upon the Lives of the few Bishops who remained, and who were all very aged: Which could not have been done sooner, nor till the other Parliament, to whom the Settlement of the Church had been referred, was dissolved. Nor could He yet give any Remedy to the License in the Practice of Religion, which in all Places was full of Scandal and Disorder, because *the Liturgy* was not yet finished; till when, the Indulgence by his Declaration was not to be restrained. But at the same Time that He issued out his Writs for convening the Parliament, He had likewise sent Summons to the Bishops, for the Meeting of the Clergy in Convocation, which is the legal Synod in *England*; against the Coming together whereof *the Liturgy* would be finished, which his Majesty intended to send thither to be examined, debated and confirmed. And then He hoped to provide, with the Assistance of the Parliament, such a Settlement in Religion, as would prevent any Disorder in the State upon those Pretences. And it was very necessary to lose no Time in the Prosecution of that Cure; for the Malignity against the Church appeared to increase, and to be greater than it was upon the Coming in of the King.

The old Bishops who remained alive, and such Deans and Chapters as were numerous enough for the Corporation, who had been long kept fasting, had now Appetites proportionable. Most of them were very poor, and had undergone great Extremities; some of the Bishops having supported themselves and their Families by teaching Schools, and submitting to the like low Condescensions. And others saw, that if They died before They were enabled to make some Provision for them, their Wives and Children must unavoidably starve: And therefore They made Haste to enter upon their own. And now an Ordinance of Parliament had not Strength enough to batter an Act of Parliament. They called their old Tenants to Account for Rent, and to renew their

29

Estates if They had a Mind to it; for most old Leases were expired in the long Continuance of the War, and the old Tenants had been compelled either to purchase a new Right and Title from the State (when the Ordinance was passed for taking away all Bishops, Deans and Chapters, and for selling all the Lands which belonged to them), or to sell their present Estates to those, who had purchased the Reversion and the Inheritance thereof: So that both the one and the other, the old Tenants and the new Purchasers, repaired to the true Owners as soon as the King was restored; the former expecting to be restored again to the Possession of what They had sold, under an unreasonable Pretence of a Tenant Right (as They called it), because there remained yet (as in many Cases there did) a Year or some other Term of their old Leases unexpired, and because They had out of Conscience forborne to buy the Inheritance of the Church, which was first offered to them. And for the Refusal thereof, and such a reasonable Fine[2] as was usual, They hoped to have a new Lease, and to be readmitted to be Tenants to the Church. The other, the Purchasers (amongst which there were some very infamous Persons), appeared as confident, and did not think, that according to the Clemency that was practised towards all Sorts of Men, it could be thought Justice, that They should lose the entire Sum They had disbursed upon the Faith of that Government, which the whole Kingdom submitted to; but that They should, instead of the Inheritance They had an ill Title to, have a good Lease for Lives or Years granted to them by them who had now the Right; at least, that upon the old Rent and moderate Fines They should be continued Tenants to the Church, without any Regard to those who had sold both their Possession, and with that all the Right or Title that They might pretend to, for a valuable Consideration. And They had the more Hope of this, because the King had granted a Commission, under the Great Seal of *England*, to some Lords of the Council and to other eminent Persons, to interpose and mediate with the Bishops and Clergy in such Cases, as ought not to be prosecuted with Rigour.

But the Bishops and Clergy concerned had not the good Fortune to please their old or their new Tenants. They had been very barbarously used themselves; and that had too much quenched all Tenderness towards others. They did not enough distinguish between Persons: Nor did the Suffering any Man had undergone for Fidelity to the King, or his Affection to the Church eminently expressed, often prevail for the Mitigation of his Fine; or if it did sometimes, three or four Stories of the contrary, and in which there had been some unreasonable Hardness used, made a greater Noise and spread farther, than their Examples of

Charity and Moderation. And as honest Men did not usually fare the better for any Merit, so the Purchasers who offered most Money, did not fare the worse for all the Villanies They had committed. And two or three unhappy Instances of this Kind brought Scandal upon the whole Church, as if They had been all guilty of the same Excesses, which They were far from. And by this Means the new Bishops, who did not all follow the Precedents made by the old, underwent the same Reproaches: And many of them who had most adhered to their Order, and for so doing had undergone for twenty Years together sundry Persecutions and Oppressions, were not in their present Passion so much pleased with the renewing it, as They expected to have been. Yet upon a very strict Examination of the true Grounds of all those Misprisions[3] (except some few Instances which cannot be defended), there will be found more Passion than Justice in them; and that there was even a Necessity to raise as much Money as could be justly done, for the repairing the Cathedrals, which were all miserably ruinated or defaced, and for the entirely building up many Houses of the Prebends, which had been pulled down or let fall to the Ground. And those Ways much more of those Monies which were raised by Fines were issued and expended, than what went into the private Purses of them, who had a Right to them, and had Need enough of them. But the Time began to be froward again, and all Degrees of Men were hard to be pleased; especially when They saw one *Classis* of Men restored to more than They had ever lost, and preferred to a Plenty They had never been acquainted with, whilst themselves remained remediless after so many Sufferings, and without any other Testimony of their Courage and Fidelity, that in the Ruin of their Fortunes, and the Sale of their Inheritance.

* * *

The Bishops were not all of one Mind. Some of them, who had greatest Experience and were in Truth wise Men, thought it best "to restore and confirm the old *Book of Common Prayer*, without any Alterations and Additions; and that it would be the best Vindication the *Liturgy* and Government of the Church could receive, that after so many Scandals and Reproaches cast upon Both, and after a bloody Rebellion and a War of twenty Years raised, as was pretended, principally against Both, and which had prevailed and triumphed in the total Suppression and Destruction of Both, they should now be restored to be in all Respects the same they had been before. Whereas any Alterations and Additions (besides the Advantage it might give to the common Adversary, the *Papist*, who would be apt to say that We had reformed and changed our Religion again), would raise new Scruples in the factious and schismatical Party, that was ashamed of all the old Arguments, which had so often been answered, and stood at present exploded in the Judgment of all sober Men; but would recover new Spirits to make new Objections, and complain that the Alterations and Additions are more grievous and burdensome to the Liberty of their Conscience, than those of which They had formerly complained."

Others, equally grave, of great Learning and unblemished Reputation, pressed earnestly both for the Alterations and Additions; said, "that it was a common Reproach upon the Government of the Church, that it would not depart from the least unnecessary Expression or Word, nor explain the most insignificant Ceremony; which would quiet or remove the Doubts and Jealousies of many conscientious Men, that they did in Truth signify somewhat that was not intended: And therefore since some powerful Men of that troublesome Party had made it their earnest Request, that some such Alterations and Additions might be made, and professed that it would give great Satisfaction to many very good Men; it would be great Pity, now there was a fit Opportunity for it, which had not been in former Times of Clamour, not to gratify them in those small Particulars, which did not make any important Difference from what was before." It may be there were some, who believed that the Victory and Triumph of the Church would be with the more Lustre, if somewhat were inserted, that might be understood to reflect upon the rude and rebellious Behaviour of the late Times, which had been regulated and conducted by that Clergy: And so both Additions and Alterations were made.

But the Truth is, what Show of Reason soever and Appearance of Charity the latter Opinion seemed to carry with it, the former Advice was the more prudent, and would have prevented many Inconveniences which ensued. Whatever had been pretended or desired, the Alterations which were made to please them did not reduce one of them to the Obedience of the Church; and the Additions raised the Clamour higher than it had been. And when it was evident that They should not be left longer without a Liturgy, They cried aloud for the same They had before, though They had inveighed against it for near a hundred Years together. . . .

Whilst the Clergy was busy and solicitous to prepare this Remedy for the present Distempers, the People of all the several Factions in Religion assumed more License than ever They had done. The *Presbyterians*[4] in all their Pulpits inveighed against the *Book of Common*

Prayer that They expected, and took the same Liberty to inveigh against the Government of the Church, as They had been accustomed to before the Return of the King; with reflections upon the Persons of the Bishops, as if They assumed a Jurisdiction that was yet at least suspended. And the other Factions in Religion, as if by Concert, took the same Liberty in their several Congregation. The *Anabaptists*[5] and the *Quakers*[6] made more Noise than ever, and assembled together in greater Numbers, and talked what Reformations They expected in all Particulars. These Insolencies offended the Parliament very much: And the House of Commons expressed much Impatience, that the *Liturgy* was so long in Preparation, that the *Act of Uniformity* might without Delay be passed and published; not without some Insinuations and Reflections, that his Majesty's Candour, and Admission of all Persons to resort to his Presence, and his Condescension to confer with them, had raised their Spirits to an Insolence insupportable; and that Nothing could reduce them to the Temper of good Subjects, but the highest Severity.

It is very true, from the Time of his Majesty's Coming into *England*, He had not been reserved in the Admission of those who had been his greatest Enemies, to his Presence. The Presbyterian Ministers He received with Grace; and did believe that He should work upon them by Persuasions, having been well acquainted with their common Arguments by the Conversation He had had in *Scotland*, and was very able to confute them. The *Independents*[7] had as free Access, both that He might hinder any Conjunction between the other Factions, and because They seemed wholly to depend upon his Majesty's Will and Pleasure, without resorting to the Parliament, in which They had no Confidence; and had rather that Episcopacy should flourish again, than that the *Presbyterians* should govern. The King had always admitted the *Quakers* for his Divertisement and Mirth, because He thought, that of all the Factions They were the most innocent, and had least of Malice in their Natures against his Person and his Government: And it was now too late, though He had a worse Opinion of them all, to restrain them from coming to him, till their should be some Law made to punish them; and therefore He still called upon the Bishops, to cause the Liturgy to be expedited in the Convocation . . .

When the *Book of Common Prayer* was, by the King's Command, presented to the House of Lords by the two Archbishops (for it had been approved by the Convocation of the Province of *York*, as well as by that of *Canterbury*) confirmed by his Majesty under the Great Seal of *England*; the Book itself took up no Debate. . . .

But then the *Act of Uniformity* depended long, and took up much Debate in Both Houses. In the House of Peers, where the Act first began, there were many Things inserted, which had not been contained in the former *Act of Uniformity*, and so seemed to carry somewhat of Novelty in them. It admitted "no Person to have any Cure of Souls or any Ecclesiastical Dignity in the Church of *England*, but such who had been or should be ordained Priest or Deacon by some Bishop, that is, who had not Episcopal Ordination; excepting only the Ministers or Pastors of the *French* and *Dutch* Churches in *London* and other Places, allowed by the King, who should enjoy the Privileges They had."

This was new; for there had been many and at present there were some, who possessed Benefices with Cure of Souls, and other Ecclesiastical Promotions, who had never received Orders but in *France* or in *Holland*; and these Men must now receive new Ordination, which had been always held unlawful in the Church, or by this Act of Parliament must be deprived of their Livelihood, which They enjoyed in the most flourishing and peaceable Times of the Church. . . .

To this it was answered, " . . . Rebaptization is not allowed in or by any Church: Yet in all Churches where it is doubted, as it may be often with very good Reason, whether the Person hath been baptized or no, or if it hath been baptized by a Midwife or lay Person; without determining the Validity or Invalidity of such Baptism, there is an hypothetical Form, *If thou hast not been already baptized, I do baptize,* &c. So in this Case of Ordination the Form may be the same, *If thou hast not been already ordained, then I do ordain*, &c. If his former Ordination were good, this is void; if the other was invalid or defective, He hath Reason to be glad that it be thus supplied." After much Debate, that Clause remained still in the Act: And very many, who had received Presbyterian Orders in the late Times, came very willingly to be ordained in the Manner aforesaid by a Bishop; and very few chose to quit or lose a Parsonage or Vicarage of any Value upon that Scruple.

There was another Clause in the Bill, that made very much more Noise afterwards, though for the present it took not up so much Time, and in Truth was little taken Notice of: That is, a Form of Subscription that every Man was to make, who had received, or before He received, any Benefice or Preferment in the Church; which comprehended all the Governours, Superiours and Fellows, in all the Colleges and Halls of either University, and all Schoolmasters and the like, who are subservient towards Learning. Every such Person was to declare "his unfeigned Assent and Consent to all and every Thing contained and prescribed in and by the Book, entitled *The Book of Common Prayer*, &c." The Subscription was generally thought so reasonable, that it scarce met with any Opposition in either House. But when it came abroad, and was to be submitted to, all the dissenting Brethren cried out, "that it was a Snare to catch them, to say that which could not consist with their Consciences." They took great Pains to distinguish and to make great Difference between *Assent* and *Consent*: "They could be content to read the Book in the Manner They were obliged to do, which shewed their Consent; but declaring their unfeigned Assent to every Thing contained and prescribed therein would imply, that They were so fully convinced in their Judgments, as to think that it was so perfect, that Nothing therein could be amended, which for their Part They thought there might. That there were many Expression in the *Rubrick*, which They were not bound to read; yet by this Assent They declared their Approbation thereof." But after many tedious Discourses of this tyrannical Imposition, They grew by Degrees ashamed of it; and were persuaded to think, that *Assent* and *Consent* had so near the same Signification, that They could hardly consent to do what They did not assent to: So that the chiefest amongst them, to avoid a very little Inconvenience, subscribed the same . . .

By this *Act of Uniformity* there was an End put to all the Liberty and License, which had been practised in all Churches from the Time of his Majesty's Return, and by his Declaration that He had emitted afterwards. The *Common Prayer* must now be constantly read in all Churches, and no other Form admitted: And what Clergyman soever did not fully conform to whatsoever was contained in that Book, or enjoined by the *Act of Uniformity*, by or before *St. Bartholomew-Day*,[8] which was about three Months after the Act was published; He was *ipso facto* deprived of his Benefice, or any other spiritual Promotion of which He stood possessed, and the Patron was to present another in his Place, as if He were dead: So that it was not in the King's Power to give any Dispensation to any Man, that could preserve him against the Penalty in the *Act of Uniformity*.

This Act was no sooner published (for I am willing to continue this Relation to the Execution of it, because there were some intervening Accidents that were not understood), than all the Presbyterian Ministers expressed their Disapprobation of it with all the Passion imaginable. They complained "that the King had violated his Promise made to them in his Declaration from *Breda*," which was urged with great Uningenuity, and without any Shadow of Right; for his Majesty had thereby referred the whole Settlement of all Things relating to

Religion, to the Wisdom of Parliament: and declared, "in the mean Time that Nobody should be punished or questioned, for continuing the Exercise of his Religion in the Way He had been accustomed to in the late Confusions."[9] And his Majesty had continued this Indulgence by his Declaration after his Return, and thereby fully complied with his Promise from *Breda*, which He should indeed have violated, if He had now refused to concur in the Settlement the Parliament had agreed upon, being in Truth no less obliged to concur with the Parliament in the Settlement that the Parliament should propose to him, than He was not to cause any Man to be punished for not obeying the former Laws, till a new Settlement should be made. But how evident soever this Truth is, They would not acknowledge it; but armed their Proselytes with confident Assertions, and unnatural Interpretations of the Words in the King's Declaration, as if the King were bound to grant Liberty of Conscience, whatever the Parliament should or should not desire, that is, to leave all Men to live according to their own Humours and Appetites, let what Laws soever be made to the contrary. They declared "that They could not with a good Conscience either subscribe the one or the other Declaration: They could not say that They did assent or consent in the first, nor declare in the second that there remained no Obligation from the *Covenant*;[10] and therefore that They were all resolved to quit their Livings, and to depend upon Providence for their Subsistence." . . .

The continued Address and Importunity of these Ministers, as *St. Bartholomew's* Day approached nearer, more disquieted the King. They enlarged with many Words "on the great Joy that They and all their Friends had received, from the Compassion his Majesty so graciously had expressed on their Behalf, which They would never forget, or forfeit by any undutiful Carriage." They confessed "that They found, upon Conference with their Friends who wished them well, and upon Perusal of the Act of Parliament, that it was not in his Majesty's Power to give them so much Protection against the Penalty of the Act of Parliament, as They had hoped, and as his great Goodness was inclined to give them. But that it would be an unspeakable Comfort to them, if his Majesty's Grace towards them were so manifested, that the People might discern that this extreme Rigour was not grateful to him, but that He could be well content if it were for some Time suspended; and therefore They were humble Suitors to him, that He would by his Letters to the Bishops, or by a Proclamation or an Act of Council, or any other Way his Majesty should think fit, publish his Desire that the Execution of the *Act of Uniformity*, as to all but the

Reading of the *Liturgy*, which They would conform to, might be suspended for three Months; and that He would take it well from the Bishops or any of the Patrons, who would so far comply with his Desire, as not to take any Advantage of those Clauses in the Statute, which gave them Authority to present as in a Vacancy. They doubted not there would be many, who would willingly submit to his Majesty's Pleasure: But whatever the Effect should be, They would pay the same humble Acknowledgements to his Majesty, as if it had produced all that They desired."

Whether his Majesty thought it would do them no Good, and therefor that it was no Matter if He granted it; or that He thought it no Prejudice to the Church, if the Act were suspended for three Months; or that He was willing to redeem himself from the present Importunity (an Infirmity He was too often guilty of): True it is, He did make them a positive Promise, "that He would do what They desired;" with which They were abundantly satisfied, and renewed their Encouragement to their Friends "to persevere to the End." And this Promise was solemnly given to them in the Presence of the General,[11] who was to solicit the King's Dispatch, that his Pleasure might be known in due Time. It was now the long Vacation, and few of the Council were then in Town, or of the Bishops, with whom his Majesty too late thought it necessary to confer, that such an Instrument might be prepared as was fit for the Affair. Hereupon the King told the Chancellor (who was not thought Friend enough to the *Presbyterians* to be sooner communicated with) all that had passed, what the Ministers had desired, and what He had promised; and bade him "to think of the best Way of doing it."

The Chancellor was one of those, who would have been glad that the Act had not been clogged with many of those Clauses, which He foresaw might produce some Inconveniences; but when it was passed, He thought it absolutely necessary to see Obedience paid to it without any Connivance: And therefore, as He had always dissuaded the King from giving so much Countenance to those Applications, which He always knew published more to be said than in Truth was ever spoken, and was the more troubled for this Progress They had made with the King; He told his Majesty, "that it was not in his Power to preserve those Men, who did not submit to do all that was to be done by the Act, from Deprivation. . . . The King demanded the Judgment of the Lawyers, "whether He could legally dispense with the Observation of the Act for three Months;" who answered, "that notwithstanding any Thing He could do in their Favour, the Patrons might present their Clerk as if the Incumbents were dead, upon their Not-performance of what They were enjoined." Upon the whole Matter the King was converted; and with great Bitterness against that People in general, and against the particular Persons whom He had always received too graciously, concluded that He would not do what was desired, and that the Connivance should not be given to any of them.

The Bishops departed full of Satisfaction with the King's Resolution, and as unsatisfied with their Friend the Chancellor's Inclination to gratify that People, not knowing the Engagement that was upon him. And this Jealousy produced a greater Coldness from some of them towards him, and a greater Resentment from him, who thought He had deserved better from their Function and their Persons, than was in a long Time, if ever, perfectly reconciled. Yet He never declined in the least Degree his Zeal for the Government of the Church, or the Interest of those Persons; nor thought They could be blamed for their Severity against those Ministers, who were surely the proudest Malefactors, and the most incapable of being gently treated, of any Men living. For if any of the Bishops used them kindly, and endeavoured to persuade them to Conformity, They reported "that They had been caressed and flattered by the Bishops, and offered great Preferments, which They had bravely refused to accept for the Preservation of a good Conscience;" And in Reports of this Kind, few of them ever observed any Rules of Ingenuity or Sincerity.

When They saw that They were to expect and undergo the worst, They agreed upon a Method to be observed by them in the leaving and parting with their Pulpits. And the last Sunday They were to preach, They endeavoured to infuse Murmur, Jealousy and Sedition into the Hearts of their several Auditories; and to prepare them "to expect and bear with Patience and Courage all the Persecutions which were like to follow, now the Light of the Gospel was so near being extinguished." And all those Sermons They called their Farewel Sermons, and caused them to be printed together, with every one of the Preachers Pictures before their Sermons; which in Truth contained all the Vanity and Ostentation with Reference to themselves, and all the Insinuations to Mutiny and Rebellion, that could be warily couched in Words which could not be brought within Penalty of Law, though their Meaning was well understood.

When the Time was expired, better Men were put into their Churches, though with much murmuring of some of their Parishes for a Time, increased by their loud Clamour, "that They had been betrayed by the King's Promise that They should have three Months longer Time," Which drew the like Clamour upon them by those who had hearkened to their Advice in continuing their Obstinacy in Confidence of a Dispensation; whereas otherwise They would have conformed, as very many of their Party did. And many of the other who were cozened by them, and so lost the Livings They had, made all the Haste They could to make themselves capable of getting others, by as full Subscriptions and Conformity as the *Act of Uniformity* required. And the greatest of them, after some Time, and after They found that the private Bounty and Donatives, which at first flowed in upon them in Compassion of their Sufferings and to keep up their Courages, every Day begun to slacken, and would in the End expire, subscribed to those very Declarations, which They had urged as the greatest Motives to their Nonconformity. And the Number was very small, and of very weak and inconsiderable Men, that continued refractory, and received no Charge in the Church: Though it may without Breach of Charity be believed, that many who did subscribe had the same Malignity to the Church, and to the Government of it; and it may be did more Harm, than if They had continued in their Inconformity.

The long Time spent in Both Houses upon the *Act of Uniformity* had made the Progress of all other publick Business much the slower; or rather, the Multitude of private Bills which depended there, (and with which former Parliaments had been very rarely troubled), and the Bitterness and Animosities which arose from thence, exceedingly disquieted and discomposed the House; every Man being so much concerned for the Interest of his Friends or Allies, that He was more solicitous for the Dispatch of those, than of any which related to the King and the Publick, which He knew would by a general Concurrence be all passed before the Session should be made;[12] whereas if the other should be deferred, the Session would quickly follow . . . and the Benefit of those Pretences would be lost, and with greater Difficulty be recovered in a succeeding Session. Then as those private Bills were for the particular Benefit and Advantage of some Persons, which engaged all their Friends to be very solicitous for their Dispatch; so for the most Part they were to the Loss and Damage of other Persons, who likewise called in Aid of all their Friends to prevent the Houses consent: And by this Means so many Factions were kindled in Both Houses, between those who drove on the Interest of their own or of their Relations, who mutually looked upon one another as Enemies, and against those who for Justice and the Dignity of Parliament would have rejected all or most of the Addresses of that Kind; that in most Debates which related to neither, the Custom of Contradiction, and the Aversion to Persons, very much disturbed and prolonged all Dispatch.

It cannot be denied, that after a civil War of so many Years, prosecuted with that Height of Malice and Revenge, so many Houses plundered and so many burned, in which the Evidences of many Estates were totally destroyed, and as many by the unskilful Providence of others, who in Order to preserve them had buried their Writings so unwarily under Ground, that they were taken up so defaced or rotted, that they could not be pleaded in any Court of Justice; many who had followed the King in the War, and so made themselves liable to those Penalties which the Parliament had prepared for them and subjected them to, had made many feigned Conveyances, with such Limitations and so absolutely (that no Trust might be discovered by those who had Power to avoid it) that they were indeed too absolute to be avoided by themselves, and their Estates become so much out of their own Disposal, that They could neither apply them to the Payment of their just Debts, or to the Provision for their Children: I say, there were many such Cases, which could be no other Way provided for but by an Act of Parliament, and to which an Act of Parliament without too much Severity and Rigour could not be denied. And against any of those there appeared none or very little Opposition to be made.

But the Example and Precedent of such drew with them a World of unreasonable Pretences; and They, who were not in a Condition to receive Relief in any Court of Justice, thought They had a Ground to appeal to Parliament. They who had been compelled, for raising the Money They were forced to pay for their Delinquency, to sell Land, and could not sell it but at a very low Value (for it was one Species of the Oppression of that Time, that when a powerful Man had an Aspect upon the Land of any Man who was to compound, and so in View like to sell it, no other Man would offer any Money for it, so that He was sure at last to have it upon his own Price); now all that monstrous Power was vanished, They who had made these unthrifty Bargains and Sales, though with all the Formalities of Law, by Fines and Recoveries and the like (which is all the Security that can be given upon a Purchase), especially if the Purchaser was of an ill Name, came with all imaginable Confidence to the Parliament, to have their Land restored to them. Every Man had raised an Equity in his own Imagination, that He thought ought to prevail against any Descent, Testament or Act of Law; and that whatever any Man had been brought to do, which common Reason would make manifest that He would never have done if He could have chosen, was Argument sufficient of such a Force, and ought to find Relief in Parliament, from the unbounded Equity They were Masters of and could dispense, whatever Formalities of Law had preceded or accompanied the Transaction. And whoever opposed those extravagant Notions, which sometimes deprived Men of the Benefit of the *Act of Oblivion*, was thought to be without Justice, or which to them was worse, to be without any Kindness to the King's Party. And without Question, upon those Motives or others as unreasonable, many Acts were passed of very ill Example, and which many Men were scandalized at in the present, and Posterity will more censure hereafter, when Infants who were then unborn shall find themselves disinherited of those Estates, which their Ancestors had carefully provided should descend to them; upon which Irregularities the King made Reflection when He made the Session.

Notes

EDWARD HYDE, First Earl of CLARENDON (1609-74), was a moderate constitutionalist throughout hs life. He became an M.P. in 1640 and opposed Charles I's extra-parliamentary taxation but supported the anglican establishment, and joined the King's forces in 1642, leaving England in 1645 with the Prince of Wales (later Charles II). He remained a faithful member of the court in exile in the 1650s, and was appointed Lord Chancellor in 1658. The Declaration of Breda reflected his beliefs. After the restoration, he would have preferred a greater degree of religious toleration than Parliament permitted, but, once the laws concerning religion had been passed, he insisted on their firm enforcement, and they came to be known in consequence as the Clarendon Code. He was effectively chief minister until 1667, when the second Anglo-Dutch war led to his downfall. He fled abroad to escape prosecution and died in exile. He had begun his *History of the Rebellion and Civil Wars in England* in 1646; this he completed abroad, adding later the *Life and Continuation* from which these extracts are taken.

1. I.e. the succession of bishops through a chain of lawful ordinations, reaching back to the apostles, one instance of the complex of the successive titles, 'Long and Dark,/Drawn from the Mouldy Rolls of *Noah's* Ark' (*Absalom and Achitophel*, 11. 301-2) on which English society was based.

2. A sum paid by a new tenant to keep the subsequent rent low.

3. A wrongful action, especially a failure of duty by an official.

4. Protestants who held that the church should be governed by presbyters or elders, not bishops; the predominant religious grouping in Scotland (see p. 73, n. 21).

5. Protestants who held that only adults should be baptised and admitted to

church membership (see p. 160, n. 6).

6. A pejorative name for the Friends who believed in the inner illumination of all believers.

7. Protestants who believed in the complete autonomy of the local congregation.

8. August 24, a singularly ill-chosen date, since it was the anniversary of the massacre of some 3,000 French protestants (Huguenots) in 1572.

9. A disingenuous reading of the Declaration of Breda which anticipated the passing of laws by Parliament 'for the full granting [of] indulgence'.

10. A solemn oath taken by the Convention of Estates, the Westminster Assembly and the House of Commons in 1643; under the Uniformity Act (1662) clergymen and others were required to declare it an unlawful oath and not therefore binding.

11. George Monck, duke of Albemarle (1608-70), whose forces secured the restoration of Charles II in 1660. He was a moderate presbyterian.

12. Concluded the parliamentary sitting.

2 From: *The History of the Royal Society of London, for the Improving of Natural Knowledge*

Thomas Sprat, 1667

From: The First Part

And now it is much to be wonder'd, that there was never yet such an Assembly erected, which might proceed, on some standing constitutions of Experimenting. There have, 'tis true, of late, in many parts of *Europe*, some Gentlemen met together, submitted to Common Laws, and form'd themselves into *Academies*. But it has been, for the most part, to a far different purpose: and most of them only aim'd at the smoothing of their Style, and the Language of their Country. Of these, the first arose in *Italy*; where they have since so much abounded, that there was scarce any one great City without one of these *combinations*. But that, which excell'd all the other, and kept itself longer untainted from the corruptions of speech, was the *French Academy* at *Paris*. This was compos'd of the noblest Authors of that Nation: and had for its *Founder*, the *Great Cardinal de Richelieu*:[1] who, amongst all his cares, whereby he establish'd, and enlarg'd that *Monarchy* so much, did often refresh himself by directing, and taking an account of their progress. And indeed in his own life, he found so great success of this Institution, that he saw the *French Tongue* abundantly purifi'd, and beginning to take place in the Western World, almost as much, as the *Greek* did of old, when it was the Language of Merchants, Souldiers, Courtiers, and Travellers. . . .

I hope now, it will not be thought a vain digression, if I step a little aside, to recommend the forming of such an *Assembly*, to the Gentlemen of our Nation. I know indeed, that the *English Genius* is not so airy, and discoursive, as that of some of our neighbors, but that we generally love to have Reason set out in plain, undeceiving expressions; as much, as they to have it deliver'd with colour, and beauty. And besides this, I understand well enough, that they have one great assistance, to the growth of Oratory, which to us is wanting: that is, that their Nobility live commonly close together in their Cities, and ours for the most part scattered in their Country Houses. For the same reason, why our streets are not so well built as theirs, will hold also, for their exceeding us in the Arts of Speech: They prefer the Pleasures

43

of the Town; we, those of the Field: whereas it is from the frequent conversations in Cities, that the Humour, and Wit, and Variety, and Elegance of Language, are chiefly to be fetch'd. But yet, notwithstanding these discouragements, I shall not stick to say, that such a project is now seasonable to be set on foot, and may make a great Reformation in the manner of our Speaking, and Writing. First, the thing itself is no way contemptible. For the purity of Speech, and greatness of Empire have in all Countries, still met together. The *Greeks* spoke best, when they were in their glory of conquest: The *Romans* made those times the Standard of their Wit, when they subdu'd, and gave Laws to the World: And from then, by degrees, they declin'd to corruption; as their valour, their prudence, and the honor of their Arms did decay: and at last did even meet the *Northern Nations* half way in *Barbarism*, a little before they were overrun by their *Armies*.

But besides, if we observe well the *English Language*; we shall find, that it seems at this time more then others, to require some such aid, to bring it to its last perfection. The Truth is, it has been hitherto a little too carelessly handled; and I think, has had less labor spent about its polishing, then it deserves. Till the time of *King Henry* the *Eighth*,[2] there was scarce any man regarded it, but *Chaucer*; and nothing was written in it, which one would be willing to read twice, but some of his *Poetry*. But then it began to raise it self a little, and to sound tolerably well. From that Age, down to the beginning of our late *Civil Wars*, it was still fashioning, and beautifying itself. In the Wars themselves (which is a time, wherein all Languages use, if ever, to increase by extraordinary degrees; for in such busie, and active times, there arise more new thoughts of men, which must be signifi'd, and varied by new expressions) then I say, it receiv'd many fantastical terms, which were introduc'd by our *Religious Sects*; and many outlandish phrases, which several *Writers*, and *Translators*, in that great hurry, brought in, and made free as they pleas'd, and with all it was inlarg'd by many sound, and necessary Forms, and Idioms, which it before wanted. And now, when mens minds are somewhat settled, their Passions allai'd, and the peace of our Country gives us the opportunity of such diversions: if some sober and judicious Men, would take the whole Mass of our Language into their hands, as they find it, and would set a mark on the ill Words; correct those, which are to be retain'd; admit, and establish the good; and make some emendations in the Accent, and Grammar: I dare pronounce, that our *Speech* would quickly arrive at as much plenty, as it is capable to receive; and at the greatest smoothness, which its derivation from the rough *German* will allow it.

Nor would I have this new *English Academy*, confin'd only to the weighing Words, and Letters: But there may be also greater Works found out for it. By many signs we may ghess, that the Wits of our Nation, are not inferior to any other; and that they have an excellent mixture of the Spirit of the *French*, and the *Spaniard*: and I am confident, that we only want a few more standing Examples, and a little more familiarity with the Antients, to excell all the Moderns. Now the best means, that can be devis'd to bring that about, is to settle a fixt, and *Impartial Court* of *Eloquence*; according to whose Censure, all Books, or Authors should either stand or fall. And above, all, there might be recommended to them one Principal Work, in which we are yet defective; and that is, the compiling of a *History* of our late *Civil Wars*. Of all the labors of mens Wit, and Industry, I scarce know any, that can be more useful to the World, then *Civil History*: if it were written, with that sincerity, and majesty, as it ought to be, as a faithful Idea of humane Actions. And it is observable, that almost in all civiliz'd Countries, it has been the last thing, that has come to perfection. I may now say, that the *English* can already shew many industrious, and worthy Pieces in this kind: But yet, I have some Prophetical imagination in my thoughts, that there is still behind, something Greater, then any we have yet seen, reserv'd for the Glory of this Age. One Reason of this my strong persuasion, is a comparison, that I make, between the condition of our *State*, and that of the *Romans*. They at first writ, in this way, not much better than our *Moncks:* onely Registring in an undigested manner, some few naked Breviaries of their Wars, and Leagues, and Acts, of their City Magistrates. And indeed they advanc'd forward by very slow degrees: For I remember, that *Tully*[3] somewhere complains, in these Words: *Historia nondum latinis literis illustrata.*[4] But it was in the peaceful reign of *Augustus*,[5] after the conclusion of thier long Civil Wars, that most of their perfect *Historians* appear'd. And it seems to me, that we may expect the same progress amongst us. There lye now ready in Bank, the most memorable Actions of Twenty years: a Subject of as great Dignity, and Variety, as ever pass'd under any Mans hands: the peace which we injoy, gives leisure and incouragement enough: The effects of such a Work would be wonderfully advantageous, to the safety of our Country, and to *His Majesties* Interest: for there can be no better means to preserve his Subjects in obedience for the future, than to give them a full view of the miseries, that attended rebellion. There are onely therefore wanting, for the finishing of so brave an undertaking, the united indeavors of some publick minds, who are conversant both in Letters and business: and if it were appointed to be the labor of one or two men to compose it, and of such an *Assembly*, to revise and correct it, it might certainly challenge all the Writings of past, or present Times. . . .

From: The Second Part

It was . . . some space after the end of the Civil Wars at *Oxford*, in *Dr. Wilkins*[6] his Lodgings, in *Wadham College*, which was then the place of Resort for Vertuous, and Learned Men, that the first meetings were made, which laid the foundation of all this that follow'd. The *University* had, at that time, many Members of its own, who had begun a *free way* of reasoning; and was also frequented by some *Gentlemen*, of Philosophical Minds, whom the misfortunes of the Kingdom, and the security and ease of a retirement amongst Gown-men, had drawn thither.

Their first purpose was no more, then onely the satisfaction of breathing a freer air, and of conversing in quiet one with another, without being ingag'd in the passions, and madness of that dismal Age. And from the Institution of that *Assembly*, it had been enough, if no other advantage had come, but this: That by this means there was a race of yong Men provided, against the next Age, whose minds receiving from them, their first Impressions of *sober* and *generous knowledge*, were invincibly arm'd against all the inchantments of *Enthu[s]iasme* . . . for such *spiritual Frensies*, which did then bear Rule, can never stand long, before a cleer, and a *deep skill* in *Nature*. It is almost impossible, that they, who converse much with the subtilty of *things*, should be deluded by such *thick deceits*. There is but one better charm in the world, then *Real Philosophy*, to allay the impulses of the *false spirit:* and that is, the blessed presence, and assistance of the *True*.

Nor were the good effects of this conversation, onely confin'd to *Oxford*: But they have made themselves known in their printed Works, both in our own, and in the learned Language: which have much conduc'd to the Fame of our Nation *abroad*, and to the spreading of profitable Light, *at home*. This I trust, will be universally acknowledg'd, when I shall have nam'd the Men. The principal, and most constant of them, were Doctor *Seth Ward*,[7] the present Lord Bishop of *Exeter*, Mr. *Boyl*,[8] Dr. *Wilkins*, Sir *William Petty*,[9] Mr. *Mathew Wren*,[10] Dr. *Wallis*,[11] Dr. *Goddard*,[12] Dr. *Willis*,[13] Dr. *Bathurst*,[14] Dr. *Christopher Wren*,[15] Mr. *Rook:*[16] besides several others, who joyn'd themselves to them, upon occasions. . . .

For such a candid, and unpassionate company, as that was, and for such a gloomy season, what could have been a fitter Subject to pitch upon, then *Natural Philosophy?* To have been always tossing about some *Theological question*, would have been, to have made that their private diversion, the excess of which they themselves dislik'd in the publick: To have been eternally musing on *Civil business*, and the distresses of their Country, was too melancholy a reflexion: It was *Nature* alone, which could pleasantly entertain them, in that estate. The contemplation of that, draws our minds off from past, or present misfortunes, and makes them conquerers over things, in the greatest publick unhappiness: while the consideration of *Men*, and *humane affairs*, may affect us, with a thousand various disquiets; *that* never separates us into mortal Factions; *that* gives us room to differ, without animosity; and permits us, to raise contrary imaginations upon it, without any danger of a *Civil War*.

Their *meetings* were as frequent, as their affairs permitted: their proceedings rather by action, then discourse; chiefly attending some particular Trials, in *Chymistry,* or *Mechanicks:* they had no Rules nor Method fix'd: their intention was more, to communicate to each other, their discoveries, which they could make in so narrow a compass, than an united, constant, or regular inquisition. And me thinks, their constitution did bear some resemblance, to the *Academy* lately begun at *Paris*: where they have at last turn'd their thoughts, from *Words*, to experimental *Philosophy*, and perhaps in imitation of the *Royal Society*. . . .

I come now to the Second Period of my Narration: wherein I promis'd, to give an account of what they did, till they were publickly own'd, incourag'd, and confirm'd by Royal Favor. And I trust, that I shall here produce many things, which will prove their attempts to be worthy of all Mens incouragement:though what was perform'd in this interval, may be rather styl'd the *Temporary Scaffold* about the building, then the *Frame itself*. . . .

I will here, in the first place, contract into few Worlds, the whole *summe* of their *Resolutions*; which I shall often have occasion, to touch upon in *parcels*. Their purpose is, in short, to make faithful *Records*, of all the Works of *Nature*, or *Art*, which can come within their reach: that so the present Age, and posterity, may be able to put a mark on the Errors, which have been strengthned by long prescription: to restore the Truths, that have lain neglected: to push on these, which are already known, to more various uses: and to make the way more passable, to what remains unreveal'd. This is the compas of their

Design. And to accomplish this, they have indeavor'd, to separate the knowledge of *Nature*, from the colours of *Rhetorick*, the devices of *Fancy* or the delightful deceit of *Fables*. They have labor'd to inlarge it, from being confin'd to the custody of a few; or from servitude to private interests. They have striven to preserve it from being over-press'd by a confus'd heap of vain, and useless particulars; or from being straitned and bounded too much up by General Doctrines. They have try'd, to put it into a condition of perpetual increasing; by settling an inviolable correspondence between the hand, and the brain. They have studi'd, to make it, not onely an Enterprise of one season, or of some lucky opportunity; but a business of time, a steddy, a lasting, a popular, an uninterrupted Work. They have attempted, to free it from the Artifice, and Humors, and Passions of Sects; to render it an Instrument, whereby Mankind may obtain a Dominion over *Things*, and not onely over one anothers *Judgements*. And lastly, they have begun to establish these Reformations in Philosophy, not so much, by any solemnity of Laws, or ostentation of Ceremonies; as by solid Practice, and examples: not, by a glorious pomp of Words; but by the silent, effectual, and unanswerable Arguments of real Productions. . . .

As for what belongs to the *Members* themselves, that are to constitute the *Society:* It is to be noted, that they have freely admitted Men of different Religions, Countries, and Professions of Life. This they were oblig'd to do, or else they would come far short of the the largeness of their own Declarations. For they openly profess, not to lay the Foundation of an *English, Scotish, Irish, Popish*, or *Protestant* Philosophy; but a Philosophy of *Mankind*.

That the *Church of England* ought not to be apprehensive, of this free converse of various Judgments, I shall afterwards manifest at large. For the present, I shall frankly assert; that our *Doctrine*, and *Discipline*, will be so far from receiving damage by it; that it were the best way to make them universally embrac'd, if they were oftner brought to be canvas'd amidst all sorts of dissenters. It is dishonorable, to pass a hard Censure on the Religions of all other Countries: It concerns them, to look to the reasonableness of their Faith; and it is sufficient for us, to be establish'd in the Truth of our own. But yet this comparison I may modestly make; that there is no one Profession, amidst the several denominations of Christians, that can be expos'd to the search and scrutiny of its adversaries, with so much safety as ours. So equal it is, above all others, to the general Reason of Mankind: such honorable security it provides, both for the liberty of Mens Minds, and for the peace of Government: that if some Mens conceptions were put in practice, that all wise Men should have two Religions; the one, a *publick*, for their conformity with the people; the other, a *private*, to be kept to their own Breasts: I am confident, that most considering Men, whatever their first were, would make ours their second, if they were well acquainted with it. Seeing therefore, our Church would be in so fair a probability of gaining very much, by a frequent contention, and incounter, with other Sects: It cannot be indanger'd by this Assembly; which proceeds no farther, then to an unprejudic'd mixture with them.

By their *naturalizing* Men of all Countries, they have laid the beginnings of many great advantages for the future. For by this means, they will be able, to settle a *constant Intelligence*, throughout all civil Nations; and make the *Royal Society* the general *Banck*, and Free-port of the World: A policy, which whether it would hold good, in the *Trade of England*, I know not: but sure it will in the *Philosophy*. We are to overcome the mysteries of all the Works of Nature; and not onely to prosecute such as are confin'd to one Kingdom, or beat upon one shore. . . .

By their admission of Men of all *professions*, these *two* Benefits arise: The *one*, that every *Art*, and every way of life already establish'd, may be secure of receiving no damage by their Counsels. A thing which all new Inventions ought carefully to consult. It is in vain, to declare against the profit of the most, in any change that we would make. We must not always deal with the violent current of popular passions; as they do with the furious *Eager*[17] in the *Severn:* Where the safest way is, to set the head of the Boat directly against its force. But here Men must follow the shore; wind about leisurably, and insinuate their useful alterations, by soft, and unperceivable degrees. From the neglect of this Prudence, we often see men of great Wit, to have been overborn by the multitude of their opposers; and to have found all their subtile projects too weak, for custom, and interest. While being a little too much heated with a love of their own fancies; they have rais'd to themselves more Enemies than they needed to have done; by defying at once, too many things in use. But here, this danger is very well prevented. For what suspicion can *Divinity, Law,* or *Physick*, or any other course of life have, that they shall be impair'd by these men's labours: when they themselves are as capable of sitting amongst them as any others? Have they not the same security that the whole Nation has for its lives and fortunes? of which this is esteem'd the Establishment, that men of all sorts, and qualities, give their voice in every law that is made in *Parliament*. But the other benefit is, that by this equal Balance of all

Professions, there will no one particular of them overweigh the other, or make the *Oracle* onely speak their *private* sence: which else it were impossible to avoid. It is natural to all Ranks of men, to have some one Darling, upon which their care is chiefly fix'd. If *Mechanicks* alone were to make a Philosophy, they would bring it all into their Shops; and force it wholly to consist of Springs and Wheels, and Weights: if *Physicians*, they would not depart farr from their Art; scarce any thing would be consider'd, besides the *Body* of *Man*, the *Causes, Signs*, and *Cures* of Diseases. So much is to be found in Men of all conditions, of that which is call'd *Pedantry* in Scholars: which is nothing else but an obstinate addiction, to the forms of some private life, and not regarding general things enough. This freedom therefore, which they use, in embracing all assistance, is most advantageous to them: which is the more remarkable, in that they diligently search out, and join to them, all extraordinary men, though but of ordinary Trades. And that they are likely to continue this comprehensive temper hereafter, I will shew by one Instance: and it is the recommendation which the *King* himself was pleased to make, of the judicious Author of *the Observations on the Bills of Mortality:* In whose Election, it was so farr from being a prejudice, that he was a Shop-keeper of *London*; that His Majesty gave this particular charge to His Society, that if they found any more such Tradesmen, they should be sure to admit them all, without any more ado. From hence it may be concluded, what is their inclination towards the manual Arts; by the carefull regard which their *Founder*, and *Patron*, has engag'd them to have, for all sorts of *Mechanick Artists.*

But, though the *Society* entertains very many men of *particular Professions*; yet the farr greater Number are *Gentlemen*, free, and unconfin'd. By the help of this, there was hopefull Provision made against *two corruptions* of Learning, which have been long complain'd of, but never remov'd: The *one*, that *Knowedge* still degenerates to consult *present profit* too soon; the *other*, that *Philosophers* have bin always *Masters, & Scholars*, some imposing, & all the other submitting; and not as equal observers without dependence. . . .

From: The Third Part

I will now proceed to the weightiest, and most solemn part of my whole *undertaking*; to make a defence of the *Royal Society*, and this new *Experimental Learning*, in respect of the *Christian Faith*. I am not ignorant, in what a slippery place I now stand; and what a tender

matter I am enter'd upon. I know that it is almost impossible without
offence, to speak of things of this Nature, in which all *Mankind*, each
Country, and now almost every *Family*, do so widely disagree among
themselves. I cannot expect that what I shall say will escape misinter-
pretation, though it be spoken with the greatest simplicity, and submission, while I behold that most men do rather value themselves, and
others, on the little differences of *Religion*, than the main substance
itself; and while the will of *God* is so variously distracted, that what
appears to be *Piety* to some *Christians*, is abhorr'd as the greatest
superstition, and heresy by others.

However to smooth my way as much as I can, and to prepare all our
several *Spiritual Interests*, to read this part with some tolerable *moderation*; I do here in the beginning most sincerely declare, that if this
design should in the least diminish the *Reverence*, that is due to the
Doctrine of Jesus Christ, it were so far from deserving *protection*,
that it ought to be abhorr'd by all the *Politic*, and *Prudent*; as well as
by the devout Part of Christendom. And this I profess, I think they
were bound to do, not only from a just dread of the *Being*, the
Worship, the *Omnipotence*, the *Love of God*, all which are to be held
in the highest veneration: but also out of a regard to the peace, and
prosperity of men. In matters that concern our *opinions* of another
World, the least alterations are of wonderful hazard: how mischievous
then would that enterprise be, whose effects would abolish the
command of Conscience, the belief of a *future life*; or any of those
Hevenly Doctrines, by which not only the *eternal condition* of men
is secur'd, but their *natural* Reason, and their *Temporal safety*
advanc'd? Whoever shall impiously attempt to subvert the Authority
of the *Divine Power*, on false pretences to better *Knowledge*, he will
unsettle the strongest foundations of our *hopes*; he will make a terrible
confusion in all the offices, and opinions of men: he will destroy the
most prevailing *Argument to virtu:* he will remove all *human Actions*,
from their firmest center: he will even deprive himself, of the prærogative of his *Immortal Soul*; and will have the same success, that the *Antient
Fables* make those to have had, who contended with their *Gods*, of
whom they report, that many were immediatly turn'd into *Beasts*.

With these apprehensions I come to examin the *Objections*, which I
am now to satisfy: and having calmly compar'd the *Arguments* of some
devout men against *Knowledge*, and chiefly that of *Experiments*; I
must pronounce them both, to be altogether inoffensive. I did before
affirm, that the *Royal Society* is abundantly cautious, not to intermeddle in *Spiritual things*: But that being only a general plea, and the

question not lying so much on what they do at present, as upon the probable effects of their Enterprise; I will bring it to the test through the chief Parts of *Christianity*; and shew that it will be found as much avers from *Atheism*, in its issue and consequences, as it was in its original purpose.

The public Declaration of the *Christian Religion*, is to propose to mankind, an infallible way to *Salvation*. Towards the performance of this happy end, besides the *Principles* of *Natural Religion*, which consists in the acknowledgement and Worship of a *Deity:* It has offer'd us the merits of a glorious *Saviour:* By him, and his *Apostles Ministry*, it has given us sufficient *Examples*, and *Doctrines* to acquaint us with *divine things*, and carry us to *Heven*. In every one of these, the *Experiments* of *Natural things*, do neither darken our eies, nor deceive our minds, nor deprave our hearts.

First there can be no just reason assign'd, why an *Experimenter* should be prone to deny the essence, and properties of *God*, the universal Sovereignty of his *Dominion*, and his *Providence* over the *Creation*. He has before him the very same argument, to confirm his judgment in all these; with which he himself is wont to be abundantly satisfy'd, when he meets with it in any of his *philosophical Inquiries*. In every thing that he tryes, he believes, that this is enough for him to rest on, if he finds, that not only his own, but the *universal Observations* of men of all times and places, without any mutual conspiracy have consented in the same *conclusion*. How can he then refrain from embracing this common *Truth*, which is witness'd by the unanimous approbation of all *Countries*, the agreement of *Nations*, and the secret acknowledgment of every mans breast?

'Tis true his *employment* is about *material things*. But this is so far from drawing him to oppose invisible *Beings*, that it rather puts his thoughts into an excellent good capacity to believe them. In every *work* of *Nature* that he handles, he knows that there is not only a gross substance, which presents itself to all men eies; but an infinit subtilty of *parts*, which come not into the sharpest sense. So that what the *Scripture* relates of the Purity of God, of the Spirituality of his *Nature*, and that of *Angels*, and the *Souls* of men, cannot seem incredible to him, when he perceives the numberless particles that move in every mans *Blood*, and the prodigious streams that continually flow unseen from every *Body:* Having found this, his own *senses* have been so far assisted by the *Instruments* of *Art*, he may sooner admit, that his mind ought to be rays'd higher, by a Hevenly light, in those things wherein his *senses* do fall short. If (as the *Apostle* says) the invisible things of *God* are manifested by the visible;[18] then how much stronger

Arguments has he for his belief, in the *eternal power*, and *Godhead*, from the vast number of Creatures, that are invisible to others, but are expos'd to his view by the help of his *Experiments?*

Thus he is præpar'd to admit a *Deity*, and to embrace the consequences of that concession. He is also from his *Experiments* as well furnish'd with *Arguments* to adore it: he has always before his eys the *beauty, contrivance*, and *order* of *Gods Works*: From hence, he will learn to serve him with all reverence, who in all that he has made, consulted *Ornament*, as well as *Use*.

From hence he will best understand the infinit distance between *himself*, and his *Creator*, when he finds that all things were produc'd by him: whereas he by all his study, can scarce imitate the least effects, nor hasten, or retard the common cours of *Nature*. This will teach him to *Worship* that *Wisdom*, by which all things are so easily sustain'd, when he has look'd more familiarly into them, and beheld the chances, and alterations, to which they are expos'd. Hence he will be led to admire the wonderful contrivance of the *Creation*; and so to apply, and direct his praises aright: which no doubt, when they are offer'd up to *Heven*, from the mouth of one, who has well studied what he commends, will be more sutable to the *Divine Nature*, than the blind applauses of the ignorant. This was the first service, that *Adam* perform'd to his *Creator*, when he obey'd him in mustring, and naming,[19] and looking into the *Nature* of all the *Creatures*. This had bin the only *Religion*, if men had continued innocent in *Paradise*, and had not wanted a *Redemption*. Of this the *Scripture* itself makes so much use, that if any devout man shall reject all *Natural Philosophy*, he may blot *Genesis*, and *Job*, and the *Psalms*, and some other Books, out of the *Canon* of the *Bible*. *God* never yet left himself without witness in the *World*: And it is observable, that he has commonly chosen the dark and ignorant *Ages*, wherein to work Miracles; but seldom or never the times when *Natural Knowledge* prevail'd: For he knew there was not so much need to make use of extraordinary signs, when men were diligent in the works of his hands, and attentive on the impressions of his footsteps in his *Creatures*.

It is almost a *proverbial* speech, *That the most* Learned Ages *are still the most* Atheistical, *and the* ignorant *most* devout. Whoever devis'd this distinction at first, the true *Piety* is little beholden to him for it: For insteed of obeying the *Jewish Law*, which forbids us to offer up to *God* a Sacrifice that has a Blemish, he has bestow'd the most excellent of all the Race of men on the Devil; and has only assign'd to *Religion* those *Men* and those *Times*, which have the greatest Blemish of *human Nature*, even a defect in their *Knowledge* and *Understanding*. . . .

But the chief part of our *Religion*, on which the certainty of all the rest depends, is the *Evangelical Doctrine* of *Salvation* by *Jesus Christ*. In this there is nothing, from which he that converses much with *Nature*, can be thought to be more avers than others; nay, to which he may not be concluded to be more inclinable, on this very account; seeing it has all bin prov'd to him his own way. Had not the appearance of *Christ* bin strengthen'd by undeniable signs of *almighty Power*, no age nor place had bin oblig'd to believe his Message. And these *Miracles* with which he asserted the *Truths* that he taught (if I might be allow'd this boldness in a matter so sacred) I would even venture to call *Divine Experiments* of his *Godhead*.

What then can there be in all this *Doctrine*, at which a Real and impartial *Inquirer* into *Natural Things*, should be offended? Does he demand a Testimony from *Heven*? he has it: He reads effects produc'd, that did exceed all mortal skill and force: And of this he himself is a better judge than others: For to understand aright what is *supernatural*, it is a good step first to *know* what is according to *Nature*.

Does he require that this should be testified, not by men of *Craft* or *Speculation*; but rather by men of *Honesty, Trades*, and *Business*? The *Apostles* were such. Will he not consent to any mans *Opinions*, unless he sees the *operations* of his hands agree with them? *Christ* himself requires no more of any of his *Followers:* For he commanded his *Disciples* not to believe him, but the *Works* that he did. Does he think that it is the most honorable Labor to study the benefit of Mankind? to help their infirmities? to supply their wants? to ease their burdens? He here may behold the whole *Doctrine* of *Future Happiness*, introduc'd by the same means; by feeding the Hungry; by curing the Lame, and by opening the eyes of the Blind.[20] All which may be call'd *Philosophical Works*, perform'd by an *Almighty hand*.

What then can hinder him from loving and admiring this *Saviour*, whose *Design* is so conformable to his own, but his *Ability* so much greater? What jealousie can he have of an imposture in this *Messias*? Who though his *Doctrine* was so pure and venerable, though his *Life* was so blameless, though he had the power of *Heaven* and *Earth* in his hands, though he knew the thoughts of men, and might have touch'd and mov'd them as he pleas'd; did yet not rely on his *Doctrine*, on his *Life*, on the irresistible assistance of *Angels*, or his own *Divinity* alone; but stoop'd to convince men by their *Senses*, and by the very same cours by which they receive all their *Natural Knowledge*.

The last *Doctrinal* part of our *Religion*, I shall mention, consists of those Doctrines which have been long since deduc'd by consequences from the *Scripture*, and are now setled in the Body of that *Divinity*, which was deliver'd down to us by the *Primitive Church*, and which the generality of *Christendom* embraces. It may here be suggested, that the sensible *knowledge* of *things* may in time abolish most of these, by insinuating into mens minds, that they cannot stand before the impartiality of *Philosophical Inquisitions*, But this surmise has no manner of foundation. These Superstructures are of two sorts: either those of which a man may have a cleer apprehension in his thoughts, upon a rational account, and which are intelligible to any ordinary Reader; or else such as exceed the common measures of our *Reason* and *Senses*. There will be no fear that an *Experimenter* should reject the first, seeing they may be conceiv'd by the meanest capacity, and have that stamp upon them, which he for the most part esteems the character of *Truth*, that they are vulgar. But now towards the consenting to the last, there is nothing better than to believe them in gross: And for this he is as well prepar'd as any other *Philosopher*. If we suppose him sufficiently convinc'd of the authority of the Deliverer (as I have already shown he may be) he cannot be suspected for disavowing his word, though never so mystical; or for resisting the voice of him, whose Arm he has found to be Omnipotent. This submission of his *judgment* he may make, notwithstanding the severity of his *Inquiries*: And the most subtil Speculative man in the world can do no more. After all his acute *Arguings* in *Divinity*, he can never render any one point, which is the proper object of *Faith*, to be plain, and equal, and expressible to our *Reason*. What good can he then do? seeing he is not able to make it any way fitter for our *Faith*, by all his *Transcendental Notions*, than it was before, on the bare account of the *wondrous Works* of the *Author*.

This is the place in which the *Peripatetic Philosophy*[21] has long triumph'd: But I canot imagine on what right. The spiritual and supernatural part of *Christianity* no *Philosophy* can reach: And in the plain things there is no need of any at all: So that it is excluded on both accounts. In some *Doctrines* it is useless, by reason of their sublimity; in others, because of their commoness. How small assistance it brings, may be seen in those very points, in which its Empire seems most to be plac'd, in *Gods Decrees*, his *Immateriality*, his *Eternity*, and the holy Mystery of the *Trinity*: In all which we are only brought into a more learned darkness by it; and in which unfathomable Depths a plain *Believing* is at last acknowledg'd by all to be our only Refuge. The truth is, notwithstanding the great stir they have made about *Religion*, if we had only follow'd their light, we had still worshipp'd the *Creator* and *Redeemer* of the *World*, under the same title by which their Prædecessors did formerly at *Athens*, as the *Unknown God*.[22]

This I have urg'd so far, because I am confident that the reducing of *Christianity* to one particular Sect of *Philosophy*, and confining it to that, is one of the most destructive Engines that ever was manag'd against it. Of this the Church of *Rome* for her share has already found the ill effects. And the danger is apparent: For by this means the benefit of *Religion* will become very narrow, seing where *Reason* takes place it will only convince them who are of the same opinions in *Philosophy* with those that convert them. And also (that which is worse) if ever by any fate of *Times*, or change of *Governments*, or succession of new *Arts*, that Sect shall chance to be quite broken, the *Doctrine* of *Christ*, relying upon it, were inevitably ruin'd, unless *God* were pleas'd to support it a supernatural way, or to restore it again by new *Miracles*. *Religion* ought not to be the subject of *Disputations:* It should not stand in need of any devices of *reason*: It should in this be like the Temporal Laws of all Countries, towards the obeying of which there is no need of *syllogisms* or *distinctions*; nothing else is necessary but a bare promulgation, a common apprehension, and sense enough to understand the Grammatical meaning of ordinary words. Nor ought *Philosophers* to regret this divorce: seing they have almost destroy'd themselves, by keeping *Christianity* so long under their guard: By fetching *Religion* out of the *Church*, and carrying it Captive into the *Schools*, they have made it suffer banishment from its proper place; and they have withal thereby very much corrupted the substance of their own *Knowledge*: They have done as the *Philistines* by seising on the *Ark*:[23] who by the same action, depriv'd the People of *God* of their *Religion*, and also brought a Plague amongst themselves.

Thus far I trust it will be confess'd, that *Experiments* are unblameable. But yet there is much more behind, of which many pious men are wont to express their jealousy. For though they shall be brought to allow, that all these *Doctrines*, which I have nam'd, may seem to remain safe amidst the studies of *Natural things*: yet they still whisper, that they may chance by degrees, to make the sincerity of devotion appear ridiculous, and to bring the strictness of holy life out of fashion: and that so they will silently, and by piece-meals, demolish *Religion*, which they dare not openly encounter. I will therefore next endeavor the removal of these scruples, though I sufficiently understand, that it is a very *difficult Work*, to confute such popular, and plausible errors, which have the pretence of the caus of *God* to confirm them.

The chief substance of Real, and Sober *Piety*, is contain'd in the devout observation of all those ways, whereby *God* has bin pleas'd to manifest his Will; and in a right separation of our minds from the lusts, and desires of the *World*. The most remarkable means, whereby he has made known his pleasure, are those, which have been fix'd, and reveal'd in his *Word*; or else the extraordinary signs of his Authority, and Command.

Concerning our acknowledgement of his *reveal'd Will* in the *Scripture*, I have already spoken. And our obedience to the later consists chiefly of two kinds: an humble submission to *Divine Prophecies*, and a careful observance of all *remarkable Providences*. In both which *Experimental Philosophy* may well be justify'd. It may perhaps correct some excesses, which are incident to them. But it declares no enmity against the things themselves.

The sum of the whole *Doctrine* of *Prophecies* is this, that the *Great Creator* of the World has the Prærogative of foreseeing, appointing, and prædicting all future Events: that he has often in former Ages made use of this power, by the Visions, and raptures of holy men inspir'd from above: that his *infinit Wisdom* has still the like ability to do the same: that whenever such prædictions are accompanied, with undeniable Testimonies of their being sent from *Heven*, they ought to be praefer'd before all *human Laws*.

The true Foundation of *Divine Prodigies*, is much of the same Nature with the other. It relyes on these suppositions, that all the Creatures are subject to *Gods Word*, by which they were made: that he can alter their *Courses*, exalt, or destroy their *Natures*, and move them to different ends from their own, according to his pleasure: that this he has often done heretofore: that still his Arm is not weaken'd, nor the same *omnipotence* diminish'd: that still he may change the wonted Law of the *Creation*, and dispose of the *Beings*, and *motions* of all things, without controul: and that when this is done, it is with a peculiar design of punishing, or rewarding, or forewarning mankind.

Notes

THOMAS SPRAT (1635-1713) was a close associate of the founding members of the Royal Society while a fellow of Wadham College, Oxford. He was a clergyman, and achieved ecclesiastical preferment in the 1660s for his royalist views. In 1684 he became Bishop of Rochester and was subsequently a member of James II's hated Ecclesiastical Commission. However, though he at first opposed the accession of William and Mary, he later assisted at their coronation.

1. Armand Jean du Plessy, Cardinal de Richelieu (1585-1642), first minister of Louis XIII of France.

2. Henry VIII (reigned 1509-47), initiator of the English reformation.

3. Marcus Tullius Cicero (106-43 BC), Roman orator.

4. 'History has not yet been illuminated by (or in) the Latin language.'

5. Gaius Octavius Caesar 'Augustus' 63 BC-14 AD), the first Roman Emperor and grand nephew and adopted son of Gaius Julius Caesar (100-44 BC), founder of the Roman Empire.

6. John Wilkins (1614-72), Warden of Wadham College, Oxford (1648-59), and subsequently Master of Trinity College, Cambridge, and Bishop of Chester: a tolerant man.

7. Seth Ward (1617-89), Bishop of Exeter (1662) and then of Salisbury (1667); a fervent opponent of dissenters.

8. Hon. Sir Robert Boyle (1627-91), celebrated chemist and fervent anglican.

9. Sir William Petty (1623-87), political economist, surveyor and inventor (see Introduction, p. 8).

10. Matthew Wren (1585-1667), Master of Peterhouse College, Cambridge (1625), and subsequently Bishop of Hereford (1634), Norwich (1635) and Ely (1638), a furious suppressor of dissenting protestant congregations.

11. John Wallis (1616-1703), distinguished mathematician.

12. Jonathan Goddard (1617?-75), Warden of Merton College, Oxford, 1651-60, and Professor of Physic at Gresham College, 1655-75, where the Royal Society was founded and incorporated in 1663.

13. Thomas Willis (1621-60), distinguished physician and Sedleian Professor of Natural Philosophy, Oxford; a very loyal anglican.

14. Ralph Bathurst (1620-1704), clergyman and physician, President of Trinity College, Oxford, 1663-1704; notable for his anglican and royalist sympathies during the interregnum.

15. Sir Christopher Wren (1632-1723), architect, Fellow of All Souls College, Oxford, 1653-61, Professor of Astronomy, Gresham College, 1657-61, Savilian Professor of Astronomy, Oxford, 1661-73.

16. Lawrence Rooke (1622-62), astronomer and close associate of Sir Robert Boyle.

17. A tidal wave of unusual height caused by the incoming tide in a narrowing estuary.

18. See 1 Corinthians 14:40.

19. Genesis 2:19, 20.

20. See Matthew 11:5.

21. The philosophy of Aristotle and of his followers, especially the medieval schoolmen. (see p. 216, n. 6.)

22. Acts 17:23

23. 1 Samuel 4:23.

3 From: *Angliae Notitia; or, the Present State of England: Together with Divers Reflections upon the Antient State Thereof*, Chapter 2

Edward Chamberlayne, 1670

England hath been possest by *five* several Nations, and coveted by many more, and no wonder so *fair* and *rich* a *Lady* should have many *Lovers*, it being a Country (as was said of the Tree in the midst of *Paradise*) *good for food, pleasant to the eyes, and to be desired;*[1] whereas the *High-lands* of *Scotland, Wales, Biscay, Switzerland,* and other like Countries, continue still in the possession of their *Aborigines,* of the first that laid claim unto them, none since judging it worth their pains to dispossess them.

The first Inhabitants of *England* are believed to be the *Britains,* descended from the *Gauls,* whose language was once almost the same; subdued afterward by the *Romans*: who, by reason of their troubles nearer home, were constrained to abandon this Country about 400 years after *Christ*: whereupon the *Picts* Inhabitants of *Scotland,* invading the *Britains,* they call to their aid the *Saxons*; who chasing away the *Picts,* soon made themselves Masters of the *Britains*: but these not able to endure the heavy yoke of the *Saxons,* after many Battels and Attempts to recover their lost Liberties and Country, retired, or were driven some of them into *Britan* in *France,*[2] from whence some think they first came; but most of them into the two utmost *Western barren,* and *mountainous* parts of this Countrey, called afterwards by the *Saxons Walishland,* instead of *Gaulishland.* . . .

The *Saxons* solely possest of all the best part of this *Isle,* were for a long time infested, and for some time almost subdued by the *Danes,* and afterwards wholly by the *Normans,* who drave not out the *Saxons,* but mixed with them; so that the *English blood* at this day is a *mixture* chiefly of *Norman* and *Saxon,* not without a *tincture* of *Danish, Romish* and *British* Blood.

The English according to several Matters and Parts of the Kingdom; are governed by several Laws, *viz. Common Law, Statute Law, Civil Law, Canon Law, Forest Law,* and *Martial Law*; besides particular Customs and *By-Laws.* . . .

The *Common Law* of *England* is the Common Customs of the King-dome, which have by length of time obtained the force of *Laws*: It is called *Lex non scripta*,[3] not but that we have them written in the old *Norman Dialect*,[4] which being no where vulgarly used, varies no more than the Latin but because it cannot be made by Charter or by Parlia-ment; for those are alwayes matters of *Record*; whereas Customs are onely matters of *Fact*; and are no where but in the *Memory of the People*: and of all Laws must be the best for the English: for the written Laws made in *England* by Kings or Privy-Councils, as *antiently*, or by Parliaments, as of *later times*; are imposed upon the Subject before any probation or trial whether they are beneficial to the Nation, or agreeable to the Nature of the People; but Customs bind not the People till they have been tried and approved time out of mind; during which time no inconvenience arising to hinder, those Customs became Laws; and therefore when our Parliaments have altered any Funda-mental points of our Common-Law, (as sometimes hath been done) those alterations have been by experience found so inconvenient, that the same Law by succeeding Parliaments hath soon been restored. This Common-Law is the Quintessence of the Customary Laws of the *Mercians*, prevailing before the Conquest in the Middle Counties of *England*, called the Kingdom of *Mercia*, and of the *Saxons* amongst the West and South parts, and of the *Danes* among the *East-Angles*, all first reduced into one body by King *Edward* the *Elder*[5] about the year 900; which for some time almost lost, were revived by the good King *Edward* the Confessor,[6] and by Posterity named his Laws. To these the Conquerour added some of the good Customs of *Normandy*, and then his Successor King *Edward* the first[7] having in his younger years given himself satisfaction in the glory of Arms, bent himself (like another *Justinian*)[8] to endow his Estate with divers notable Fundamental Laws, ever since practised in this Nation. The excellent conveniency and con-naturalness of the Common Law of *England* to the temper of English Men, is such, that the serious consideration thereof induced King *James*[9] in a Solemn Speech to prefer it as to this Nation, before the Law of *Moses*.

Where the *Common-Law* is silent, there we have excellent *Statute Laws* made by the several Kings of *England*, by and with the Advice and Consent of all the Lords Spiritual and Temporal, and with the Consent of all the Commons of *England*, by their Representatives in Parliament; whereunto the *English* easily submit, as made at their own earnest desire and request . . .

Lex Castrensis Anglicana, is that Law that dependeth upon the Kings

Will and Pleasure, or his Lieutenant in time of actual War; for although in time of Peace the King for the more equal temper of Laws towards all his Subjects, makes no Laws but by the consent of the Three Estates in Parliament: yet in times of War, by reason of great dangers arising suddenly and unexpectedly upon small occasions, he useth absolute Power, insomuch as his word goeth for a Law. Martial Law extends onely to Soldiers and Mariners, and is not to be put in practice in times of Peace, but only in times of War, and then and there where the Kings Army is on foot.

By the Kings Royal Charter granted to divers Cities of *England*, the Magistrates have a Power to make such Laws as may be beneficial for the Citizens, and not repugnant to the Laws of the Land; and these are binding only to the Inhabitants of the place, unless such Laws are for a general good, or against a general inconvenience; for then they bind Strangers.

Because Humane Laws can promote no other good, nor prevent any other evil but what is open to publick cognizance, it is very necessary for the Society of Mankind and it is the great Wisdom of God so to ordain, That by Religion a Tribunal should be erected in every mans soul, to make him eschew evil and do good, when no Humane Law can take notice of either.

Of all Religions in the World, antiently only the Jews worshipt the true God in the true manner.

The Jews Religion in process of time by Traditions and Superstitions much corrupted, was partly abrogated, and the rest reformed, refined, and sublimated by our Saviour Christ, and since called the *Christian Religion*, which was planted in *England*, *Tempore ut scimus* (saith *Gildas*) *Summo Tiberii Cæsaris*,[10] which by computation will fall to be 5 years before *St. Peter* came to *Rome*, and about 5 years after the death of Christ.

It is also affirmed by Antient and Modern Grave Authors expressly, That in the 12th year of the Emperour *Nero*, St. *Peter* preached here, baptized many, and ordained Bishops, Priests, and Deacons: That immediately after St. *Stephen*'s death and the Jews dispersion, *Joseph* of *Arimathea* with 12 others here preacht and died: That the first Fabrick of a Christian Church or Temple in all the World, was at *Glastenbury* in *Somerset-shire*, 31 years after Christs death: And that St. *Paul* was permitted to preach here, before he was suffered so to do at *Rome*. Afterwards *Anno* 180 the Christian Faith was here first professed by publick Authority under King *Lucius*[11] the first Christian King in the World; and with Christianity no doubt came in the Episcopal

Government, as may be seen in the Catalogue of *British Bishops*, and it is certain that at the Council of *Arles Anno* 347 there were three British Archbishops, *viz.* of *London, York*, and *Caerleon*; whereof the first had for his Province under him the *South*, the second all the *North*, and the third all beyond *Severn*, or the *West* part of this Island. Under these three Archbishops there were reckoned about that Age 28 Bishops, all which did observe the Customs and Orders of the Greek or Eastern Churches, and particularly that of *Easter* different from the Custom of the Latine or Western Churches: nor did they acknowledge *Rome* to be the Mother Church of the *Britannick* Church. *Britain* was then a Patriarchal Jurisdiction in substance,[12] though perhaps not in name, until about the year 596. When *Austin* the Monk[13] assisted by the fraud of 40 other Monks, and by the Power of the then Heathen *Anglo-Saxons* (who had long before driven the Britains into *Wales*) constrained the British Bishops to submit themselves to the Bishop of *Rome*, after which, by the Connivence or Concessions of the successive *Saxon* and *Norman* Kings, this Church was in some things subjected to the Bishop of *Rome* as its Patriarch or Primate; until *Henry* the Eighth[14] by his Royal Authority (as he and all other Kings might remove their Chancellours or other Officers, and dispose of their Offices to others) did remove the Primacy or Metropolitanship from the See of *Rome* to the See of *Canterbury*; as being far more agreeable to Civil Policy and Prudence; that such a high Power should be placed rather in a Subject of our own Nation than in a Soveraign Prince (for so is the Pope over several Territories in *Italy*) and he far remote beyond the Seas: Which ejection of the Popes Authority was not done, as in other Nations, by popular Fury and Faction, but by the mature deliberate Counsel of Godly and Learned Divines assembled in Convocation, with the express Authority of the King, and ratified by the Three States in Parliament.

The minds of English Christians thus delivered from the Spiritual Tyranny, and the Dignity of English Kings from the Spiritual Slavery of *Rome*, the King and Clergy took this occasion to reform the many abuses and errors crept into the Church in length of time by the great negligence and corruption of Governours; wherein the Wisdom of the English Reformers is to be admitted to all Posterity: which was briefly thus:

First, Care was taken lest that (as it oft happens in indiscreet Purges, and where ever the People only hath been the Reformer) the good should be taken away with the bad: It was therefore resolved not to separate farther from the Church of *Rome* in Doctrine or Discipline than that Church had separated from what she was in her purest Times.

For Doctrine they embraced that excellent Counsel of the Prophet, *State super vias antiquas & videte quænam sit via recta & ambulate in ea*;[15] they made a stand and took a view of the purest Primitive Christian Times, and thence saw which was the right way, and followed that. For the Discipline of this Reformed Church they considered what it was in the purest Times of the first good Christian Emperours, for the Times of Persecution (before Temporal Princes embraced the Christian Faith) as they were most excellent Times for Doctrine and Manners; so very improper and unfit for a Pattern or example of outward Government and Policy.

The Doctrine of the Church of *England* is contained in the 39 Articles of the Book of Homilies.

The Worship and Discipline is seen in the Liturgy and Book of Canons, by all which it will appear to impartial forreign eyes, that the Church of *England* may warrantably be said to be the most exact and perfect Patern of all the Reformed Churches in the World: and whosoever shall be so happy as to be a true Son of that Church, must confess that it is the most incorrupt, humble, innocent, learned, the most Primitive, most Decent; and Regular Church in *Christendome*; that her Doctrine is built upon the Prophets and Apostles, according to the explication of the Antient Fathers; the Government truly Apostolical, and in all essential parts thereof of Divine Institution; the Liturgy an extract of the best Primitive Forms; the Ceremonies few but necessary, and such as tend onely to Decency and increase of Piety: That she holds the whole truly Catholick Foundation according to the Scripture and the Four first General Councils,[16] that she adheres closely to Tradition truly Universal, that is, doth willingly receive *quod ab omnibus, quod ubique, quod semper receptum fuit*;[17] which is the Old Rule of Catholicisme: so that none can say more truly with *Tertullian*[18] than the English, *In ea regula incedimus quam Ecclesia ab Apostolis, Apostoli a Christo, Christus a Deo accepit*;[19] Search all the Religions in the World; none will be found more consonant to Gods Word for Doctrine, nor to the Primitive Examples for Government. None will be found that ascribes more to God, or that constitutes more firm Charity amongst Men; none will be found so excellent not only in the Community as Christian, but also in the special Notion as Reformed, for it keepeth the middle way between the Pomp of Superstitious Tyranny, and the meanness of Fanatick Anarchy.

In two Points the Church of *England* is truly Transcendent. First, It hath the Grand Mark of the true Church, which most *European* Churches seem to want, and that is Charity towards other Churches;

for it doth not so engross Heaven to its own Professors, as to damn all others to Hell. Secondly, It is the great glory of the English Protestant Church; that it never resisted Authority, nor engaged in Rebellion, a Praise that makes much to her advantage in the minds of all those who have read or heard of the dismal and devillish effects of the Holy League in *France*, by Papists,[20] of the holy Covenant in *Scotland* by Puritans,[21] and of the late Solemn League and Covenant in *England*[22] by Presbyterians.

As for the Scandal begotten by the late Troubles and Murder of the late King, which some of the *Romish* endeavour to throw upon the English Religion; it is sufficiently known, that not one person that was a known Favourer and Practiser of that Religion by Law establisht in *England*, was either a Beginner or active Prosecuter of that Rebellion, or any way an Abettor of that horrid Murther; for that our Religion neither gives such Rules, nor ever did set such Examples: nor indeed can that be truly said to be an Act either of the Parliament or People of *England*, but only of a few wretched Miscreants, Sons of *Belial*,[23] that had not the feare of God before their eyes.

About the year 1635 or 1636 the Church of *England*, as well as the State, seemed to be in her full Stature of Glory; shining in Transcendent Empyreal Lustre and Purity of Evangelical Truth: Her Religious Performances, Her Holy Offices, ordered and regulated agreeably to the expedient of such Sacred Actions; Her Discipline-Model suitable to the Apostolick Form; the Set and Suit of Her Holy Tribe[24] renowned for Piety and Learning; and all these in so Supereminent a Degree that no Church on this side the Apostolick can hardly or ever could compare with her in any one. And in this Felicity she might probably have continued, had she not been disturbed by a Generation of Hypocritical or at least blind Zealots; whose Predecessors in Queen *Elizabeth*'s[25] time began to oppose that excellent begun Reformation, and then to contrive the Alteration of Government; beginning first very low at Caps and Hoods, Surplices, and Episcopal Habits; but these flew higher, proceeding at length to the height of al Impiety; subverted even Liturgy, Episcopacy, and Monarchy it self: all which our Most Gracious King upon his Restauration hath most wisely and piously restored, after the example of that good King *Hezekiah*[26] *2.Chr. 29. 2, 3*. Since which we are able to render this joyful acount of the Religion and Church of *England*, *viz*. That there is nothing wanting in order to Salvation: We have the Word of God, the Faith of the Apostles, the Creeds of the Primitive Church, the Articles of the Four First General Councils, a Holy Liturgy, Excellent Prayers, Due Administration of the Sacraments, the Ten Commandements, the Sermons of Christ, and all the Precepts and Councels of the Gospel. We teach Faith and Repentance, and the Necessity of Good Works,[27] and strictly exact the severity of a Holy Life. We live in Obedience to God, ready to part with all for his Sake; we honour His Most Holy Name;[28] we worship Him at the mention of his Name; we confess his Attributes; we have Places, Times, Persons, and Revenues, consecrated and set apart for the Service and Worship of our Great God Creator of Heaven and Earth; we honour this Vicegerent the King, holding it damnable to use any other Weapons against him or his Army but Prayers and Tears:[29] we hold a charitable respect toward all Christians: we confess our sins to God and to our Brethren, whom we have offended, and to Gods Ministers the Priests, in Cases of Scandal or of a troubled Conscience; and they duly absolve the Penitent Soul. We have an uninterrupted succession of Reverend, Learned, and Pious Bishops,[30] who Ordain Priests and Deacons, Consecrate Churches, Confirm the Baptised at a due age, Bless the People, Intercede for them, Visit oft their respective Dioceses; taking Care of all the Churches, that they be served with as good and able Pastors as the small Maintenance can invite; they defend the Church Liberties, confer Institutions, inflict Ecclesiastical Censures, dispence in certain Cases, keep Hospitality, as St. *Paul* admonisheth,[31] and Preach as oft as necessity requireth. *Hodie enim neque Concionatorum paucitas uti olim, neque Infidelium multitudo hoc exigere videtur.*[32] For now neither that scarcity of Preachers as was amongst the Primitive Christians nor multitude of Heathens as dwelt among them doth seem to require it very oft.

Ever since the beginning of our Reformation, there are some few Families in several parts of *England*, have persisted in the Romish Religion, and are usually called *Papists* from *Papa*, the old usual Name of the Bishop of *Rome*. Against these there are divers severe Laws still in force, but their number being not considerable, nor their Loyalty of later years questionable, those Laws are more rarely put in execution: besides the Clemency and gentle usage shewn them here, begets in *Romish* States and Potentates abroad the like gentle treatment of their Protestant Subjects, and of the English, living within their Dominions.[33]

As for those other Perswasions whose Professors are commonly called *Presbyterians, Independents, Anabaptists, Quakers,*[34] *Fifth-Monarchy-Men,*[35] *Ranters,*[36] *Adamites,*[37] *Behmenists,*[38] *Family of Love,*[39] and the rest of those Mushromes of *Christianity*; as most of them sprang up suddenly in the late unhappy Night of Confusion, so it is to be presumed that they may in a short time vanish in this blessed Day of Order; and therefore not worthy to be described here as Religions professed

in *England*: for as the State of *England* doth account them no other
Members then the *Pudenda* of the Nation, and are ashamed of them,[40]
*Quippe ubi cætera Membra moventur ad arbitrium hominis, hæc sola
tam turbida, inordinata ac effrœnata sunt ut prœter & contra voluntatem
commoveri solent;*[41] so neither doth the Church of *England* look upon
those Professors as Sons but Bastards: or make account of any other
interest in them then a man makes of those Vermin which breed out of
his excrementitious sweat, or those *Ascarides*[42] which come sometimes
in his most uncleanly parts . . .

As some years before the late Troubles, no people of any Kingdom in
the World enjoyed more freedom from *Slavery* and *Taxes*, so generally
none were freer from evil tempers and humors: none more *devoutly
religious, willingly obedient to the Laws, truly loyal to the King, lov-
ingly hospitable to Neighbours, ambitiously civil to Strangers*, or more
liberally charitable to the Needy.

No Kingdom could shew a more *valiant prudent Nobility*, a more
learned and *pious Clergy*, or a more *contented loyal Commonalty*.

The *Men* were generally honest, the *Wives* and *Women* chast and
modest, *Parents loving, Children obedient, Husbands kind, Masters
gentle*, and *Servants faithful*.

In a word, the *English* were then according to their *Native Tempers*,
the best *Neighbours*, best *Friends*, best *Subjects*; and the best *Christians*
in the World.

Amongst these excellent *Tempers*, amongst this goodly *Wheat*, whilst
men slept, the Enemy came and sowed *Tares*,[43] there sprang up of later
years a sort of People *sowre sullen, suspitious, querulous, peevish,
envious, reserved, narrow-hearted, close-fisted, self-conceited, ignorant,
stiff necked Children of Belial* (according to the genuine signification
of the *word*) ever prone to *despise Dominion*, to *speak evil of Dignities*,
to *gain-say Order, Rule* and *Authority*, who have accounted it their
honour to contend with *Kings* and *Governors*, and to *disquiet* the peace
of *Kingdoms*: whom no *deserts*, no *clemency* could ever oblige, neither
Oaths or *Promises* bind, breathing nothing but *sedition* and *calumnies*
against the Establisht Government: *aspiring* without measure, *railing*
without reason, and making their own *wild fancies* the Square and Rule
of their *Consciences*; hating, despising, or disrespecting the *Nobility,
Gentry*, and *Superiour Clergy* &c.

These lurking in all quarters of *England*, had at length with their
pestilential breath infected some of the *worse natured* and *worse
nurtured Gentry*, divers of the *inferiour Clergy*, most of the *Tradesmen*,
and very many of the *Peasantry*, and prevailed so far, as not only to

spoil the best governed State, and ruin the purest and most flourishing Church in *Christendome*, but also to corrupt the *minds*, the *humors*, and very *natures* of so many English, that notwithstanding the late happy Restauration of the *King* and *Bishops*, the incessant joynt endeavours and studies of all our Governnours to reduce this people to their *pristine* happiness, yet no man now living can reasonably hope to see in his time the like blessed dayes again; without a transplantation of all those Sons of *Belial* (as King *James* in his grave Testament to his Son did intimate) without an utter extirpation of those Tares, which yet the Clemency and meekness of the Protestant Religion seems to forbid.

The *Nobility* and chief *Gentry* of *England* have been even by Strangers compared to the *finest Flowre*, but the lower sort of common People to the *coursest bran*; the innate good nature, joyned with the liberal education and converse with Strangers in forreign Countries, render those exceeding civil; whereas the wealth, insolence, and pride of these, and the rare converse with Strangers, have rendred them so distasteful, not only to the few Strangers who frequent *England*, but even to their own Gentry, that they could sometimes wish that either the Country were less plentifull, or that the Impositions were heavier; for by reason of the great abundance of *Flesh* and *Fish*, *Corn*, *Leather*, *Wooll*, *&c.* which the Soil of its own bounty with little labour doth produce, the *Yeomanry*[44] at their ease and almost forgetting labour, grow rich, and thereby so proud, insolent, and careless, that they neither give that humble respect and awful reverence which in other Kingdoms is usually given to *Nobility*; *Gentry*, and *Clergy*, nor are they so *industrious* or so *skilful* in *Manufactures* as some of our Neighbour Nations; so that in *England* it is no *Paradox* to affirm, that as too much *indigency* in the inferior sort of people doth *depress* the spirits and dull the minds of them, so too *plentiful* and *wanton* a fortune, causeth in them a *laziness* and *less industry*, that State commonly enjoying most *peace* and *order* and *happiness*, where either the *moderate barrenness* of the Countrey, or *want* of *ground*, or *multitude* of *Imposts* (as in *Holland*) do necessitate the common people to be industrious in their Callings, and so to mind their own, as not to disturb the State and Church affairs.

Moreover, of the *English* especially it hath been formerly and unhappily observed, that then it is *happiest* with them, when they are somewhat *pressed*, and in a *complaining* condition; according to that old Riming Verse,

Anglica gens est optima flens & pessima ridens.[45]

The *English* Common people anciently were, and at this day are very apt to hearken to *Prophesies*, and to create *Prodigies*; and then interpret them according to their own extravagant conceits: to invent and then maintain any the most prodigious Opinions and Tenets in Divinity: some of the inferiour sort of late holding abominable opinions, unworthy even of men and such as in no Age were ever broacht before.

The *English National vices* were antiently *Gluttony* and the effects thereof *Lasciviousness*, (when they made four Meals in a day and most excessive *Feasting*, with great plenty of *French Wine*) when Women of *professed incontinency* were permitted to proffer their Bodyes to all Comers, in certain places called *Stews* or *Stoves*, or *Bathing places*; because men were wont to *bath* themselves there (as still in other Countreyes) before they adrest themselves to *venereous acts*. Moreover *Pride* in *Apparel*, wherein they were antiently so extravagant and foolish, so superfluous and obscene, that divers *Statutes* before our *Reformation* in *Religion*, and *Homilies* since, have been made against that Excess, and an English Man was wont to be pictured naked with a pair of *Taylors Sheers* in his hand; and a piece of Cloth under his arme, with Verses annext, intimating, that he knew not what fashion of Clothes to have.

Excess of drinking was anciently more rare in *England*, as appears by an old Poet.

> *Ecce Britannorum mos est laudabilis iste*
> *Ut bibat arbitrio pocula quisque suo.*[46]

The *Danes* in the time of King *Edgar*[47] first brought it in, but it was afterward banisht hence, so that we find no ancient Statute since the Conquest against it; for though the Statutes heretofore made against Excess in *Apparel* and *Dyet* are ancient, yet those against *Drunkenness* are but of late date.

As the *English* returning from the Wars in the *Holy Land*, brought home the foul disease of *Leprosie*, now almost extinct here, though not yet in our neighbouring Countries: so in our Fathers days the *English* returning from the service in the *Neatherlands*,[48] brought with them the foul Vice of *Drunkenness*, as besides other Testimonies the Term of *Carous*, from *Gar anz*, *All out*, learnt of the *High Dutch* there in the same service; so *Quaffe*, &c. This Vice of late was more, though at present so much, that some persons, and those of quality may not safely be visited in an afternoon, without running the hazard of excessive drinking of *Healths* (whereby in a short time twice as much liquor is consumed as by the *Dutch*, who sip and prate) and in some places it is esteemed a piece of wit to make a man drunk; for which purpose some *swilling insipid Trencher-Buffoon* is alwayes at hand.

However it may be truly affirmed that at present there is generally less Excess in *Drinking* (especially about *London*, since the use of *Coffee*) less excess in *Dyet*, but principally in *Apparrel* than heretofore; insomuch that the poor Tradesman is much pincht thereby; for as it is expedient for the benifit of the whole Common-wealth, that divers *unnecessary* and *superfluous* Commodities should be allowed; as *Tobacco*, *Coffee*, *Spices*, *Sugars*, *Raisins*, *Silks*, *Fine Linnen*, *&c.* so some less hurtful excesses (as in *Apparrel*, *Diet*, *Building*, *Coaches*, *Lacqueys*, *&c.*) must either be connived at, or much of all the money of the Nation must lie dead and unimployed (as it now doth in the *private, sullen, niggardly Non-Conformists* hand[49]) and Tradesmen must either starve or be sustained by Almes . . .

The English according to the *Climate*,[50] are of a *middle temper*. The *No[r]thern Saturnine*, and the *Southern Mercurial temper* meeting in their Constitutions, render them so *genious* and *active*, yet *solid* and *persevering*, which nourisht under a sutable liberty, inspires a courage *generous* and *lasting*.

Their *Ingenuity* will not allow them to be excellent at the *Cheat*, but subject in that point rather to take than give, and supposing others as open-hearted as themselves, are many times in Treaties overmatcht by them, whom they overmatcht in *Arms* and *true Valour*: which hath been very eminent in all ages, and almost in all Lands and Seas too of the whole world.

The *English* since the Reformation are so much given to Literature, that all sorts are generally the most knowing people in the World. They have been so much addicted to writing, and especially in their own Language, and with so much licence or connivence, that according to the observation of a Learned Man, there have been during our late Troubles and Confusions *more good* and *more bad Books* printed and published in the English Tongue, than in all the vulgar Languages of *Europe*.

For solidity of Matter, for elegancy of Style in their *Sermons*, *Comedies*, *Romances*, as also in their Books of *Philosophy*, *Physick*, *History*, and all other solid Learning, no Nation hath surpassed the English, and few equalled them.

The English, especially the *Gentry*, are so much given to *Prodigality* and *Slothfulness*, that Estates are oftner *spent* and *sold* than in any other Countrey: They think it a piece of frugality beneath a Gentleman to *bargain* before-hand, or to *count* afterward, for what they eat in any place, though the rate be most *unreasonable*; whereby it comes to pass, that *Cooks*, *Vintners*, *Inn-keepers*, and such mean fellows enrich themselves, and begger and insult over the Gentry. In a word, by *their prodigality* it comes to pass, that not only those, but *Taylors*, *Dancing-Masters*, and such *Trifling Fellows*, arrive to that riches and pride as to ride in their *Coaches*, keep their Summer-Houses, to be served in Plate, &c. an insolence insupportable in other well-governed Nations.

Because the several *punishments* inflicted for several Crimes are different in most Countryes, and those of *England* much different from those of all other Countreys; a brief account of them may probably not be unacceptable to Forreigners especially.

All Crimes in *England* that touch the life of a Man, are either *High-Treason*, *Petit-Treason*, or *Felony*. Although some *High-Treasons* are much more heinous and odious than others; yet the punishment by Law is the same for all sorts (except for Coyning of Money) and that is that the Traitor laid upon a Hurdle or Sledge be drawn to the Gallows, there hanged by the Neck, presently cut down alive, his entrails to be suddenly pulled out of his Belly and burnt before the face of the Criminal, than his Head to be cut off, his Body to be divided into 4 parts; and lastly, that the Head and Body be hung up or impaled where the King shall command.

Besides all this, he shall forfeit all his Lands and Goods whatsoever, his Wife shall lose her Dower, his Children their Nobility, and all their Right of Inheriting him or any other Ancestor: Our Law thinking it most reasonable, that he who endeavoured to destroy the King, the Breath of our Nostrils, and thereby to rend the Majesty of Government, his Body, Lands, Goods, and Posterity, should be rent torn and destroyed. For Coining of Money, though adjudged *High-Treason*, the Punishment having been onely drawing and hanging before the Statute of 25 *Ed.* 3. it remains so still.

Petit-Treason is either when a Servant killeth his Master or Mistriss, or a Wife killeth her Husband, or a Clergy-man his Prelate, to whom he oweth obedience; and for this Crime the Punishment is to be drawn (as before) and to be hanged by the Neck till he be dead. The punishment for a Woman convicted of *High-Treason* or *Petit-Treason*, is all one; and that is to be drawn and burnt alive . . .

For *Petit Larceny* or *Smal Theft*, that is of the value of $12.d^{st}$ or under, the punishment antiently was sometimes by loss of an Ear, sometimes by Cudgeling, but since *Edw.* 3. onely by Whipping; but if such *Petit Thief* be found by the Jury to have fled for the same, he forfeiteth all his Goods.

Perjury, by bearing false witness upon Oath, is punisht with the Pillory called *Collistrigium*, burnt in the Fore-head with a *P*. his Trees growing upon his Ground to be rooted up, and his Goods confiscated.

Forgery, *Cheating*, *Libelling*, *False Weights* and *Measures*, *Forestalling the Market*, *Offences* in *Baking* and *Brewing*, are commonly punished with standing in the Pillory, and sometimes to have one or both Ears naled to the Pillory, and cut off, or there bored through the Tongue with a hot Iron ...

The Punishment of *Petit Jurors*[52] attainted of giving a Verdict contrary to Evidence wittingly is severe and terrible; they are condemned to lose the Franchise or Freedom of the Law, that is, become infamous and of no credit, uncapable of being a Witness or of a Jury; their Houses, Lands, and Goods shall be seised into the Kings hands, their Houses pulled down, their Meadows ploughed up, their Trees rooted up, and their Lands layd waste, and their Bodies imprisoned.

The like Punishment is also for those who shall conspire to indict an Innocent falsely and maliciously of *Felony*.

Any Man or Woman convicted, in the Bishops *Court* of *Heresie*, is to be delivered over to the Secular Power, and to be burnt alive.

Felo de se, that is one who wittingly killeth himself; is to be buried out of *Christian* Burial with a Stake driven thorow the Corps, and to forfeit his Goods.

Drunkards, Vagabonds, &c. are punished by setting their Legs in the Stocks for certain hours.

Scolding Women are to be placed in a *Trebuchet*, commonly called a *Cucking stool*, placed over some deep water, into which they are let down and plunged under water thrice, to cool their choler and heat.

Other Misdemeanors are commonly punisht with Imprisonment or Fines, and sometimes with both.

Notes

EDWARD CHAMBERLAYNE (1616-1703) was an deeply conservative royalist. He spent the years between 1642 and the restoration abroad. A founding member of the Royal Society, he was appointed tutor to one of Charles II's illegitimate sons, and subsequently to Prince George of Denmark, husband of the Duke of York's second daughter, Anne, who succeeded to the throne on the death of William of Orange in 1702. *Angliæ Notitia*, with additions, sometimes by other hands, was published in twenty editions from 1669 until 1702, and thereafter, as

Magnæ Britanniæ Notitia, or the Present State of Great Britain, until 1755. As an apparently authoritative work of reference, its political and social bias was offensive to many of different views.

1. Genesis 2:17; 3:6. These are singularly inept scriptural references.
2. Brittany.
3. 'unwritten law'.
4. Norman French was abolished as the official legal language in England by Cromwell in 1650, but was revived after the restoration, being finally abolished in 1731.
5. Edward the Elder (reigned 899-924); son of Alfred the Great.
6. Edward the Confessor (reigned 1042-66). All claims to the throne of England after his reign derive from his choice of William, Duke of Normandy, as his successor, and the latter's victory over King Harold, at the battle of Hastings in 1066. Royalists held this victory to be an expression of the divine will; their opponents argued that the conquest had initiated an unEnglish tyranny which they described as 'the Norman yoke'.
7. Edward I (reigned 1272-1307).
8. Justinian I (reigned 529-65); Byzantine emperor celebrated for his codification of roman law.
9. James VI of Scotland (reigned 1567-1625) and I of England (reigned 1603-25).
10. 'at the end, as we know, of the reign of Tiberius Caesar.' The quotation is from *The Overthrow and Conquest of Britain (De excudio et conquestu Britanniae)* by St Gildas (500?-70), the first known work of English history (see p. 238, n. i). Tiberius died in AD 37. The story has no foundation.
11. See *The Ecclesiastical History of the English People (Historia Ecclesiastica gentis Anglorum)*, I, v, by St Bede the Venerable (d. 735).
12. I.e. as independent as the patriarchate of Constantinople.
13. St Augustine of Canterbury (d. 604?), sent by Pope St Gregory the Great (reigned 590-604) to convert the English.
14. See p. 58, n. 2.
15. 'Stand ye in the ways, and see, and ask for the old paths where is the good way and walk therein.' Job 6:16.
16. The Councils of Nicaea (325), Constantinople (381), Ephesus (435) and Chalcedon (451) which sought to resolve disputes about the divine and human natures of Christ. (See pp. 112-13, nn. 35, 36, 40, 51-4.)
17. 'that which has been accepted by everyone, everywhere and at all times.'
18. Tertullian (155?-220?), early Christian theologian.
19. 'We go according to the rule which the church has received from the apostles, the apostles from Christ and Christ from God.'
20. A party of militant catholic aristocrats, formed in 1576 and led by Henry Duke of Guise, head of the House of Lorraine, against the concessions granted by King Henry III of France to the Huguenots. The League moved inexorably towards a constitutionally revolutionary position in its efforts to prevent the French crown passing to Henry of Navarre, at the time a protestant, who was later to reign as Henry IV of France, and was Charles II's maternal grandfather. As master of Paris, the Duke of Guise appealed to the mob over the head of the King. Henry III had him assassinated in 1588, together with his brother, the Cardinal of Lorraine, but was himself assassinated a year later by a fanatical Jacobin friar, Jacques Clément. The League then proclaimed Charles, Cardinal of Bourbon, Henry III's successor, but he died in 1590. Paris held out against Henry of Navarre until his conversion to catholicism in 1693. These events were

thought to parallel the constitutional crises in England from 1640 to 1685.

21. Scottish presbyterians who subscribed to a National Covenant in 1638.

22. See p. 42, n. 10.

23. Literally 'not profitable', 'wicked'. The word is used generally in the Old Testament, in phrases such as 'son of' and 'daughter of', to designate a wicked, sometimes subversive character (Deuteronomy 13:13, Judges 19:22, etc.). In restoration England it was frequently applied to anti-royalist radicals (see *Absalom and Achitophel*, *l*.598).

24. The anglican priesthood; the Levites were the priestly tribe of Israel.

25. Elizabeth I (reigned 1558-1603).

26. Hezekiah, King of Judah (reigned 715-687 BC), who purified the religion of his kingdom and to whom some of the ritual in the Second Temple is attributed in the passage from Chronicles cited here.

27. An insistence on the necessity of good works reflecting Chamberlayne's high church views. Antinomian theories of grace, according to which election or faith, irrespective of human efforts to live righteously, was alone efficacious in securing salvation, were justifiably thought to be politically subversive.

28. A reference to the practice of bowing at the name of Jesus, which strict protestants found very offensive.

29. A classic affirmation of the anglican doctrine that Christians were forbidden to resist sovereign authority.

30. See p. 41, n. 1.

31. Hebrews 13:2.

32. 'Indeed today neither scarcity of preachers as formerly, nor a great number of unbelievers, seem to require this.'

33. See Bethel's reply, p. 134.

34. See pp. 41-2, nn. 4-7.

35. A radical sect which anticipated the imminent establishment of 'the fifth monarchy', i.e. the rule of Christ.

36. Successors to the Levellers who taught an extreme form of antinomianism (see n. 27).

37. A fundamentalist sect practising nudity and free love.

38. Disciples of the protestant mystic Jacob Boehme (1575-1624); they later merged with the quakers.

39. A group with affinities with the quakers.

40. See Bethel's protest, p. 134.

41. 'To be sure, where other parts of the body are moved by man's free will, these alone are so disturbed, disordered, and unbridled that they are commonly put into violent motion independently of, or against our will.' Propaganda against dissenters – in Dryden's *Mr Limberham, or The Kind Keeper* (1680), for example – frequently associated religious fervour with sexual excitement. Swift further develops the idea in *The Tale of a Tub*.

42. Intestinal worms.

43. Matthew 13:24-30.

44. A view very different from Baxter's account of the lot of the tenant farmer (pp. 224ff).

45. 'The English populace is best when it weeps and worst when it laughs.'

46. 'A praisworthy custom of the British is that every man drinks as much as he chooses.'

47. Possibly Edgar, King of Mercia and Northumbria (reigned 957-75), but his reign was peaceful.

48. A reference to the involvement of English forces in the struggle in the Low Countries for independence from Spain during the reign of Elizabeth I. This was

perceived then and later as the sign of a genuinely protestant foreign policy.

49. A common charge against dissenters (see p. 138, n. 5).

50. A commonplace rehearsal of the theory that national character resulted from the influence of the climate. Temple begins his Essay with speculations on this topic. See also Dryden, *The Medall*, *ll*.248-9.

51. 12 pence.

52. Members of a trial jury. Grand juries sent an accused prisoner for trial. Juries were usually under the control of sheriffs in the seventeenth century, so that control of local government often meant control over local justice. Whig and tory sheriffs frequently secured the return of perverse verdicts in the 1670s and the 1680s and judges as frequently sought to browbeat juries.

4

From: *The Rehearsal Transpos'd: or, Animadversions Upon a late Book, Intituled, A Preface Shewing What Grounds there are of Fears and Jealousies of Popery*

Andrew Marvell, 1672

The grand Thesis upon which he[1] stakes not onely all his own Divinity and Policy, his Reputation, Preferment and Conscience, of most of which he hath no reason to be prodigal; but even the Crowns and Fate of Princes, and the Liberties, Lives and Estates, and, which is more, the Consciences of their Subjects, which are too valuable to be trusted in his disposal, is this, pag. 10. *That it is absolutely necessary to the peace and government of the World, that the supream Magistrate of every Commonwealth should be vested with a Power to govern and conduct the Consciences of Subjects in affairs of Religion.* And . . . P. 92 . . . he determines *Christian Liberty* to be *founded upon the Reasonableness of this Principle.* P. 308. *In cases and disputes of Publick concernment, Private men are not properly* sui Juris,[2] *They have no power over their own actions. they are not to be directed by their own judgments, or determined by their own wills, but by the commands and determinations of the publick Conscience; and if there be any sin in the Command, he that imposed it shall answer for it, and not I whose whole duty it is to obey. The Commands of Authority will warrant my Obedience, my Obedience will hallow, or at least excuse my action, and so secure me from sin, if not from error: and in all doubtful and disputable cases, 'tis better to err with Authority than to be in the right against it: not only because the danger of a little error (and so it is if it be disputable) is outweighed by the importance of the great duty of Obedience, &c.*
   Another of his Corollaries is, *That God hath appointed* (p. 80) *the Magistrates to be his Trustees upon Earth, and his Officials to act and determine in Moral Virtues and Pious Devotions according to all accidents and emergencies of affairs: to assign new particulars of the Divine Laws to declare new bounds of right and wrong, which the Law of God neither doth nor can limit.* P. 69. *Moral Virtue being the most material and useful part of all Religion, is also the utmost end of all its other duties.* P. 76. *All Religion must of necessity be resolved into Enthusiasm*

*or Morality. The former is meer Imposture; and therefore all that is true
must be reduced to the latter.* Having thus enabled the Prince, dispensed
with Conscience, and fitted up a Moral Religion for that Conscience; to
show how much those Moral Virtues are to be valued, P. 53. of the
Preface to his *Ecclesiastical Policy* he affirms, that *'tis absolutely necessary to the peace and happiness of Kingdoms, that there be set up a
more severe Government over Mens Consciences and Religious Perswasions, than over their Vices and Immoralities.* And, pag. 55. of the
same, that *Princes may with less hazard give liberty to mens Vices and
Debaucheries than their Consciences.* But for what belongs particularly
to the use of their Power in Religion; he first (p. 56. of his Book) saith,
that *the Protestant Reformation hath not been able to resettle Princes
in their full and natural rights in reference to its concerns:* & 58. *most
Protestant Princes have been frighted, not to say hector'd out of the
exercise of their Ecclesiastical jurisdiction.* P. 271. *If Princes will be
resolute (and if they wil govern so they must be) they may easily make
the most stuborn Conscience bend to their resolutions.* P. 221. *Princes
must be sure to bind on at first their Ecclesiastical Laws with the straitest
knot, and afterward keep them in force by the severity of their execution.* 223 speaking of honest and well meaning men: *So easy is it for
men to deserve to be punished for their Consciences, that there is no
Nation in the World, in which were Government rightly understood and
duly managed, mistakes and abuses of Religion would not supply the
Galleys with vastly greater numbers than Villany.* Pag. 54. of the Preface
to Ecclesiast. Policy. *Of all Villains the well-meaning Zealot is the most
dangerous.* P. 49. *The Fanatick-Party in Country Towns and Villages
ariseth not (to speak within compass) above the proportion of one to
twenty. Whilst the publick peace and settlement is so unluckily defeated
by quarrels and mutinies of Religion, to erect and create new Trading
Combinations, is only to build so many Nests of Faction and Sedition,
&c. For it is notorious that there is not any sort of people so inclinable
to seditious practices as the Trading part of a Nation.* And now though
many as material passages might be heap'd up out of his Book on all
these and other as tender Subjects, I shall conclude this imperfect
enumeration with one Corollary more to which indeed his grand Thesis
and all the superstructures are subordinate and accommodated. P. 166.
*Princes cannot pluck a pin out of the Church, but the State immediately
shakes and totters.* This is the *Syntagm*[3] of Mr. *Bayes* his Divinity, and
System of his Policy: . . .

And here, for brevity and distinction sake, I must make use of the
same priviledge by which I call him Mr. *Bayes*, to denominate also his

several Aphorisms or Hypotheses: and let him take care whether or no they be significant.

First, The *Unlimited Magistrate*.

Secondly, *The Publick Conscience*.

Thirdly, *Moral Grace*.

Fourthly, *Debauchery Tolerated*.

Fifthly, *Persecution recommended*.

And lastly, *Pushpin-Divinity*. . . .

As for his first Hypothesis of the *Unlimited Magistrate*, I must for this once do him right, that after I had read in his 12th page, that *Princes have power to bind their Subjects to that Religion they apprehend most advantagious to publick Peace and Tranquillity*; a long time after, not as I remember till pag. 82. when he bethought himself better, he saith, *No Rites nor Ceremonies can be esteemed unlawful in the Worship of God, unless they tend to debauch men either in their practices or their conceptions of the Deity*. But no man is in Ingenuity obliged to do him that service for the future; neither yet doth that limitation bind up or interpret what he before so loosly affirmed. However, take all along the Power of the Magistrate as he hath stated it; I am confident if Bishop *Bramhall*[4] were alive (who could no more forbear *Grotius*,[5] than Mr. *Bayes* could the Bishop, notwithstanding their friendship) he would bestow the same Censure upon him that he doth upon *Grotius*, p. 18. *When I read his Book of the Right of the Sovereign Magistrate in Sacred things, he seem'd to me to come too near an Erastian,*[6] *and to lessen the power of the Keys too much, which Christ left as a Legacy to his Church. It may be he did write that before he was come to full maturity of judgment: and some other things, I do not say after he was super-annuated, but without that due deliberation which he useth at other times.* . . .

But one thing I must confess is very pleasant, and he hath past an high Complement upon his Majesty in it: that he may, if he please, reserve the Priesthood and the Exercise of it to himself. Now this indeed is surprising; but this onely troubles me, how his Majesty would look in all the Sacerdotal habiliments, and the Pontifical Wardrobe. I am afraid the King would find himself incommoded with all that furniture upon his back, and would scarce reconcile himself to wear even the Lawn-sleeves and the Surplice. But what? even *Charles the fifth*,[7] as I have read, was at his Inauguration by the Pope, content to be vested, according to the Romane Ceremonial, in the habit of a Deacon: and a man would not scruple too much the formality of the drest in order to Empire.

But one thing I doubt Mr. *Bayes* did not well consider; that, if the King may discharge the Function of the Priesthood, he may too (and 'tis all the reason in the world) assume the Revenue. It would be the best Subsidy that ever was voluntarily given by the Clergy. But truly otherwise, I do not see but that the King does lead a more unblamable Conversation, and takes more care of Souls than many of them, and understands their Office much better, and deserves something already for the pains he hath taken.

The next is *Publick Conscience*. For as to mens private Consciences he hath made them very inconsiderable, and, reading what he saith of them with some attention, I only found this new and important Discovery and great Priviledge of Christian Liberty, that *Thought is free*. We are however obliged to him for that, seing by consequence we may think of him what we please. And this he saith a man may assert against all the Powers of the Earth: And indeed with much reason and to great purpose; seeing, as he also alledges, the Civil Power is so far from doing violence to that liberty, that it never can. But yet if the freedom of thoughts be in not lying open to discovery, there have been wayes of compelling men to discover them; or, if the freedom consist in retaining their judgments when so manifested, that also hath been made penal. And I doubt not but beside *Oaths* and *Renunciations*, and *Assents* and *Consents*, Mr. *Bayes*, if he were searched, hath twenty other tests and picklocks in his pocket. Would Mr. *Bays* then perswade men to assert this against all the Powers of the Earth? I would ask in what manner? To say the truth I do not like him, and would wish the Non-conformists to be upon their guard, lest he trepan them first by this means into a Plot, and then peach, & so hang them: . . .

The third is *Moral Grace*. And whoever is not satisfied with those passages of his concerning it, before quoted, may find enough where he discourseth it at large, even to surfeit. I cannot make either less or more of it than that he overturns the whole fabrick of Christianity, and Power of Religion. For my part, if Grace be resolv'd into Morality, I think a man may almost as well make God too to be only a Notional and Moral Existence. . . . [8]

The fourth is *Debauchery tolerated*. For supposing, as he does, that 'tis better and *safer to give a Toleration to mens Debaucheries than to their Religious Perswasions*, it amounts to the same reckoning. This is a very ill way of discoursing; and that a *greater severity ought to be exercised over mens Consciences than over their Vices and Immoralities*. For it argues too much indiscretion, by avoiding one evil to run up into the contrary extream. And Debauch'd Persons will be ready hence to conclude, although it be a perverse way of reasoning, That where the Severity ought to be less, the Crime is less also: nay, even that the more they are debauch'd, it is just that the Punishment should still abate in proportion; but however, that it were very imprudent and unadvisable to reform and erre on the Religious hand, lest they should thereby incur the greater penalties. . . .

But Mr. *Bayes* nevertheless is for his fifth; *Persecution recommended*: and he does it to the purpose. *Julian*[9] himself, who I think was first a Reader, and held forth in the Christian Churches before he turned Apostate and then Persecutor, could not have outdone him either in Irony or Cruelty. Only it is God's mercy that Mr. *Bayes* is not Emperour. You have seen how he inveighs against Trade: *That whilst mens Consciences are acted by such peevish and ungovernable Principles, to erect Trading-Combinations is but to build so many Nests of Faction and Sedition.* Lay up your Ships, my Masters, set Bills on your Shop-doors, shut up the Custom-house; and why not adjourn the Term, mure up *Westminster*-hall, leave Plowing and Sowing, and keep a dismal Holyday through the Nation; for Mr. *Bayes* is out of humour. But I assure you it is no jesting matter. For he hath in one place taken a List of the Fanatick Ministers, whom he reckons to be but about an hundred *Systematical Divines*: though I believe the *Bartlemew*-Register or the *March*-Licences would make them about an hundred and three or an hundred and four, or so: But this is but for rounder number and breaks no square. And then for their People, either *they live in greater Societies of men* (he means the City of *London* and the other Cities and Towns-Corporate, but expresses it so to prevent some inconvenience that might betide them) *but there their noise is greater than their number*. Or else in *Country-Towns and Villages, where they arise not above the proportion of one to twenty*. It were not unwisely done indeed if he could perswade the Magistrate that all the Fanaticks have but one neck, so that he might cut off Nonconformity at one blow. I suppose the Nonconformists value themselves tho upon their Conscience and not their Numbers: but they would do well to be watchful, lest he have taken a List of their Names as well as their Number, and have set Crosses upon all their Doors against there should be occasion. But till that *happy juncture*, when Mr. *Bayes shall be fully avenged of his new Enemies the wealthy Fanaticks* (which is soon done too, for he saith *there are but few of them men of Estates or Interest*) he is contented that they should only be exposed (they are his own expressions) to the *Pillories, Whipping-posts, Galleys, Rods,* and *Axes*; and moreover and above, to all other Punishments whatsoever, provided they be of a severer nature than those that are inflicted on men for their immoralities. . . .

But Mr. *Bayes* his sixt, is that which I call his *Push-pin Divinity*. For he would perswade Princes that *there cannot a Pin be pull'd out of the Church but the State immediately totters*. That is strange. And yet I have seen many a Pin pull'd out upon occasion, and yet not so much as the Church it self hath wagg'd. It is true indeed, and we have had sad experiments of it, that some Clergy-men have been so opiniastre that they have rather exposed the State to ruine than they would part with a Pin, I will not say out of their Church, but out of their Sleeve. There is nothing more natural then for the Ivy to be of opinion that the Oak cannot stand without its support: or, seeing we are got into Ivy, that the Church cannot hold up longer than It underprops the Walls: whereas it is a sneaking insinuating Imp, scarce better than Bindweed, that sucks the Tree dry, and moulders the building where it catches. But what, pray Mr. *Bayes*, is this Pinne in *Pallas's* buckler?[10] Why 'tis some Ceremony or other, that is *indifferent in its own nature*, that *hath no antecedent necessity* but *only as commanded*, that *signifies nothing in it self but what the Commander pleases*, that even by the Church which commands it, is *declared to have nothing of Religion in it, and that is in it self of no great moment or consequence, only it is absolutely necessary that Governours should enjoyn it to avoid the evils that would follow if it were not determined*. Very well, Mr. *Bayes*. This I see will keep cold: anon perhaps I may have a stomach. But I must take care lest I swallow your Pin.

*   *   *

I know a medicine for Mr. *Bayes* his Hiccough (it is but naming *J.O.*[11]) but I cannot tell certainly, though I have a shrew'd guess what is the cause of it. For indeed all his Arguments here are so abrupt and short, that I cannot liken them better, considering too that frequent and perpetual repetition. Such as this, *Why may not the Soveraign Power bestow this Priviledge upon Ceremony, as well as Use and Custom, by virtue of its prerogative? What greater Immortality is there in them when determined by the Command and Institution of the Prince, than when by the consent and institution of the people?* This the Tap-lash of what he said, p. 110. "When the Civil Magistrate takes upon him to determine any particular Forms of outward Worship, 'tis of no worse Consequence than if he should go about to define the signification of all words used in the Worship of God." And p. 108.of his first Book. "So that all the Magistrates power of instituting significant Ceremonies, &c. can be no more Usurpation upon the CONSCIENCES of Men, than

if the Sovereign Authority should take upon it self, as some Princes
have done, to define the signification of words . . . [‟]. But though I
therefore will not dispute against that Flower of the Princes Crown, yet, I
hope that without doing much harm, I may observe that for the most
part they left it to the People, and seldom themselves exercised it. And
even *Augustus Cæsar,*[12] though he was so great an Emperour, and so
valiant a man in his own person, was used to fly from a new word though
it were single, as studiously as a Mariner would avoid a Rock for fear of
splitting. . . . And had I a mind to play the Politician, like Mr. *Bayes,*
upon so pleasant and copious a Subject, I would demonstrate that
though the imposition of Ceremonies hath bred much mischief in the
world, yet (shall I not venture too on a word once for tryal) such a
Penetration or Transubstantiation of Language would throw all into
Rebellion and Anarchy, would shake the Crowns of all Princes, and
reduce the World into a second *Babel.*[13] Therefore Mr. *Bayes* I doubt
you were not well advised to make so close an Analogy betwixt imposing of significant words and significant Ceremonies: for I fear the
Argument may be improved against you, and that Princes finding that
of words so impracticable, and of ill consequence, will conclude that
of Ceremonies to be no less pernicious. And the Nonconformists (who
are great Traders, you know, in Scripture, and therefore thrown out of
the Temple) will be certainly on your back. For they will appropriate
your pregnant Text of *Let all things be done decently and in order,*[14]
to preaching or praying in an unknown Tongue,[15] which such an imposition of words would be: and then, to keep you to your Similitude,
they will say too that yours are all Latine Ceremonies, and the Congregation does not understand them. But were not this Dominion of
words so dangerous, (for how many millions of men did it cost your
Roman Empire to attain it!) Yet it was very unmannerly in you to
assign to Princes, who have enough beside, so mean a trouble. When
you gave them leave to exercise the Priesthood in person, that was
something to the purpose. That was both Honorable, and something
belongs to it that would have help'd to bear the charge. But this Mint
of words will never quit cost, nor pay for the coynage. This is such a
drudgery; that, rather than undergo it, I dare say, there is no Prince but
would resign to you so Pedantical a Soveraignty. I cannot but think
how full that Princes head must be of Proclamations. For, if he published but once a Proclamation to that purpose, he must forthwith set
out another to stamp and declare the signification of all the words contained in it, and then another to appoint the meaning of all the words
in this, and so on: that here is work cut out in one Paper of State for

the whole Privy Council, both Secretaries of State, and all the Clerks of
the Council, for one Kings Reign, and *in infinitum*. But, I cannot but
wonder, knowing how ambitious Mr. *Bayes* is of the power over words,
and jealous of his own Prerogative of refining Language, how he came
to be so liberal of it to the Prince: Why, the same thing that induced
him to give the Prince a power antecedent and independent to *Christ*,
and to establish what Religion he pleased, &c. Nothing but his spight
against the Non-conformists. I know not that thing in the world, except
a Jest, that he would not part with to be satisfied in that particular. He
hoped doubtless by holding up this Maxim, to obtain that the words of
the Declaration of the 15th *March*[16] should be understood by contraries.
You may well think he expected no less an equivalent, he would never
else have permitted the Prince even to define the signification of all
words used in the Worship of God, and to determine the proper signification of all Phrases imploy'd in Divine Worship. . . .

One Argument I confess remains still behind, and that will justifie
any thing. 'Tis that which I call'd lately *Rationem ultimam Cleri*;[17]
Force, Law, Execution, or what you will have it. I would not be mistaken, as though I hereby meant the body of the *English* Clergy, who
have been ever since the Reformation (I say it without disparagement
to the Foraign Churches) of the Eminentest for Divinity and Piety in
all Christendom. And as far am I from censuring, under this title, the
Bishops of *England*, for whose Function, their Learning, their Persons
I have too deep a veneration to speak anything of them irreverently.
But those that I intend only, are a particular bran of persons, who will
in spight of Fate be accounted the Church of *England*, and to shew
they are Pluralists,[18] never write in a modester Stile than *We, We*; nay,
even these, several of them, are Men of parts sufficient to deserve a
Rank among the Teachers and Governors of the Church. . . . They are
the *Politick Would-be's*[19] of the Clergy. Not Bishops, but Men that have
a mind to be Bishops, and that will do any thing in the World to compass it. And, though Princes have always a particular mark upon these
Men, and value them no more than they deserve, yet I know not very
well, or perhaps I do know, how it oftentimes happens that they come
to be advanced. They are Men of a fiery nature that must always be
uppermost, and so they may increase their own Splendor, care not
though they set all on flame about them. You would think the same
day that they took up Divinity they divested themselves of Humanity,
& so they may procure & execute a Law against the Non-conforminsts,
that they had forgot the Gospel: They cannot endure that Humility,
that Meekness, that strictness of Manners and Conversation, which is

the true way of gaining Reputation and Authority to the Clergy; much less can they content themselves with the ordinary and comfortable provision that is made for the Ministry: But, having wholly calculated themselves for Preferment, and Grandeur, know or practise no other means to make themselves venerable but by Ceremony and Severity. Whereas the highest advantage of promotion is the opportunity of condescention, and the greatest dignity in our Church can but raise them to the Title of *Your Grace*, which is in the Latine *Vestra Clementia*. But of all these, none are so eager & virulent, as some, who having had relation to the late times, have got access to *Ecclesiastical Fortune*, and are resolved to make their best of her. For so, of all Beasts, none are so fierce and cruel as those that have been taught once by hunger to prey upon their own kind; as of all Men, none are so inhumane as the *Canibals*. But whether this be the true way of ingratiating themselves with a generous and discerning Prince, I meddle not; nor whether it be an ingenuous practice towards those whom they have been formerly acquainted with: but whatsoever they think themselves obliged to for the approving of their new Loyalty; I rather commend. That which astonishes me, and only raises my indignation is, that of all sorts of Men, this kind of Clergy should always be, and have been for the most precipitate, bruitish, and sanguinary Counsels. The former Civil War cannot make them wise, nor his Majesties Happy Return, good natured; but they are still for running things up unto the same extreams. The softness of the Universities where they have been bred, the gentleness of Christianity in which they have been nurtured, hath but exasperated their nature, and they seem to have contracted no *Idea* of wisdom, but what they learnt at School, the Pedantry of Whipping. They take themselves qualified to Preach the Gospel, and no less to intermeddle in affairs of State. Though the reach of their Divinity is but to persecution, and an Inquisition is the height of their Policy.

And you Mr. *Bayes*, had you lived in the days of *Augustus Cæsar* . . . His Father[20] too was murdered. Or (to come nearer both to our times, and your resemblance of the late War, which you trumpet always in the Ear of his Majesty) had you happen'd in the time of *Henry* the *fourth* of *France*,[21] should not you have done well in the Cabinet? His Predecessor too was assassinated. No, Mr. *Bayes*, you would not have been for their purpose: They took other measures of Government, and accordingly it succeeded with them. And His Majesty, whose Genius hath much of both those Princes, and who derives half of the Blood in his Veins from the latter, will in all probability not be so forward to hearken to your advice as to follow their Example. For these Kings,

Mr. *Bayes*, how negligent soever or ignorant you take 'em to be, have I doubt, a shrewd understanding with them. 'Tis a Trade, that God be thanked, neither you nor I are of, and therefore we are not so competent Judges of their Actions.[22] I my self have often times seen them, some of them, do strange things, and unreasonable in my opinion, & yet a little while, or sometimes many years after, I have found that all the men in the world could not have contrived any thing better. 'Tis not with them as with you. You have but one Cure of Souls, or perhaps two, as being a Noblemans Chaplain, to look after: And if you make Conscience of discharging them as you ought, you would find you had work sufficient, without writing your *Ecclesiastical Policies*. But they are the Incumbents of whole Kingdoms, and the Rectorship of the Common people, the Nobility; and even of the Clergy, whom you are prone to *affirm when possest with principles that incline to rebellion and disloyal practises, to be of all Rebels the most dangerous, p. 49.* the care I say of all these, rests upon them. So that they are fain to condescend to many things for peace-sake, and the quiet of Mankind, that your proud heart would break before it would bend to. . . . If a man have an Antipathy against any thing, the Company is generally so civil, as to refrain the use of it, however not to press it upon the person. If a man be sick or weak the Pope grants a Dispensation from *Lent*, or Fasting dayes: ay, and from many a thing that strikes deeper in his Religion. If one have got a cold, their betters will force them to be covered. There is no end of Similitudes: but I am led into them by your calling these Ceremonies Pins of the Church. It would almost tempt a Prince that is curious, and that is setled (God be praised) pretty fast in his Throne, to try for experiment, whether the pulling out of one of these Pins would make the State totter. But, Mr. *Bayes*, there is more in it. 'Tis matter of Conscience: and if Kings do, out of discretion, connive at the other infirmities of their People; If great persons do out of civility condescend to their inferiours, and if all men out of common humanity do yield to the weaker; Will your Clergy only be the men, who, in an affair of Conscience, and where perhaps 'tis you are in the wrong, be the onely hard-hearted and inflexible Tyrants; and not only so, but instigate and provoke Princes to be the ministers of your cruelty? But, I say, Princes, as far as I can take the height of things so far above me, must needs have other thoughts, and are past such boyes-play to stake their Crowns against your Pins. They do not think fit to command things unnecessary, and where the profit cannot countervail the hazard. But above all they consider, that God has instated them in the Government of Mankind, with that incumbrance (if it may so be called) of Reason, and that incumbrance upon Reason of Conscience. That he might have given them as large an extent of ground and other kind of cattle for their Subjects: but it had been a melancholy Empire to have been only Supreme Grasiers and Soveraign Shepherds. And therefore, though the laziness of that brutal magistracy might have been more secure, yet the difficulty of this does make it more honourable. That men therefore are to be dealt with reasonably: and conscientious men by Conscience. That even Law is force, and the execution of that Law a greater Violence; and therefore with rational creatures not to be used but upon the utmost extremity. That the Body is in the power of the mind; so that corporal punishments do never reach the offender, but the innocent suffers for the guilty. That the Mind is in the hand of God, and cannot correct those perswasions which upon the best of its natural capacity it hath collected: So that it too, though erroneous, is so farr innocent. That the Prince therefore, by how much God hath indued him with a clearer reason, and by consequence with a more enlightned judgment, ought the rather to take heed lest by punishing Conscience, he violate not only his own, but the Divine Majesty.

Notes

ANDREW MARVELL (1621-78) was a poet, a friend of Milton's, an anti-royalist satirist and an M.P. He did not take part in the civil war but by 1653 had become tutor to the daughter of the parliamentary general, Lord Fairfax. He was subsequently tutor to a ward of Cromwell's and became Milton's colleague in the Secretaryship for Foreign Tongues in 1658. In the 1660 Parliament he was elected M.P. for Hull. His satires against Clarendon, the King and royal government were published anonymously, as was *The Rehearsal Transpos'd*, though more openly. It is an attack on Samuel Parker's *A Discourse of Ecclesiastical Polity* (1670), *A Defence and Continuation of Ecclesiastical Polity* (1671) and a preface to Bishop Bramhall's *Vindication of Himself and the Episcopal Clergy* (1672). All three of these texts are mentioned in these extracts. Marvell's title derives from a play by the Duke of Buckingham, *The Rehearsal*, in which Dryden is satirised under the name of Bayes. Marvell 'transposes' this device, addressing Parker as Bayes throughout. Parker was eventually silenced by the publication of *The Rehearsal Transpos'd: The Second Part* (1673). Marvell did not long remain an ally of the King's, publishing his ferocious *Account of the Growth of Popery and Arbitrary Government* in 1677, the year before his death.

1. Samuel Parker (1640-88): he was brought up a strict puritan but under the influence of Ralph Bathurst (see p. 58, n. 14) he became a fervent anglican. He was appointed Archdeacon of Canterbury in 1670. He wrote copiously in favour of royal absolutism and was made Bishop of Oxford in 1686 by James II. He was much disliked and he increased this unpopularity by writing in favour of religious toleration in line with royal policy at the time. In 1687 he was installed as President of Magdalen College, Oxford, against the wishes of the fellows, and admitted catholics to the college. He died shortly before the collapse of James's government.

2. 'in lawful control of their own affairs.'

3. Series of propositions.

4. John Bramhall (1594-1663), Bishop of Derry (1634-60), Archbishop of Armagh (1660-3). He was a strong supporter of Charles I's 'thorough' policy in Ireland, and in consequence was in danger of his life during the civil war. His *Vindication* was published posthumously. He was involved in a celebrated controversy with Hobbes.

5. Hugo Grotius (1583-1645), celebrated Dutch writer on jurisprudence.

6. Follower of Thomas Erastus (1524-83), Swiss physician and religious controvertialist, who defended the thesis that churches did not have the power of excommunication since only magistrates had the right to punish. His teaching was subsequently and erroneously taken to mean that kings ought to govern the church and even to subordinate religious to state interests.

7. Charles V (reigned 1519-56), Holy Roman Emperor.

8. A response to Parker's argument that 'Religion must of Necessity be resolved into Enthusiasm or Morality' which Marvell sees as implicitly denying the reality of a supernatural order and therefore as atheistic. He thereby distances himself from the tendency of latitudinarian anglicanism to naturalise religion.

9. Julian 'the apostate' (reigned 361-3), Roman Emperor who attempted to restore paganism and persecuted Christianity.

10. The shield or aegis of Zeus (originally a goathide cloak), frequently carried by his daughter, the goddess Pallas Athene, and used by her to protect those fighting in her cause. She was goddess of wisdom and of Athens. To unpin her buckler, therefore, is to leave the state defenceless against the forces of unreason and anarchy.

11. John Owen (1616-83) who wrote a reply to Parker's *A Discourse of Ecclesiastical Polity*. He was Vice-Chancellor of Oxford University under Cromwell, and refused a bishopric at the restoration. He was subsequently indicted for holding illegal religious conventicles. He was an associate of Baxter's and his intellectual distinction, integrity and tolerant spirit indicate something of what English culture lost by the exclusion of nonconformists from full participation in national life.

12. See p. 58, n. 5.

13. See Genesis: 11:1-9.

14. Corinthians 14:40.

15. A reference to protestant objections to the use of Latin in the catholic liturgy.

16. The first Declaration of Indulgence issued by the King on 15 March 1672 and withdrawn under pressure from Parliament on 24 February 1673.

17. 'the last argument of a clergyman.'

18. Holders of more than one ecclesiastical living, an abuse much attacked by nonconformists.

19. A self-important would-be politician in Jonson's *Volpone*.

20. See p. 58, n. 5.

21. See p. 72, n. 20.

22. An ironic reference to the traditional belief that only anointed kings understood the mysteries of statecraft (*arcana imperii*).

From: *The Narrative of the Persecution of Agnes Beaumont in 1674*

Agnes Beaumont, [1674]

Soe about the midle of the day, which was Saterday, I said to my Sister, "Will yow goe with me to my ffathers, to see what he will say to me now"; and she said yes, she would goe with mee. Soe wee went, and when wee came to the doore, we found the doore lockt, and my father in the house; for he would not goe out, but he would locke the doore, and put the key in his pocket. Neither would he goe into the house but he would lock the door after him.

Soe we went to the window, and my Sister said, "ffather, where are yow?" And he came to the window, and spake to vs. Said my Sister, "ffather, I hope now yor Anger is over, and that yow will let my Sister come in." Soe I prayed him to be reconsiled to mee, and fell A Crying very much, for indeed at y^t[1] time my heart was full of greife and sorrow to see my ffather soe Angrye with me still, and to heere what he said, which now I shall not mention; Only this one thing Hee said, he would never give mee A penny as long as he lived; nor when he dyed, but he would give it to them he never saw before.

Now to tell you the truth, these was very hard sayings to me, and at the heareing of it my heart began to sinck. Thought I to my selfe, "What will be come of mee? To goe to service and worke for my liueing is a new thing to me; and soe young as I am too. What shall I doe?" thought I. And these thoughts came suddenly into my mind, "Well, I haue a good God to goe to still"; and y^t word did Comfort me "when my father and mother forsooke mee, then the Lord took me vpp"; but my heart sanck quickly. Soe my Sister stood pleading with him, but all in vaine. Then I prayed my father, if he did not please to let me come in, that he would give me my Bible and my pattings.[2] But he would not, And said Againe he was resolued I should neuer haue one peny, nor pennyworth, as long as he lived; nor when he dyed.

As I said, I was very much Cast downe at this. Now did my thoughts beginn to worke. Thought I, "what shall I doe? I am now in A miserable Case," for I went home with my Sister Againe Crying bitterly, for indeed vnbeleefe and Carnall reasoning was gott in at A great rate, Notwithstanding god had beene soe wonderfull good to me but the last night in the barne.

Soe away I went vp Staires to Crye to the Lord that afternoone, whoe gaue me hopes of an Eternall inheritance; and I was lett to see I had a better portion then silver or gold. Oh, then I was willing to go to service or be striptt of all for Christ. Now I was vnconcerned Againe at what my father had said. I was made to beleeve I should never want.

Soe at night I had a mind to goe Againe to my fathers; "but," thought I, "I will goe alone"; for I see he was more Angry with my brother that morneing and with my Sister at noone then he was with mee. "And," thought I, "now he hath beene Alone one night, and hath noe body to do anything for him, it may be he will let me come in."

And soe I considered wch way to goe. Thought I, "I will goe such A bye way that he shall not see mee till I come to the doore; And if I find it open, I will goe in. He will thincke I will come noe more to night, and soe it may bee the doore may be opened. And if it is," thought I, "I will goe in, let my father doe with mee what he pleases when I am in. If he doth through me out, he does; I will venture."

Soe in the Evening I went; and when I came at the doore, it stood a Jarr, wth the key o'th' out side, and my father in the house. Soe I shoved it soughly³ and was goeing in. But my father was A Comeing through the Entry to come out, whoe see me A Comeing in; soe he came hastily to the doore and clapt it too; and if I had not beene very quicke one of my leggs had beene between the doore and the thresshold. Soe he Clapt the door too wth the key o'th' out side, for he had not time to take the key out, and then pin^d the door within side, for he could not Lock it, the key being o'th' out side of the door. Soe I would not be soe vncivill to locke my father in the house; but I tooke the key out of the doore and put it in my pocket, and I thought to my selfe, "it may be my father will come out presently to serue the Cowes"; for I see they was not serued vp for all night. And thincke I, "when he is gone vpp in the yard, I will goe in." And thought I, "I will goe stand behind the house, and when I heare him come out, I will goe in; and when I am in, I will lye at his mercy."

Soe their I stood lissening, and after A while I heard him come out. But before he would goe vp in the yard to serue the Cowes, he comes and lookes behind the house, and thier he sees mee stand. Now behind the house was A pond, Only a narrow path betweene the house and the ponde, and their I stood close vp to the wall. Soe my fath^r comes to mee, and takes hould of my Arme.

"Hussiff," said hee "giue me the key quickly, or I will through yow in the pond."

Soe I very speedily pull^d the key out of my pocket and gaue it to
him, and was very sad and silent; for I see it to be in vaine to say any
thing to him. Soe I went my way down into one of my fathers closess[4]
to a wood side, sighing and groaneing to god as I went along. And as I
was A goeing wth my heart full of sorrow, that Scripture came in vpon
my mind, "Call vpon me and I will Answere thee, and shew thee greate
and mighty things that thou knowest not."[5]

Soe away I went to the Wood side (and it was very darke night),
Where I powred out my soul wth plenty of teeres to thee Lord; and still
this Scripture would often dart in vpon my mind, "Call vpon me and
I will Answere the, and shew thee greate and mighty things y^t thou
knowest not." And sometimes I should bee ready to say in my heart,
"Lord what mighty things wilt thou shew me?" Soe their I remained
some time, Crying to ye Lord very bitterly.

As any rationall body must needs thincke, these was harde things
for me to meet with. But that was a blessed word to mee, "the Eyes of
the Lord are over the righteous, and his eares are open to their Cryes."[6]
Oh, I did beleeue, his Eares was open in heaven to heare the Cryes of a
poore disolate afflict^d Creature, and that his heart did yearne towards
mee. That was A wonderfull word to mee, "in all their afflictions hee
was afflicted."[7] Soe staying soe long, my brother and Sister was much
concern^d for mee, and sent some of their men to my fathers on some
Arrand, on purpose to see whither my father had let me come in. But
they returned thier master that Answere that their old m^r was alone; I
was not their.

Soe my brother and some of his family went About seekeing for mee
but found mee not. At last I came to my Brothers, when I had spread
my Complaints before ye Lord. And now I began to resolue in my mind
what to doe, for this was the Case — That if I would promise my father
never to goe to A meeting againe, he would let me come in. Soe, thought
I to my selfe, that I will never doe, If I begg my bread from doore to
doore. And I thought I was soe strongly fixed in this resolution that
nothing could moue mee; what ever I mett with from my father, I
should neuer yeild vpon that Account. But poore weake Creature y^t I
was, I was peeter like,[8] as yow will heare afterwards.

Well, this was Saterday night. Soe when Sabboth day morning came,
I said to my Brother, "Let vs goe to my ffathers as wee goe to the meeting." But he said noe, "It will but provoake him." Soe wee did not.
And as my brother and I went to the meeting, he was talkeing to me
as wee went.

"Sister," said hee, "yow are now brought vpon the Stage to Act for

Christ and his wayes." Said he, "I would not haue yow Consent to my
father vpon his termes." "Noe, Brother," said I, "if I begg my bread
from doore to doore." Thought I, "I doe not want any of y^r Cautions,
vpon that Account." Soe wee went to the meeting; but as I sat in the
meeting my mind was very much hurried and afflicted, as noe wonder
Considering my Curcumstances. Soe when it was night, I said to my
Brother as we went from the meeting, "Let vs goe to my fathers." Soe
he consented to it.

And we went and found him in the yard A serueing ye Cowes, but
before we came into the yard, my Brother warned mee Againe that I
did not Consent to promise my father to forsake the wayes of god; but
I thought I had noe need of his Counsell vpon that Account. Soe my
Brother talked with him very mildly, and pleaded with him to bee
reconsiled to mee. But he was soe Angry with him that he would not
heare him. Soe I whispred to my Brother, and bid him goe hence.
"Noe," said he, "I will not goe with out yow." Said I, "Goe, I will
come p^rsently." But, as he afterwards said, he was afraid to leaue mee
for feare I should yeild. But I thought I could as soone part from my
life.

Soe my Brother and Sister went on their way home. Soe their I remained in the yard, talkeing to my father whoe then had the key in his
pocket. And I was pleading with him to let me goe in; "ffather," said
I, "I will serue yow in any thing that lyes in me to doe for yow as long
as you liue and I liue; And father," said I, "I desire time to goe noe
whether but to heare gods word, if yow will but let me goe A Sabbath
dayes to the meeting; And I desire noe more. Father," said I, "yow
Cant Answere for my Sins, nor stand in my steed before god; I must
looke to the Saluation of my Soul, or I am vndone for ever."

Soe he told me if I would promise him never to goe to a meeting as
long as he lived, I should goe in, and he would doe for me as for his
other Children; but if not I should never haue A farthing.

"ffather," said I, "my Soul is of more worth then soe; I dare not
make such A promise"; And my poore Brothers heart Ackt that he did
not see me ffollow him. Soe my father began to be very Angry And bid
me begone, and not trouble him, for he war resolu^d what to doe; "And
therfore tell mee; if yow will promise mee Never to goe to A meeting
Againe, I will give yow the key and yow shall goe in."

Soe many times together [he] held the key out to mee, to see if I
would promise him; And I as often refused to yeild to him.

Soe at last he began to be Impatiant; "Hussiff," said hee, "what doe
you say? If yow will promise me never to goe to A meeting Againe As

long as I live, heare is the key; take it, and goe in"; And held the key
out to mee.

Said he, "I will never offer it to yow more, and I am resolved yow
shall never come within my doore Againe while I live." And I stood
Crying by him in the yard. Soe he spake hastily to me, "What doe yow
say, hussiff," said hee, "will yow promise me or noe?"

"Well fath^r," said I, "I will promise yow that I will never goe to A
meeting Againe, as long as yow live, without your Consent"; not thinking what doler and misery I brought vpon my selfe in soe doeing. Soe
when he heard me say soe he gaue me the key to goe in. Soe I vnlockt
the doore and went in; And soe soone as I gott within the doore, that
dreadfull Scripture came vpon my mind, "They y^t deny me before men,
them will I deny before my father and ye Angells that are in heauen",⁹
And y^t word, "he y^t forsaketh not ffather and mother and all y^t he
hath, is not worthy of me."¹⁰ "Oh," thought I, "what will become of
mee now? What haue I done this night?" Soe I was A goeing to runn
out of ye house Againe; but, thought I, that wont helpe what I haue
done if I doe. Oh, now all my Comforts and Injoyments was gone! In
the roome of which I had nothing but terrour and gillt and rendings of
Contience. Now I see whatt all my resolutions was Come too. This was
Sabbath day night, A Black night.

Soe my poore father comes in and was very loveing to mee, And bid
me gitt him some Supper; which I did. And when I had done soe, he
bid mee come and eate some. But oh, bitter Supper to mee! Soe my
poore brother was mightily troubled that I did not come to his house.
He wondred that I stayed soe long. He did feare and thincke what I had
done; but to be satisfied he sent one of his men on some Arrand to see
if I was in the house wth my ffather. And he returned his master that
Answere, that I was in the house with their Old master, and he was
very Chearfull with mee; which, when my Brother heard, was much
troubled, for he knew that I had yeilded, Else my father would not
haue let me goe in. But noe tong can Express what a dolefull Condition
I was in, Neither durst I hardly looke vp to god for mercy. Oh, now I
must heare gods word noe more. Thought I, "Oh, what A rech am I,
that I should deny Christ and his wayes; he y^t had soe often visited my
Soul, and had beene soe gratious to me in all my troubles. But now I
haue turned my backe vpon him. Oh, black night! Oh, dismall night!"
thought I, "in which I haue denyed my dere Saviour." Soe I went to
bed, when I had my father to bed; but it was a sadd night to mee.

Soe on the next morne, which was munday morneing, Came, my
Brother; And the first Salutation that he gaue mee, "Oh, Sister," said

hee, "what haue you done? What doe yow say to that Scripture, 'he that denyes mee before men, him will I deny before my father and the Angells that are in heaven?'" "Oh," thought I, "it is this that cutts my heart; but I said litle to him only wept bitterly.

Soe my father Comeing in, hee said noe more, Only said, "good morrow, father'; And went Away. But I canot Express with words the doler I was in; I filled every Corner of the house and yard that day with bitter sights[11] and groanes and teires. I went Crying About as if my very heart would haue burst in sunder with greiffe and horrour. But now and then one blessed promise or other would dropp vpon my mind; but I could take litle Comfort in them; As that word, "Simon, Sathan hath desired to haue thee that he may sift the as wheat, but I haue prayed for thee."[12] But oh, this lay vppermost, I must heare gods word noe more. "Now," thought I, "if my father Could give me thousands of gold what good would it doe mee?"

Thus I went groaneing about till I was almost spent; and when my father was but gone out of the house, I made ye house ring wth dismall Cryes, but tould not my greife to my brother, for I thought he would not pitty mee. Neither did I ever tell him what I went through vpon that Account. And when my father came into the house, then I would goe out into the barnes or outhousen to vent my sorrowfull groanes and teires to the Lord.

Soe before night, as I stood sighting and Crying like a poore distracted body, leaneing my head Against something in the house, saying, "Lord, what shall I doe? what shall I doe?" them words dropt vpon my mind, "Their shall be A way made for yow to Escape, that yow may be able to beare it."[13] "Lord," said I, "what way shall be made? wilt thou make my father willing to let me goe to thine Ordinances?" But if it should be soe, thought I, yet what A wrech was I to deny Christ. Oh, now hopes of the pardon of my sinns was worth A world; for the forgiveness of my sins was that I Cryed much for, saying, "Lord, pitty and pardon pitty and pardon."

Soe at Night as my father and I sat by the fire, he Asked me what was the matter with mee; for he tooke notiss of me in what A sorrowfull Condition I was in all day. Soe I burst out A Crying, "Oh, father," said I, "I am soe afflicted to thincke that I should promise yow never to goe to A meeting Againe without yor Consent; and the feares yt I haue least yow should not be willing to let me goe"; and I tould him what trouble I was in.

And he wept like a Child.

"Well, dont let that trouble yow," said hee, "we shall not disagree."

At this I was a litle Comforted. Said I, "Pray, father, forgive mee wherein I haue beene vndutyfull to you, or dissobedient in Anything." Soe he sat weeping, and tould me how troubled he was for me that night he shutt me out, and could not Sleepe. But he thought I had bene gone to my Brothers. But it was my rideing behind John Bunyan, he said, y^t vext him; for that enemy in the towne had often beene in Censing of him Against Mr Bunyan, though sometime before my father had heard him preach gods word, & heard him with a broaken heart as he had done severall others. For when I was first awakened, he was mightily concernd, Seeing me in such distress about my Soul, and would say to some neighbours that came some times to the house; said he, "I thincke my daughter will bee distracted, She scarse Eates, drincks, or sleepes; and I haue lived these three score yeares And scarse ever thought of my Soul." And afterwards would Crye to the Lord in Secret, as well as I, and would goe to meetings for A greate while together, and hath heard gods word with many teires. But that evill minded man in the towne would set him against the meetings. I haue stood and heard him say to my father, "Haue you lived to these yeares to be led away with them? These be they that lead silly women Captive into houses, and for A pretence make long prayers"; and soe neuer leaue till he had set him Against me and the meetings; and would I suppose Counsell him not to let me goe. And laterly I mett wth A great deale from him vpon that Acc^tt.

Well, this was munday night; but notw^thstanding what my father had said to mee, I was full of Sorrow, and gilt of Contience; and my worcke was still to Crye to ye Lord for pardon of Sin and to humble my selfe before him for what I had done. And much time I spent y^t night in Crying to the Lord for mercy; now was I made to Crye for pardon of Sin, and that god would keep me by his grace for time to come, As if I never prayed before; and y^t he would keepe me from denying of him and his wayes. I see now what all my stronge resolutions came too, and y^t I was but a poore weake Creature if god did not keepe me by his grace.

And the next day came, wch was Tuesday, in wch I still remained in a sorrowfull frame, Weeping and Crying bitterly. But, as I remember, god brought me vp out of this horrible pitt before night, and set my feet vpon A Rock, and I was helped to beleeue the forgiueness of my sinns; and many a good word I had come in vpon my heart, wch I haue forgott.

But now I began to looke backe with Comfort vpon fryday night in the barne, And to thincke of that blessed word "Beloved," and I did beleeue that Jesus Christ was ye same yesterday, and today, and for ever.[14] But all day I spent in praying and Crying to god in Corners, vnless it was to doe my worke about house, and gitt my father his dinner. And he did eate as good A dinner as ever I see him eate.

Well, night came on, which indeed was a very dismall night to me, And had not the Lord stood by me, and strengthened me, I had Certainly sancke downe vnder gods hand that night. But he was faithfull, whoe did not suffer me to be tempted and afflicted aboue what I was able. Towards night that Scripture would often run in my mind, "In six troubles I will be with thee, and in seauen I will not leaue thee."[15] And y^t was A mighty word to mee, "The Eternall god is thy Refuge, and vnderneath are the everlasting Armes."[16]

Soe in the Euening, my father said, "It is A very cold night; we will not sitt vpp too long to night." He, when the nights ware long, would sitt vpp with me A Candles burneing, as I haue satt A spinning or at other worke. But then he said he would haue his Supper and goe to bed because it was soe could.

Soe after Supper, as he sat by the fyre, he tooke A pipe of Tobacco. And when he had done, he bid me take vp the Coales and warme his bed; which I did. And as I was Covering of him, them words runn through my mind, "The End is Come, The End is Come, the time drayeth neere."[17] I could not tell what to make of these words, for they was very darke to mee. Soe when I had done, I went out of the Chamber into the Kitching.

Now the Chamber where my ffather and I lay had too beds, and it was A lower roome, soe y^t I could heare my ffather when hee was A sleepe as I sat by the fyre in ye next roome; for when he was A sleep, he vsed to snore soe in his sleepe that one might heare him all over the house. Now when I haue heard him doe soe, I often tooke liberty to sitt vp the longer, wher god gaue me A heart to improve my time. And that night he slept very sound as he vsed to doe. And although he bid me make hast to bed, yet I did not, But went to the throne of grace, where I found my heart wounderfully drawne out in prayre for severall things for which I had not found it in such A violent maner for some time before. And one thing y^t I was soe Importunate wth god for was y^t he would shew mercy to my deare father, and saue his Soul. This I could not tell when to haue done pleading wth god for. And y^t word still run thro my mind, "The End is Come, the End is Come, the time draweth neare"; And y^t word, "The sett time is Come." But not one thought I had that it had respect to my fathers death. And Anothing[18] I was Crying to the Lord for was that he would please to stand by me, and be wth mee, in whatsoever I had to meet wth in this World; not thinckeing what I had to meet wth that night and weeke. But I was soe helped to direct my Cryes to ye Lord as if I had knowne what had beene A Comeing vpon mee, which I did not. And it was A very sweet season to my poore soul.

Soe after a greate while I went to bed. and when I came into the Chamber, my father was still A sleepe, which I was glad of; which I often vsed to bee, when I had sat vp A greate while, for if he hath happened to heare me come to bed, he would often chide mee for sitting vp soe late.

Soe I went to bed, I hope wth A thanckefull heart to god for what he had given me y^t night. And after I had beene A bed A while, fell A sleepe; but I suppose had not beene A sleepe long But heard a very dolefull noyse. I thought it to be in the yard, not being quite awake. At last it wakened me more and more, and I perceived it was my father. Soe hereing of him make such a dolefull noise I start vp in my bed.

"ffather, said I, "are you not well?" And he said, "No." Said I, "How long haue you not beene well, pray?" Said he, "I was strucke wth A paine at my heart in my sleepe; I shall dye p^rsently."

Soe I start out of my bed and slipt on my pettycoates & shoes, and ran and light A Candle, and came to his bed side. And he sat vpright in his bed, Crying out to the Lord for mercy. "Lord," said he, "haue mercy on me. I am A poore miserable Sinner; Lord Jesus, wash me in thy pretious blood."

Soe I stood by him trembling to heare him in such distress of Soul for Christ, and to see him looke soe pale in the face. Soe I knelt downe by his bed side And spent a litle time in prayre by him, soe well as god helped me; and he seemed to Joyne wth me soe Earnestly. Soe when I had done, which was more then ever I did wth him before, "ffather," said I, "I must goe Call some body, for I dare not stay with you Alone"; for I had noe body wth mee, nor noe house very neere.

Said he, "Yow shall not goe out at this time of the night; dont be afraid of mee." And he still made the house ring wth Cryes for mercy. Soe he said he would rise, and he put on his Cloths himselfe. And I ran and made a good fire Against he came out; and he all the while Cryed and prayed for mercy; And Cryed out of a paine at his heart. Thought I, may bee it is Cold that is settled about his heart, for want of takeing of hott things when he would not let me come in, and had noe body to doe Any thing for him.

Soe I run and made him something hott, hopeing he might be better. "Oh, I want mercy for my Soul," said hee, "Oh, Lord shew mercy to mee; I am A greate Sinner. Oh, Lord Jesus, if thow doest not show mercy to me now, I am vndone for ever."

"ffather," said I, "their is mercy in Jesus Christ for Sinners; Lord helpe yow to lay hould of it."

"Oh," said hee, "I haue beene Against yow for seekeing after Jesus Christ; the Lord forgiue me, and lay not y^t Sinn to my Charge."

Soe, when I had made him something hot, I prayed him to drincke some of it; and he drancke A litle of it, and straind to vomitt, but did not. Soe I run to him to hold his head, As he sat by the fyre; and he Changed black in ye face, As if he was A dying. And as I stood by him to hold his head, he leant Against me with all his Weight. Oh, this was A very frightfull thing to me indeed! Thought I, "if I leaue him, he will dropp in fier; And if I stand by him, he will dye in my Armes, And noe body neare mee. Oh," I cryed out, "Lord helpe me, what shall I doe?" Them words darted in vpon my mind, "Feare not, I am wth thee; be not dismaied, I am thy god, I will helpe the, I will vp hold thee."[19]

Soe after A litle it pleased god my father revived againe, And came to himselfe; And Cryed out Againe for mercy, "Lord, haue mercy vpon mee, I am a sinfull man; Lord spare me one weeke more, one day more." Oh, these was peirsing words to mee! Soe sitting a while by the fier after hee came to himselfe, for I thincke he did swound Away for A time, he said, "Give me the Candle to goe in to the Chamber, for I shall haue A stoole."

Soe he tooke the Candle & went into the Chamber; And I see him stagger as he went over the threshould. Soe I made A better fier Against he came out, and when I had done I went into the Chamber to him p^{r}sently, and when I came wthin the doore, I see him lye vpon the grownd. And I run to him, scremeing and Crying, "ffather, father"; and I put my hands vnder his Armes, and lift at him to lift him vpp, and stood lifting at him, and Cryin till my strength was gone, first at one Arme, then at Another. As some afterwards said, my dreameing of the Aple tree did signifie something of this.[20] Their I stood, lifting, and Crying, till I was almost spent and Could perceiue noe life in him. Oh, now I was in a streight indeed. Soe I see I could not lift him vpp, I left him and run through the house, Crying like A poore afflicted Creature y^t I was, And unloct the doore to goe call my Brother.

Now it was the dead time of the night and noe house neere. And as I ran to the doore, these thought mett mee at the doore, that their stood rouges ready at the doore to knocke me o'th head, at which I was sadly frighted; but thinckin that my poore father lay dead in the house, I see I was now surrounded wth trouble. Soe I opened the doore, and rusht out much Affrighted. And it had snowed Aboundance that night; it lay very deepe, and I had noe stockins on Soe y^t the snow got into my shoues that I could not run A pace, and goeing to the stile, that was in my fathers yard, I stood Crying and Calling to my Brother. At last god helped me to Consider that it was Impossible to make them heare soe fer off. Then I gatt over the stile, and the snow water Caused my shoues that they would not stay on my feete for want of stockins; but I ran as fast as I could. And About the midle of the Close, as I was runing to my brothers, I was suddainly surprised wth these thoughts, that there was rouges behind mee, that would kill mee. With that I hastily lookt behind mee, and those word dropt vpon my mind, "ye Angels of thee Lord In-campeth round About them that feare him."[21]

Soe Comeing to my Brothers, I stood Crying out in A dolefull manner, vnder his Chamber window, to the sad surprising and frighting of the whole family, they being in their midnight sleepe. My poore brother was soe afrighted that he did not know my voyce. He start out of his bed, and put his head out at window, and said, "Whoe are yow? what is ye matter?" "Oh, Brother," said I, "my father is dead; Come away quickly." "Oh, wife," said hee, "this is my poore Sister. My father is dead."

Soe he Called vp his Servants, but they was soe frighted y^t they could scarse put on their Cloths. And when they came downe out of doores, they did not know me at first. Soe my Brother and too or three of his men ran, and was their before mee. And when my Brother came into the Chamber my father was risen from the ground And layde vpon ye bedd.

Soe my Brother spake to him, and stood Crying over him, but he could speake but one word, or too, to him.

Soe when I came in, they would not let me goe in to him, for they said he was Just a departing. Oh, dismall night to mee! Indeed, as I said, had not the Lord beene good to mee, I had beene frighted to death almost.

Soe presently one of my brothers men Came to me, and tould me he was departed. But in the midest of my trouble I had some hopes my father was gone to heaven notwithstanding. Soe I sat Crying in a dismall manner, thincking what a greate Chang death had made vpon my poore father of A suddaine, whoe went well to bed and was in eternity by midnight. I said in my heart, "Lord, give me one Seale more that I shall goe to heaven when death shall make this greate Chang vpon mee." That Scripture Came suddainly vpon my mind, "The Ransomed of the Lord shall returne, and Come with singin to Sion, and everlasting Joy shall be vpon their heads; they shall obtaine Joy and gladness, & sorrow and sigthing shall flye away."[22] Oh, I longed to be gone to heaven I had such a sence of the worke of the Saints was now About in heaven. Thinck I, they are singing and I am sorrowing; but I see it to be A mercy that I had Any hopes through grace of goeing thither.

Soe my Brother, quickly after he came, sent some of his men to call in neighbours. Soe Among the rest Came M[r] ffary and his Sonn, who soe soone as they came in house, asked if my father was departed; and somebody tould him yeas. And he Answered it was noe more then he lookt for. Now noe body tooke notise of them words till afterwards. Soe some women Came in, who see me sett w[th]out my stockings and scarse any thing on mee, bewailed my sorrowfull Case, and the terrifying things I had mett with that night.

Notes

AGNES BEAUMONT (1652-1720) was a member of John Bunyan's meeting in Bedford, which she joined in 1672. In 1669 her brother John had been accused by the churchwardens of Edworth of refusing to take the sacrament in his parish church. Agnes's father, also called John, was scandalised by her decision, and in particular by her riding to meetings behind Bunyan on his horse. John Beaumont the elder put his daughter out of his house and threatened to disinherit her. Her subsequent heart-broken reconciliation with him and his sudden death shortly thereafter led to her being accused of his murder. However, the coroner's jury exonerated her quickly enough. She subsequently married (twice), and her Narrative became a classic nonconformist text, though it was not published until 1760. It went through various printings, not all of them very accurate. More recently an edition based on the manuscript in the British Museum (Egerton 2414) was published by G. B. Harrison in *Constable's Miscellany of Original & Selected Publications in Literature*, from which this extract is taken.

1. 'that'.
2. Overshoes.
3. 'softly'?
4. Enclosures.
5. Jeremiah 33:3
6. Psalm 34:15 (slightly misquoted).
7. Isaiah 63:9.
8. Like the apostle Peter in denying Christ (Matthew 26: 69-75, etc.).

9. Matthew 10:33.

10. Matthew 10:37; the Authorised Version reads: 'He that loveth father and mother more than me . . .'

11. Sighs.

12. Luke 22:31-2 (slightly misquoted).

13. Not a quotation from scripture.

14. See Hebrews 13:8.

15. Job 5:19 (slightly misquoted).

16. Deuteronomy 33:27.

17. Probably a misquotation of Ezekiel 7:12.

18. 'another thing'.

19. Isaiah 41:10 (slightly misquoted).

20. Agnes had dreamt that a richly fruiting apple tree was growing in her father's yard, and that one night it was uprooted in a storm, to her great distress and that of her brother, who with her tried in vain to raise it to 'growe in its place again'. She believed that this, like other dreams she had at the time, 'was of God'.

21. Psalm 34:7 (very slightly misquoted).

22. Isaiah 35:10 (slightly misquoted).

6 From: *The Miscellaneous Works of Charles Blount, Esq; containing . . . I. The Oracles of Reason, &c.*

Charles Blount, 1695

To the Right Honourable and most ingenious Strephon,[1] *giving a Political human account of the Subversion of* Judaism, *Foundation of* Christianity, *and Origination of the* Millenaries.[2]

Ludgate Hill, Decemb. 1678.

My Lord, I humbly ask your Lordships pardon for this presumption; but when I had the last honour of waiting upon you, your Lordships candour gave me the freedom of Venting my own Thoughts; and then, as the Subject of our discourse was, about the great Changes and Revolutions that from time to time had happen'd in the Universe, so I made bold to assert, that in all Mutations, as well Ecclesiastical, as Civil, I would engage to make appear to your Lordship, that a Temporal Interest was the great Machine upon which all human Actions moved; and that the common and general pretence of Piety *and* Religion, *was but like Grace before a Meal: accordingly, I have presumed to trouble your Lordship with these ensuing Remarques, to justifie the same Assertion.*[3]

There was never any Republick which dwindled into a Monarchy, or Kingdom altered into an *Aristocracy* or Commonwealth, without a *Series* of preceding Causes that principally contributed thereunto; had not other Circumstances concurr'd, never had *Cæsar* establish'd himself, nor *Brutus*[4] erected a Senate: And if you enquire, why the first *Brutus* expell'd *Tarquin*, and the second could not overthrow *Augustus* and *Anthony*? Or why *Lycurgus*,[5] *Solon*,[6] and *Numa*,[7] could establish those Governments, which others have since in vain attempted to settle in *Genoa, Florence*, and other places, you will find it to arise from hence: that some considering those antecedent Causes, which secretly and securely encline to a Change, took advantage thereof; whilst others did only regard the Speciousness or Justice of their Pretensions, without any mature examination of what was principally to be observed;

for nothing is more certain, than that in these Cases, when the previous dispositions all intervene, but a very slight occasion, nay, often times, a meer Casualty, opportunely taken hòld on, and wisely pursued, will produce those revolutions, which (otherwise) no humane Sagacity or Courage could have accomplished.

I cannot find any Authentic Ground to believe, that the Sects among the *Jews* were more ancient than the days of the *Maccabees*, but arose after that *Antiochus* had subdued *Jerusalem*,[8] and reduced the generality of the *Jews* to Paganism; when (the better to confirm his Conquests) he erected therein an Academy for the *Pythagorean*, *Platonic* and *Epicurean Philosophers*. This I conceive, (and so do others) was the Original of the *Pharisees*, *Sadduces* and *Essenes*;[9] tho' afterwards, when the *Maccabees* had anathematized all that taught their Children the *Greek* Philosophy, one Party did justifie their Tenets, by entituling them to *Sadoc* and *Raithos*, and the other to a *Cabala*[10] derived successively from *Ezra* and *Moses*. The Introduction of those Sects, and of that *Cabala*, occasion'd that Exposition of the Prophecy of *Jacob*, viz. *The Scepter shall not depart from* Judah, *nor a Lawgiver from between his Feet, until* Shilo *come, and unto him shall the gathering of the People be.*[11] From whence they did (according to that fantastic *Cabala*) imagine, That whensoever the Scepter should depart from *Judah*, and the Dominion thereof cease, that then there should arrive a Messiah. But as for his being of the Line of *David*, this was no general Opinion;[12] for how then could any have imagined *Herod* the Great[13] to have been the Messias? Or how could *Josephus*[14] fix that Character upon *Vespasian*,[15] as him who should restore the Empire, and Glory of *Israel*, to whom all Nations should bow, and submit unto his Scepter? I do not read that the *Jews* harbor'd any such Exposition during their Captivity under *Nebuchadnezzar*;[16] albeit that the Scepter was at that time so departed from the Tribe of *Judah*, and the House of *David*, that it never was re-setled in it more. After their return to *Jerusalem*, no such thing is spoken of; when *Antiochus Epiphanes* subdued them, prophaned their Temple, destroyed their Laws, and left them nothing of a Scepter or Lawgiver; during all which time, notwithstanding they had the same Prophecies and Scriptures among them, there is no News of any expected Messiah. But after the Curiosity of the Rabbins had involved them in the pursuance of mystical Numbers, and Pythagorically or Cabalistically to explain them according to the *Gematria*,[17] then was it first discover'd, that *Shiloh* and Messiah consisted of Letters which make up the same Numerals, and therefore that a mysterous promise of a Redeemer was Insinuated thereby: as also, that the Prophecy of

Balaam[18] concerning a Star out of *Jacob*, and a Scepter rising out of
Israel, with a multitude of other Predictions, (which the condition of
their Nation made them otherwise to despair of) should be accomplish'd
under this Messiah. I name no other Prophecies, because they are either
general and indefinitely exprest as to the time of their Accomplishment,
or inexplicable from their obscurity, or uncertain as to their Authority:
such as are the Weeks of *Daniel*,[19] which Book the *Jews* reckon among
their *Hagiographa* or Sacred, but not Canonical Books.

This Prophecy likewise had a contradictory one, where 'tis said of
Coniah,[20] *That no man of his seed shall prosper sitting upon the Throne
of* David, *and ruling any more in* Judah *Jer.* 22. 30. Also *Ezek.* 22. 26,
27. *Thus saith the Lord God, Remove the Diadem, and take off the
Crown, this shall not be the same,* &c. Now the aforesaid obscure
Prophecy, which did not take effect at first, until the Reign of *David*,
and which suffer'd such a variety of Interruptions, seemeth to have
fallen under this Interpretation in the days of *Herod* the Great, whom
the *Jews* so hated for his Usurpation over the *Macchabees* Levitical
Family, and for his general Cruelties, that he was particularly detested
by the cabalistical *Pharisees*, who, to keep up the Rancor against him
and his Linage, as well as to alienate the People from him, I could
easily imagine the Exposition of this Prophecy to have been for no
other purpose. Neither perhaps was *Herod* much displeased with the
said Interpretation of the Prophecy, after the *Herodians* had accommodated it to him, and made him the Messiah, who (after their Conquest and Ignominy under *Pompey*[21]) having restor'd the *Jews* to a
great reputation and strength, and rebuilt their Temple, found some
who could deduce his Pedigree from the thigh of *Jacob*, as directly as
David's and *Solomon*'s were.

Now this Construction of the Prophecy being inculcated into the
People, and into all those *Jews*, Strangers or Proselytes which resorted
to *Jerusalem* at their great Festivals, (from *Alexandria*, *Antioch*, *Babylon*, and all other parts where the *Jews* had any Colonies) there arose
an universal expectation of a Messiah to come, (excepting amongst the
Herodians, who thought *Herod* the Messias) and afterwards possest the
Jews (for our *Jews* are but the Remains of the *Pharisees*) to this very
day. But their impatience for his appearance, seems to have been less
under *Herod* the Great, than ever since the first Interpretation of the
Prophecy, (there being no mention of false Messiahs at that time) perhaps, because the Prophecy was not so clear and convincing whilst that
Herod was King: Since under him the Scepter and Legislative Power
seem'd to be still in *Juda*, though sway'd by an *Idumæan* Proselyte, the

Priesthood continu'd, the Temple flourish'd, and there was a Prince of the *Sanhedrin, Rabbi Hillel*,[22] of the Lineage of *David*. But ten Years after the Birth of Christ, when *Archelaus*[23] was banish'd to *Vienna*, and *Judea* reduced into the form of a Province, the Scepter then seem'd to be entirely departed from *Judah*; the Kingdom was now become part of the Government of *Syria*, and ruled by a Procurator, who taxed them severely, then the sense of their Miseries made the People more credulous; and whether they more easily believ'd what they so earnestly desired might happen, or whether the Malecontents (taking the advantage of their afflictions) did then more diligently insinuate into the multitude that opinion, it so hapned, that there arose at that time sundry false Messiahs, and the World was big with expectation, (rais'd in every Country by the *Jews*, who had receiv'd the intelligence from their common Metropolis *Jerusalem*) that the great Prince was coming, who should reestablish the *Jewish* Monarchy, and bring peace and happiness to all the Earth.

Now these Circumstances made way for the reception of Christ, and the Miracles he did, (for Miracles were the only Demonstrations to the *Jews*) convincing the People that he was the Messiah, they never staid till he should declare himself to be so: (for I think he never directly told any he was so, but the Woman of *Samaria*[24]) or evinced his Genealogy from *David*; (for tho' some mean persons call'd him the Son of *David*, and the Mobb by that Title did cry *Hossanna*[25] to him, yet did he acquiesce in terming himself the Son of Man) but esteem'd him a Prophet, *Elias, Jeremiah,* and even the very Messiah. Also when he made his Cavalcade upon an *Asinego*, they extoll'd him as the Descendant of King *David*: but his untimely apprehension and death (together with his neglect to improve the Inclination of the People to make him King) did allay the Affections of the *Jews* towards him, disappoint all their hopes, and so far exasperated them against him, that they who had been part of his Retinue at his entrance, did now call for his Execution, and adjudge him by common Suffrage to be crucify'd: insomuch that his Disciples fly, the Apostles distrust, and sufficiently testify their unbelief, by not crediting his Resurrection. But after that he was risen again, and they assur'd thereof, they reasume their hopes of a temporal Messias, and the last Interrogatory they propose unto him, is, *Lord, wilt thou at this time restore the Kingdom to* Israel?[26]

After his Assumption into Heaven, they attended in *Jerusalem* the coming of the Holy Ghost, which seized on them, and gave them *the Gift of Tongues*[27] (as 'tis written) *for a season*; whereby they preached to the *Jews, Elamites, Parthians, Alexandrians,* &c. (whom *Salmasius*[28] shews, not to be absolute Strangers to the Natives of those Countries, but *Jews* planted there) as also to the Proselytes. These being surpriz'd with the Miracle of the *Cloven Tongues*, and *Gift of Languages*, as likewise being possest with the desire and hopes of a Messiah, and being Further ascertain'd by the Apostle *Peter*, *That Jesus* (whom *Pilate* had crucify'd) *was the Lord and Christ*,[29] were, to the number of 3000, immediately baptized into his Name; and such as were to depart, when they came to their Colonies, did divulge the tydings, and engage other *Jews* and Proselytes to the same Belief: the Apostles themselves going about, and ordaining likewise others to preach the glad tydings of a Messiah come; who (though dead) was risen again (according to the obscure Prediction of *David*) for the Salvation of *Israel*: and whose second appearance would compleat the happiness of all Nations, as well *Jews* as *Gentiles*.

Having thus therefore given your Lordship an account of the subversion of *Judaism*, as well as of the foundation of Christianity, the origination of the *Millenaries* is only the consequence of the fall of the one, and rise of the other; for it is apparent, that not only the *Jews*, but also the *Christians* were *Millenaries*, and did believe and expect the temporal Reign of a Messiah, together with the Union of the *Jews* and *Gentiles* under one most happy Monarchy. Not one of the two first Ages dissented from this Opinion; and they who oppose it, never quote any for themselves before *Dionysius Alexandrinus*,[30] who liv'd (at least) 250 years after Christ. Of this Opinion was *Justin Martyr*,[31] and (as he says) all other Christians that were exactly Orthodox. *Irenæus*[32] sets it down exactly for a Tradition, and relates the very Words which Christ us'd when he taught this Doctrine; so that if this Tenet was not an universal Tradition in the Primitive Times, I know not what Article of our Faith will be found to be such: This Doctrine was taught by the Consent of the most eminent Fathers of the first Centuries, without any Opposition from their Contemporaries; and was deliver'd by them, not as Doctors, but Witnesses: and not as their own Opinion, but as Apostolick Tradition. Moreover, it was with this pretence of Christ's being a coming to reign with them here in Glory, that stopt the Mouths of the unbelieving *Jews*, who before, upon his Death and suffering like other Men, began to doubt very much of the Power of his Messiaship, which made them distrust his reigning in Glory amongst them here on Earth, as it was foretold the Messiah should do; wherefore this *Millenary* Invention of his coming again to reign in Glory salv'd all.[33]

And thus your Lordship sees, the wickedness of Mens Natures is such, that all Revolutions whatever both in Church and State, as well

Explaining Revom to Rock

as all Mutations both in Doctrine and Matters of Faith, be they never
so pious and sacred, or never so beneficial and useful to Mankind, both
in their Souls and Bodies, yet they must be still seconded by some
private temporal Interest, and have some humane Prop to support
them, or else all will not do. My Lord, I am sensible I have a thousand
Pardons to ask your Lordship for this tedious impertinence, but to do
so at this time, were but to lengthen, and consequently add to my
Crime: So I shall only beg the honour to subscribe my self at present,

> *(My LORD) Your Lordship's most obedient humble Servant,*

> BLOUNT.

For Mr. Hobbs,[34] *to be left with Mr.* Crook, *a Bookseller, at the
Sign of the* Green Dragon *without* Temple-Bar, near St. Clement's
Church.

Ludgate-Hill, 1678.

Concerning the Arrians,[35] Trinitarians *and Councils.*

SIR, By your Permission, and Mr *Crook*'s Favour, I have had the Happiness to peruse your incomparable Treatise of Heresie in Manuscript,
wherein you have certainly given us a more accurate and faithful Account of the *Nicene* Council, together with their particular Grounds and
Reasons for each distinct Article of their Faith in the *Nicene* Creed,[36]
than is any where else to be met with. How grateful this Discourse of
yours will be to the *Quicunque-men*[37] I shall not Presume to determin,
since I am sure Mr *Hobbs* is as much above their Anger, as they are
below his Resentments. You yourself have very well observed, *When
Reason is against a Man a Man will be against Reason*; and therefore
'tis no wonder to see, from several Interests, so many several Opinions
and Animosities arise. This made the *Arrians* and *Trinitarians* so zeal-
ously endeavour to supplant one another; this made *Constantine*[38] at
first espouse the *Arrian* Interest to mount the Throne, as the present
Lewis XIV.[39] did the Interest of the *Hugonots*, and afterwards thinking
to weaken or at least to ballance that Power that raised him, strike in
with *Athanasius*[40] and the *Trinitarians* for a time, as our present *Lewis*
hath since done the like with the Popish and Jesuitical Party against his
Protestant Subjects. For Mankind ever lived and died after one and the
same Method in all Ages, being governed by the same interests and the

same passions at this time, as they were many Thousand Years before us, and will be many Thousand Years after us.

It must be confessed,[41] the *Arrians* were so powerful a Sect in the *Roman* Empire, (especially the *Eastern* Part of it) that the Followers of the *Nicene* Council were not equal to them, either in Number, Splendor, interest or Riches. If you will believe the learned *Petavius*[42] and others, they did offer to be try'd by the Fathers that preceded the *Nicene* Council: For at that Council they were rather condemn'd by a Party, than by the general Consent of the Christian Church; because *Constantine,* out of above Two thousand Bishops then assembled, excluded all but Three hundered and eighteen; nor were those perhaps (for Accounts vary) all Bishops, that made up this great Council. They were all of a Judgment at first, and so rather Parties than Judges; the *Arrians* had not the Freedom to dispute their Cause: And the Emperour *Constantine* was afterwards so ill satisfied with their proscription, that he soon recalled *Arrius*, and a little before his Death was baptized by an *Arrian* Bishop. *Constantius*[43] and *Valens*[44] were professed *Arrians* (and not to mention the *Goths*) *Valentinian,*[45] *Theodosius*[46] and other Emperors protected and honoured them, both with civil and military Commands.

The *Arrian* Doctrin was not only confirmed by Eight Councils several times assembled at *Tyre, Sardis, Syrmium, Milain, Selucia, Nice, Tarsis,* and particularly at *Ariminum* (where six hundred Bishops were of their Opinion, with only three which held the contrary) but they also punished others their Adversaries, who were of a contrary Opinion to them, with Confiscations, Banishments, and other grievous Punishments. Now whether the Power of their Party, the Riches of their Churches, the Magnificence of their Worship (as the first that brought Musick into the Church)[47] or the fame of their Learning, and pretensions to Reason (which is always an inviduous plea) did raise Jealousie & Hatred in the Emperors against them, as also rendred them odious to the *Trinitarians*: or what most contributed so their first Depression and Persecution, I know not: Since to persecute for Religion, was by the *Trinitarians* (*Athanasius, Hillary*[48] & others) then accounted an *Arrian* an unchristian Tenet. It is not to be doubted, but that, after the days of *Theodosius*, Reason of State did most prevail towards their Subversion, lest they should joyn with the *Goths*, who at that time possessed of *Italy, Spain, Afric* & other Provinces, were formidable to the *Bizantine* Empire. Notwithstanding whatsoever it was, 'tis easie to comprehend that the Depression of them did facilitate the Conquest of the *Goths*; and if you will credit *Salvian,*[49] the *Goths* were very pious in their Way, mild to the conquer'd, just in their Dealings; so that the Wickedness of the Christian Rulers of Provinces, their Exactions upon the People, and Insolence of the Foreign Souldiers, whereby they ruled, made even the *Trinitarians* themselves willingly submit to their Dominion, and prefer it before that of the *Eastern* Emperors.

As for the *Trinitarians* of those Times, I must confess, I cannot but esteem them as Enemies to all human Learning; for they had Canons forbidding them to read any Ethic[50] Books, and a Zeal which disposed them to destroy all they met with of that kind. Thus we may well suppose them universally Ignorant, except some few; and as the Pastors, so were the People. Their Religion also consisted rather in an out-side Service, than inward Piety and Knowledge; their Faith was in a manner implicit, the Mysteries of Religion (for such I call the Doctrin of the Trinity and its Dependencies) were scarce ever mentioned to them in Sermons, much less explicated. Hence the Vulgar became prone to Embrace Superstition, and credit Miracles, how ridiculous and fabulous soever. Visions, Allegories and Allusions to Texts, were convincing Arguments, and no Demonstration like to a feigned Story and Legend, or what might be interpreted a Judgment upon an Heretic.

Amongst the *Trinitarians* were a sort of People who followed the Court Religion, and believed as their Prince ordained, living then unconfined by the Dictates of the then declining Church: And though the *Trinitarians* had resolv'd upon, and subscrib'd to the *Nicene* Council, and embraced those Forms of Speech which are now in use, yet did they not understand what was meant by them. The *Latin* Church allow'd of Three Persons, and not of three Hypostases;[51] the *Greek* Church allow'd of three Hypostases, and not of three Persons. As difficult was it for them to Explicate *Usia*[52] or *Essence*, which hard words produc'd a subdivision amongst them, consisting of *Nestorians*[53] and *Eutychians*.[54] The *Nestorians* believing the Deity of Christ, held that he was made up of two distinct Persons, and so perfect God, and perfect Man. The *Eutychians* averr'd, that Christ had but one Nature, and that upon the Hypostatical Union, the Deity and Humanity were so blended together by Confusion of Properties and Substances, that one person endued with one Will, did emerge thence. Now these two Sects were of great Power in the *Eastern* Church, and though they were both condemn'd in the third and fourth General Councils, yet did they spread far and near, through *Palestine Egypt*, the Kingdom of *Abyssines*, and all *Persia* over: Each of them had their Patriarchs, Bishops and Churches contradistinct from the *Melchites*, who adhering and subscribing to the Council of *Chalcedon* (which all the Imperial Clergy did) were called *Melchites*, that is to say, Men of the King's Religion. The Authors of the *Nestorian* and *Eutychian* Sects were Learned and potent Bishops. *Eutychius* was Patriarch of *Constantinople*, and with him joyned *Dioscorius* Patriarch of *Alexandria*, *Severus* Patriarch of *Antioch*, and *Jacobus Baradœus*, from whom the *Jacobites* are at this day denominated. *Nestorius* was also Patriarch of *Constantinople*, and his Sect very much diffused.

The Truth is, such were the Ignorance of the People, and Debaucheries of the Ages at this time, that if a Man did but live a pious strict Life, with great Mortification, or outward Devotion, and were but an Eloquent Preacher, he might in any place of the *Eastern* Empire have made a potent Sect instantly. And to shew how ignorant the Clergy were at the General Council of *Chalcedon*, in the time of *Marcianus*[55] the Emperor; we find that the *Greek* Tongue was then so little understood at *Rome*, and the *Latin* in *Greece*, that the Bishops of both Countries (in all 630) were glad to speak by Interpreters. Nay, in this very Council of *Chalcedon*, the Emperor was fain to deliver the same Speech in *Greek* to one Party, and in *Latin* to the other, that so both might understand him. The Council of *Jerusalem*, for the same Reason, made certain Creeds both in *Greek* and *Latin*. At the Council of *Ephesus*, the Pope's Legates had their Interpreter to Expound the Words; and when *Cœlestine*'s[56] Letters were there read, the Acts tell us, how the Bishops desired to have them Translated into *Greek* and read over again, insomuch, that the *Romish* Legates had almost made a Controversie of it, fearing lest the papal Authority should have been prejudiced by such an Act; alledging therefore, how it was the ancient Custom to propose the Bulls of the Sea Apostolick in Latin only, and that that might now suffice. Whereupon, these poor *Greek* Bishops were in danger not to have understood the Popes *Latin*, till at length the Legates were content with Reason, when it was evidenced to them, that the major part could not understand one word of *Latin*. But the pleasantest of all is, Pope *Cœlestine*'s Excuse to *Nestorius*, for his so long delay in answering his Letters, because he could not by any means get his *Greek* construed sooner. Also Pope *Gregory* the First[57] ingeniously confesseth to the Bishop of *Thessaly*, that he understood not a Jot of his *Greek*; wherefore 'tis probable, the Proverb of honest *Accursius*[58] was even then in use, – *Grœcum est, non legitur*,[59] – and this was the Condition of Christianity in which *Justinian*[60] the Emperour found, it *A.C.* 540. So that as Mounsieur *Daille*[61] has demonstrated with how little certainty we can depend upon the Fathers, I think I may safely averr there is as little Trust to be reposed in General Councils who have been Guilty of so much ignorance and interest, as well as so frequently contradicting one another.[62] And to say, that Councils may not err, though private

Persons may, is as (as Mr. *Hales*[63] well observes) all one as to say, that every single Souldier indeed may run away, but the whole Army cannot.

Sir, Your Treatise having reviv'd these Meditations in me, I hope you'll pardon if I have been too prolix; and though I am not so vain to pretend to offer these Collections, or Indeed any, for Mr. *Hobbs*'s instruction, who is of himself the great Instructor of the most sensible part of Mankind in the noble Science of Philosophy; yet I may hope for the Honours of your Correction wherein I am Erroneous, the which will for ever oblige,

SIR, Your most unfeigned Humble Servant,

C. BLOUNT.

Notes

CHARLES BLOUNT (1654-93) was a friend and defender of Dryden and also of Hobbes, to whom he sent a copy of his sceptically inclined *Anima Mundi* in 1678. His relations with Dryden are difficult to assess. It is probable that his dedication of *Religio Laici*, following the publication of Dryden's poetic defence of anglicanism with the same title, was an exercise at once in friendship and irony. His defence of press freedom is taken largely from Milton's *Areopagitica*, just as the two 'letters' published in this volume are borrowed from Stubbe and much of *Religio Laici* derives from Lord Herbert of Cherbury's *De Religione Laici*. It is hard to acquit Blount entirely of plagiarism, but the publication of radical views was, after all, a dangerous business between 1660 and 1688. He died as a result of a suicide attempt brought about by his being unable in law to marry the sister of his dead wife. *The Oracles of Reason* were first published in 1693 and republished two years later in *The Miscellaneous Works*.

HENRY STUBBE (1632-76) was a protégé of Sir Henry Vane. He was ejected from his position as second keeper in the Bodleian Library, Oxford, on account of his anti-clerical writings. He conformed at the restoration, practising medicine in Jamaica and Warwickshire. Previously most celebrated for his apparently reactionary attacks on the Royal Society, he has been shown by recent scholarship, and in the light of his *An Account of the Rise and Progress of Mohametanism with the Life of Mohamet*, which was not published until 1911, to have been a circumspect but consistent, and in some respects a notorious radical.

1. John Wilmot, second Earl of Rochester (1647-80), poet, libertine and free thinker, who referred to himself by this name in some of his poems. He was converted, virtually on his deathbed, to latitudinarian Christianity by Gilbert Burnet (1643-1714), Fellow of the Royal Society, whose tolerant religious views and association with political radicals before 1688 (he advised William of Orange during the 1680s) led to his appointment as Bishop of Salisbury after the revolution.

2. Believers in the imminent and literal Second Coming of Christ and his thousand-year reign as prophesied in Revelation.

3. See Shairani, 1911, 2-12 for the original of the remainder of all but the final paragraph of this letter.

4. Lucius Junius Brutus (6th century BC), First Consul of Rome and legendary ancestor of Marcus Junius Brutus (85?-42 BC), assassin of Julius Caesar (see p. 58 n. 5). The first Brutus drove the last of the Etruscan kings of Rome from the city and established a republic ('erected a Senate') but his descendant's attempt to save that republic from monarchic rule was a failure; he was defeated at the battle of Philippi in 42 BC by the forces of Gaius Octavius Caesar (Augustus) (see p. 58 n. 5) and Marcus Antonius (83-30 BC).

5. Lycurgus, traditional author of the laws of Sparta.

6. Solon, archon of Athens (594 BC), and reorganiser of the city's laws and constitution.

7. Numa, traditionally the second King of Rome and founder of its ancient institutions.

8. Jerusalem was conquered by Antiochus IV 'Epiphanes', Seleucid King of Syria, in 167 BC. The following year the Maccabean family began a successful revolt against Antiochus, ultimately recapturing Jerusalem, cleansing the Temple and paving the way for an independant Jewish state.

9. The Maccabees were resisting the cultural assimilation of the Jews into the Greek world. Stubbe suggests that the Jews were, nevertheless, influenced by Greek traditions. It is possible that the Saducees did derive their name from Sadoc, Solomon's High Priest, but, sympathetic as they were to the Greeks, they were not influenced by Pythagorean philosophy. The Pharisees did indeed first appear at the time of the Maccabees, and were the ancestors of modern rabbinical Judaism, but they had no connection with Plato or his disciples. The Essenes also dated from the Maccabean period. They were a separatist group, awaiting (like Christian millenaries) a divine intervention in history. They were certainly not Epicureans. Stubbe's speculations are, therefore fanciful, but they, nonetheless, represent an important attempt to understand biblical history in secular terms.

10. The Jewish mystical tradition claiming to be based on the unwritten law revealed by God to Moses and Adam; it probably dates from the first century AD (see n. 17 below).

11. Genesis 49: 10.

12. There were indeed conflicting conceptions of the Messiah, not all of them Davidic.

13. Herod the Great (reigned 40-4 BC), King of Judea; his family was not of Jewish origin.

14. Josephus (37-100? AD), Jewish historian; a military commander opposing the Roman invasion of Judea in 66 AD, he surrendered to the armies of Vespasian, who subsequently became his patron.

15. Vespasian (reigned 69-79 AD), Roman Emperor.

16. Nebuchadnezzar (reigned 605-562 BC), King of Babylon; he captured Jerusalem in 597 BC, carrying many Jews into captivity. The concept of the Messiah did indeed develop in the post-Maccabean period.

17. A cabalistic method of interpreting the scriptures by assigning numerical values to words and exchanging words of the same value (see n. 10 above).

18. Numbers 24:17.

19. Daniel 10:22-7; the Book of Daniel is thought by most modern scholars to refer to the desecration of the Temple by Antiochus Epiphanes.

20. Côniah, son of Jehoiakim (reigned 609-597 BC), King of Judah. Stubbe is challenging literalist readings of the Bible which assume its detailed inerrancy and, therefore, its consistency.

21. Cnaeus Pompeius Magnus (106-48 BC), who annexed Syria and imposed effective Roman control over Judea in 62 BC.

22. Rabbi Hillel (30 BC - AD 9), first president of the Jewish Sanhedrin, and founder of talmudic Judaism.

23. Archelaus (reigned 34 BC - AD 17), King of Cappadocia.

24. John 4:25-6: modern scholars tend to the view that Jesus did not make messianic claims, and that some early Christians denied his Davidic descent.

25. Matthew 21:9; Mark 11:9-10.

26. Acts 1:6.

27. Acts 2:4-11; the aside, 'as 'tis written', circumspectly undercuts a literal reading of this episode.

28. Claudius Salmasius (1588-1653), French scholar.

29. Acts 2:36-41.

30. St Dionysius of Alexandria (190-264).

31. St Justin the martyr (105?-165).

32. St Irenaeus (130?-200?).

33. The remainder of the letter is by Blount.

34. Thomas Hobbes (1588-1679), the philosopher whose absolutist theories frightened libertarians and whose materialist and determinist arguments frightened conservatives. He believed in complete subordination of church to state. He made unsuccessful attempts to establish himself in geometry, and was excluded from the Royal Society. (See also Introduction, pp. 2, 8 and 13.)

35. Followers of Arius (256-336) who denied the equality of the Son with the Father and the perfect humanity of Christ. His teaching was condemned at the Council of Nicaea (see p. 72, n. 16).

36. The creed as recited in the anglican liturgy, which differs in some respects from the creed formulated at Nicaea.

37. Believers in the Athanasian creed which begins with these words ('Whosoever wishes'). See n. 40 below.

38. Constantine the Great (reigned 312-36), the first Christian Roman Emperor (see Introduction, p. 10).

39. Louis XIV (reigned 1643-1715), King of France, the embodiment of royalist absolutism and catholic intolerance, particularly after the withdrawal in 1685 of the Edict of Nantes which granted toleration to the Huguenots and had originally been issued in 1598. It had been confirmed by Cardinal Mazarin on behalf of the infant King at the beginning of Louis's reign.

40. St Athanasius (298?-373), the principal opponent of Arianism in the years after Nicaea.

41. See Shairani, 1911, 44-50 for the original of all but the final paragraph of the remainder of this letter; Blount omits some material.

42. Dionysius Petavius (1583-1652), French historian and catholic theologian.

43. Constantius II (reigned 337-61), Roman Emperor, second son of Constantine the Great.

44. Valens (reigned 363-78), Emperor of the East.

45. Valentinian (reigned 364-75), Emperor of the West.

46. Theodosius (reigned 379-95), Emperor of the East; he in fact submitted to St Ambrose and campaigned against arianism.

47. A jibe at the anglican liturgy.

48. St Hilarius (d. 388), celebrated for his opposition to arianism.

49. Salvianus of Marseilles (400-80), historian of the decline of Rome (see p. 238, n. 1).

50. A misreading of Stubbe who has 'Ethnick' – i.e. pagan (Shairani, 1911, 46).

51. 'Persons' as distinct from 'substances' and 'natures'; before Nicaea, however, 'hypostasis' was frequently used in the sense of the Latin 'substantia' and the Greek 'usia' (see n. 52).

52. In most orthodox theology the word used to signify the being or substance in which the Three Persons of the Trinity are one.

53. Followers of Nestorius (d. 451), who was condemned at the Council of Ephesus for holding that there were two hypostases or persons in Christ.

54. Followers of Eutyches (378?-454), who was condemned at the Council of Chalcedon for holding that the human nature of Christ was wholly absorbed into his divinity. Stubbe was justified in praising the learning of the nestorians and eutychians.

55. Marcianus (reigned 450-7), Emperor of the East..

56. Pope Celestine I (reigned 422-32).

57. See p. 72, n. 13.

58. Franciscus Accursius (1182?-1260), Italian jurist.

59. 'It is Greek and unreadable.'

60. See p. 72, n. 8. .

61. Jean Daille (1594-1670), French protestant divine.

62. A view of the four great Councils very different from Chamberlayne's (see p. 63).

63. John Hales (1584-1656), a Laudian divine deprived of his livings under the Commonwealth.

7 From: *Religio Laici, written in a Letter to John Dryden, Esq.* [1]

Charles Blount, 1683

The Occasion of this Treatise.

There is not any Meditation hath given me greater trouble, than when I think, That a Doctrine so necessary, as the Knowledge of God, with the true Way to serve and worship him, together with the Means to attain everlasting Salvation, should be so variously deliver'd and taught in divers Ages and Countries; as also urged in such perplext and difficult terms; (which by the many Volumes of this Argument, in several Languages, may appear;) and after all this, yet to find it presented to me under such terrible Menaces and Execrations, as if, among the many Churches in the World, I did not adhere to the right, (which each claimed to be theirs) I could not justly hope for salvation; but, on the contrary, expect eternal Torture, without any prospect of Relief.

Being therefore in this doubtful and dangerous condition, I did at last conclude with my self, that one of these two things was to be done:

Methods of Enquiry into Religion.

First, That (notwithstanding the Affronts and Threats wherewith the Priests on every side would deter us from all other Religions, as well as Invitations, Promises, and comfortable Doctrines, by which they would draw us to their own, in any particular Church,) I was bound, either to study with an impartial mind, not only all the several Religions; but likewise the Controversies amongst them in divers Ages, Languages and Countries. And for this purpose, not only to acquire the Tongues used heretofore, or at this present time throughout the Universe: But also to read the several Authors that have written upon these Arguments; and together with them to confer those Learned men, who (though they had not published any thing in writing) might yet be no less able to edifie me, than the former. Or,

Secondly, To fix upon some Fundamental Articles agreed upon by all that I could meet with, and consider afterwards how far they might conduce to my salvation.

The former of these two I soon perceiv'd to be impossible; for, whose private Affairs at home, or publick Duty to his Native Country, will pemit him to take such Journies to all the Quarters of the World? Whose Estate or Revenue will furnish him with Money for so long and great an Undertaking? Or whose Constitution is of that strength and ability, that, were he to escape all the Dangers he must inevitably meet with, could yet undergo so immense a travel and labour? Whose Memory could either contain all the Works of the several Languages and Religions; or Judgment decide the different Opinions and Faiths pretended under the Authority of so many great Churches? which course yet unless he pursued to the end, he could not with Justice say he had performed his Duty. For since the determining finally of any matter of Importance, where Parties are not heard on all sides, is not only against common Reason, but contrary even to the ordinary practice of Justice in all other cases; he must think himself, in that the most important and serious business that can befall Mankind, obliged to make as particular and exact a search and examination of Religions, as is possible.

But here we will suppose, that after diligent Enquiry, one might learn what was taught in this or that Country, under some general Notions; (though no where sufficiently according to all the Tenents, Rites, and Ceremonies taught or practised amongst them,) yet how could the knowledge of any one Religion alone give him satisfaction, especially when he should find it controverted in some other Country, and where as able men, at least in all other points of Learning, might in great numbers be found? Shall he, because his Birth or Affection enclines him to one Country or Religion more than another, so factiously embrace it, as to think no other to be good or acceptable to God, where men do the best they can to serve him, and live well? Must he prejudge all other Religions as erroneous and false, when as yet he hath not heard what they can alledge for the justifying of their Faith? . . . so that whereas I thought my self obliged for the discharge of my Conscience to study not only all Religions that have been or are in the World, I found the *Romanish* Religion in its divers Sects alone of greater Intricacie, than that I could by any Reason or Authority dissolve or unty the many Scruples or Knots in them: since flying somtimes from *Reason* to *Faith*, and then again from *Faith* to *Reason*, with a singular agility in both, I found my self unable to follow them in any one certain way. I confess, that if they had adhered singly to either of these two, nothing could have scandalized me; since that which was delivered upon *Reason*, I should have examined, and finally accepted upon the same ground: and as well should I have believed those Points of *Faith*, which were delivered me upon the Reverend Authority of the *Church*; especially, when it could have been proved, that any former *Church* or *Congregation* had under their hands and Seals, or in any other Authentick manner subscribed, as eye-Witnesses to that they consign'd unto Posterity, and not as Hearers only; it being of great moment in the affirmation of things past, to set down what they knew certainly, and to come afterwards to what was told them by others, which they again had from others, and so perhaps from many descents; especially, if such things were related, as neither they from whom they heard it, nor indeed any mortal man by Natural Means could know. Neither would it be sufficient to say, that their *Knowledge* was *Supernatural* or *Divine*, since as that is more than could be known in following times, so, when it were granted, it would inferr little to me, but that which I would believe without it: For if any under the name of a *Prophet* should bid me do a Sin, or be Impenitent for Sins done, I should not believe him, though he pretended a thousand *Revelations* for it: And on the other side, if he bid me be Vertuous and Penitent, though he had not any shadow of *Revelation* for it, I should give entire Credit to him.

The Validity of Revelation proved by its Doctrine.

That therefore the Certainty of that Doctrine, which is called *Revealed*, or the word of God in any Age or Country, comes not to me simply either from the Authority of him that said the holy Spirit did so dictate the word to him: No, nor from the Authority of them that believed it: (how many or great soever:) but from the Goodness of the Doctrine it self; without which, I should believe but little in any extraordinary kind. Every man, in what Age or Country, that teacheth goodness, speaks the word of God to me; and if the Contrary, he shall never make me believe, he knoweth God, or heard him speak so much as one syllable, much less that he is so familiar with God, as to know him by his Voice. . . .

A Dialogue concerning Revelations.

Therefore in the first place, I should demand in a Rational and

Judicial way, how I could be assured, that the Priests *had received a* Revelation, *and what was the time, place, and manner thereof? In Answer to which, I conceive the* Priests *would tell me; That* Laicks *ought not further to enquire into such* Mysteries *than becomes them; that if this their* Revelation *were not accepted as an unquestionable and necessary Truth, there could be no cause thereof, but an* obdurate heart, *and want of* Divine Grace *in me; that if the* Sacerdotal *word might not be taken concerning the* Truth *of the said* Revelation, *there was no other way to inform me thereof: It being* Gods *manner to speak to his beloved Servants, and not to such gross* Sinners *as I was; and to be brief, that if I did not give entire credit to this* Revelation *of theirs, it was for want of* Faith: *And therefore, that no better counsel could be given me, than to pray that all obstructions might be taken away, and instead of my* heart *of* stone, *that I might receive an* heart *of* flesh,[2] *such as may be capable of this* heavenly Illumination. Finally, *They would reply nothing concerning the* time *or* manner *of their* Revelation, *but only in general say, that the* Place *was* God's *holy* Temple, *where none could be partakers of the* Word of God, *but such only as were his near Servants, and did ordinarily take their rest and sleep therein.*

Now to this I should Answer, That if I might not know the time *and* manner, *when and how this their* Revelation *was made, I would yet gladly be informed, what* Language *was used betwixt them, and whether the* words *were of* God's *immediate invention, or that there were only certain* Notes *and* Characters *in use betwixt them, whereby they understood one another? Or otherwise, if they had not a particular* Language *betwixt them, which was intelligible; whether* God *spake the ordinary* Language *of that Country, and in what* Tone; *whether the same were* lowder *than* Thunder, *or only the* ordinary *heighth, or whether* lower *yet, by* some close *or* secret expression, *somewhat less than a* whisper? *To which I believe the* Priests *would Reply, That if a* King *or* Principal Magistrate *did send me a Message or* Command *by some one of his* known *Officers, I would not then presume to make all these* Questions, *they being not only uncivil, but also impertinent and derogatory to the* Supreme *Authority, and therefore that they who were* known Ministers *of* God, *did without giving further account, require Obedience from me in his* Name. *But not withstanding all this, I should again take the boldness to ask them, (supposing they heard such words) how yet they could know that* God *spake them, and whether they were so familiar with the person of that* God, *as to know him by his* Voice, *and distinguish him from all others? How they could assure*

themselves firmly, that it was no inferiour Spirit *that gave them this*
Revelation, *there being* Spirits *of both sorts, both* good *and* bad, *which
use to deliver* Oracles *and* Revelations, *according to the* Doctrine *of
the* Manichees,[3] *who founded their Opinions upon that sentence, viz.*
that the Devil is the God of this world.[4] *But again, supposing it was a
good* Spirit *that spoke, whether* Camillus, *or his* Boy *who waited on
him in the* Temple, *did hear or understand the* Voice *as well as
himself?*[5] *Here I know the* Priests *Answer should be, That neither
himself, nor any else could come to the knowledge of* God's *Will, but
by their means and conveyance: And for the rest would again require
my Obedience, on peril of my being condemn'd as an* Infidel; *thinking
by these words at least to overawe me.*

*But this would be so far from terrifying me, that it would but put
into my head more Scruples, concerning the Truth of their* Revelation?
*when pursuing my way, I should gladly demand of him, how yet I
could be assured, that in the repeating of this their* Oracle *or* Revelation, *they had omitted no part thereof through forgetfulness; or added
anything to it by a* Paraphrase, *or* Explication; *And briefly, whether
nothing were interweaved or changed therein?*

The Priests *would here assuredly reply, That it was but a prophane
part in me to doubt anything were either added to, or taken from the*
Divine Revelation, *much less any thing mixed or interwoven with it:
and that the same* God, *who gave them this* Revelation, *did and would
preserve it entire in their memory; for further proof whereof, they were
ready to set it down, and sign it under their Hands and Seals, that so it
might be transmitted to Posterity, as an* Authentick Record: *To which
also, the* Amanuenses *or* Coppiers *of it might repair to correct all that
should be depraved, either by their carelesness, or wilful perversion of
the Sense thereof, that so their Errors might afterwards be rectified,
attested and subscribed by sufficient Witnesses, as agreeing with the*
Original; *there being no other Means so good to ascertain us* Laicks,
*that nothing therein was counterfeit, &c. Which Method (I confess) if it
had been used in all* Ages *and* Countries *where* Revelations *are said to
have been made in private to* Priests, *would have been much approved;
since* Copies *of* Copies, *through many Descents, may be subject to
many* Corruptions, *especially among those who would draw all things
to their own* Interest; *which might as well have become these latter
Times, as the former; since our Modern* Priests *(for the most part) turn*
Religion *into* Faction, *striving to render all others of different
Perswasions (though in the last matters) odious. Which Bitterness of
Spirit we find not evidently remarked among the* Heathen Priests; *so*

that how Ignorant and False soever they were, yet are they not recorded to have been Incendiaries, *and* Persecutors *of one another even unto* Death, *for* Religion *and* Conscience *sake: No, they had no such* hellish *Contrivances as the* Parisian[6] *and* Hibernian Massacres;[7] *no such Instruments of the* Devil, *as* Ravilliac,[8] Clement,[9] *and the* Priest *that poyson'd our* English Monarch *in the Eucharist;*[10] *no such* Traiterous Conspiracies *as the* Powder-plot[11] *Nor did they use to convert one another to their Opinions by* Fire *and* Fagot, *and* Rosting Kings *alive, as the* Spaniards *did in the* Indies. *He that compares but the Behaviour of those of the Religious among the* Heathens, *with the Carriage of our* Popish Bishops *here in* England *before the* Reformation, *as related by our own* Christian *Writers, would take the* Heathen Priests *for much the better* Christians *of the two.*

So that, notwithstanding all this, I should not give the Priests *over so, but at least tell them, I could have wished they had proceeded more clearly with me; since the more they debased my Understanding in* Divine Mysteries, *the more was I obliged to stand to my* Common Reason, *until they had made all things manifest or intelligible to me, without going about to convince me of* Infidelity, *because I believed not more than I understood: or when a further Belief were required, I hoped they would not charge me to believe it any otherwise than as a thing possible, or at most but likely, since this was all I could do, when God had given me no sufficient Revelation for the confirming of theirs. And to affirm it a good Plea in the Court of Heaven, to say, That a Man began at the Faith that was taught in his Native Country: Who might not then excuse himself for adhering to the grossest Superstition that can be imagined in any Age or Country whatever, where no less Esteem and Veneration was given publickly to their Sacerdotal College, than is now paid to the present Church of Rome in Italy and Spain. Finally, therefore, I should ask them, How any Priest could assure and satisfie my Conscience, that the Revelation made to him did so concern me, that I must embrace it as an undoubted Axiom, or Truth? To which (I am confident) they would answer, as formerly, That they had discharged their Duty in delivering Gods Word, and that I ought to take heed lest I be severely punished for want of Faith, and so leave me, after having with much gravity expressed their sorrow for my incorrigible stubborn Heart, &c.*

But, notwithstanding all this, I do not yet deny, but that *Revelations* may be made to Men either *sleeping* or *waking;* but where, I suppose, (as we find in *Holy Writ)* earnest *Prayers* have been made before-hand, and some *publick* and *miraculous Confirmation* of the thing *revealed* hath followed. However, unless the thing in it self be right *good* and *honest*, I should not conceive it was *God* that spake, but some *Evil Spirit* that would deceive me; it having pleased God so to implant the Love of *Goodness* and *Truth* in the *Soul*, that he hath made them a part of *Common Reason*, and conspicuous by their own *Light;* from which therefore if we recede, we shall find our selves cast not onely into much Errour and Darkness, but even in the Court of our own *Consciences* criminal and condemned: For which Cause also I believe *God* is so sparing in making publick *Revelations*, because if Men did wholly trust to them, it might be a means of making them neglect their proper Duties. . . .

Now All these Points having been for a long time debated and examined by me, to the best of my Understanding, I did think fir the rather to study and inquire out those *Common Principles* of *Religion* I could any where meet with; onely before I undertook this great Task, I thought it not amiss to advise upon what Grounds the Controverted Points amongst them did move. But, as here I observed nothing but matter of *Faith*, or *Belief* concerning Things past, questioned in any Age or Country; so did I the more easily pass by it, to come to those *Articles* which were grounded not onely upon *Reason* and *Universal Consent* of *Religions*, but are (I believe) extant and operative in the Hearts of all Men, which are not prepossess'd and obstructed with erroneous *Doctrines*, and (I am sure) most deeply engraven in mine. Which being done, I thought it my Duty to inquire, Whether by an apt Connexion of the Parts thereof, I might fix so solid a Foundation, that I might repose thereon, as the first and principal Ground of all *Religious Worship*.

The *Articles* which I propose, are *Five* in number; and the same which the great Oracle and Commander of his Time, for Wit, Learning, and Courage, *tam Marti quam Mercurio*,[12] the *Lord Herbert, Baron of Cherbury*,[13] delivered; and which (I am confident) are *so Catholique* or *Universal*, that all the *Religions* that ever were, are, or (I believe) ever shall be, did, do, and will embrace them. The Articles are these.

The Five Catholick or Universal Articles of Religion.

   I. *That there is One onely Supreme God.*
   II. *That He chiefly is to be Worshipped.*
   III. *That Vertue, Goodness, and Piety, accompanied with Faith in,*

and Love to God, are the best ways of Worshipping Him.
IV. *That we should repent of our Sins from the bottom of our Hearts, and turn to the Right Way.*
V. And lastly, *That there is a Reward and Punishment after this Life.* . . .

As to the Fourth Article: Tho *Sacrifices* for the abolishing of Sin of more than one sort, as also *Expiations, Lustrations,* and divers other *Rites* invented by the *Sacerdotal Order,* were used for the *purging* of Men from *Sin;* yet was there no *Universal Consent* or Agreement concerning them. But that *Repentance* is a certain Sign of *God's Spirit* working in us, and the onely Remedy for Sin that is declared publickly to all Mankind, and the most rational way to return to *God* and *Vertue,* is by Universal Consent established every where, without so much as the least Contradiction. Not that I think *God's* Justice can be satisfied by meer *Repentance,* and turning to a good Life; but that a further *Satisfaction* or *Reparation* for our Offences against the *Divine Majesty* is required.[14] Yet as there is no Universal Agreement concerning the Means how this is effected, (it being of greater Scrutiny than Mans Reason can attain unto) so I shall in part wave this Discourse; and the rather, for that many do not see why (according to the ordinary Rules of Justice) God should punish one Man for the Sins of another: or, to go further, for that Frailty of our own Nature, which without our Consent was bestowed upon us? To which, give me leave to add these few Remarques. I. *Decipimur specie recti.*[15] We have not a true Judgment of *Good* and *Bad*; esteeming many things Evil, which in themselves are not so. An History drawn in a Picture may have in it Representations of Battels, Slaughters, Drunkards, Harlots, and Firing of Cities, Shipwracks, or the like; and yet may be as lovely a Piece of Painting, as if it represented an *Assembly* of *Divines*: And so, perhaps, in a Natural Consideration, may be thought an Age that produces such Actions, as well as if it brought forth none but Examples of *Vertue.* 2. We denominate *Good* and *Evil* onely from our particular Interest; so that perhaps our *Vertues* may prove but *False Money,* of no *intrinsick Value,* although it bear the Stamp of our Approbation upon it. 3. A Wellbeing is the primary Appetite of Nature in all things; and so as we judge any thing more or less agreeing or contrary thereto, so are we more or less inclining or averse thereto: whereupon our Will, either for or against any thing, to do or forbear any thing, doth always follow our Judgment; which Judgment is framed by several things, *viz.* the Temper of our Brain, & our Education, together with the various

Encounters, Successes, and Experiments in the Course of our Lives: all which (it is manifest) are not in our own power, but [proceed] from the Temper of our Parents, the Diet, Climate, and Customs of our Country, with diversity of Occurrents and Conjunctures of the Times; which are produced with opportune Interventions of one another, in a continued Series of *God's Providence* in the disposal of them, and of such *Idea's* as he thereby sets before our Fansie. 'Tis apparent that he does thereby lead and guide all our Thoughts, Words, and Actions; yet not by any violent Protrusion, but by our own Consent, either by way of Delight, or as to the lesser Evil; and ever by Opinion, whether true or erroneous. So that our Consent not being violated, but led on by our own Choice, we justly become liable to Praise or Blame, and yet are in all our Ways under the Infallible Conduct of God. 4. As our *Body* is a Portion of the *Body* of the *World*, so is our *Spirit*, which guides and acts us, a *Beam* of the *Spirit* of *God*; which also, tho in its own Nature clear, yet is that Clearness in us more or less, according to our Temper whereinto it shines: Thus we find our selves of different Fancies, when we are Phlegmatick, or when our Blood is Black and Gross, from what we are when our Blood and Brain is Pure and Thin; and accordingly our Judgment grows more or less perspicacious and rectified; and by consequence the Inclinations of our Will better or worse: yet therein no violence is offer'd us. . . . Again, The Alteration of our Judgment from outward Occurrences is also of great importance to present us with new *Idea's*, which divert us this way or that way, and so into Mischief or Preservation, yet always by our own *election*: As for example, A Man going to *London*, perhaps finding the way dirty, leaves it, and takes into a Bie way, whereby he misses *Thieves*, who were then on the *Road*, although he knew not of them; or, perhaps, lights upon another Mischance in this Way, which he had missed in the other: Here is *God's Conduct* of him, either to his *Good* or *Harm*, leading him by that *Idea* of avoiding Dirt, yet without *Compulsion*, and by his *Free Election*; wherefore he cannot complain but of himself: Yet *God* did undoubtedly from all Eternity both *foresee* and *decree* this Election, with the Event which should follow thereon. For thus *God* doth ever manage us by the Temper of our *Body*, with his inoperating Spirit therein; and by meeting us from without in such Encounters and Occurrences, as will infallibly carry us by our own *Choice* into such things as from all Eternity he had ordained. 5. Some will here object, That if God gives us to *will* or to *refuse*, and that it were not in our own *power* to *will* or to *refuse*, then how could we be praised or punished for ought we *do*, or neglect to do? To which I *answer*, Just as well as it

befals us for having *Flesh* and *Blood*: Our having *Flesh* and *Blood*
makes us subject to much *Pain* and *Pleasure*; and yet this our *Body*
of *Flesh* and *Blood* was given us of *God*, when we had no power to
refuse it: And if we put our Finger or any Living Creature by force into
the *Fire*, it will smart and suffer as much, as if it had gone in by its
own desire; for the ground of its *suffering* is not in the being *willing*,
or *unwilling*, but in its *disagreeableness* to *Fire*. And so when a Man
takes into debauched intemperate Courses, he falls into Diseases; and
whether God or himself drive him, that is not the Point; the true Cause
is, the venomous and oppressive Humours which by these Courses he
puts into his Body, destructive to its own Nature. 6. *And lastly*, It was
well said of one, who having contrived and put in execution a great and
politick Business, and being asked, Whether it was his own Care, or
Divine Providence, that had brought this great Work to pass? he replied,
Fuit certe Providentia Divina, sed quæ per me transiit.[16] For if we should
see a *Sun-beam* in at a Hole enlightning a *dark Room*, 'twould be a very
shallow Conception, to suppose that this *Beam* did move or enlighten
one way or other, otherwise than as it self was continually enlightned and
carried about by its *Original* the *Sun*, from whom it can never be separated, nor have any Vertue apart: And the very same Relation and Condition has each particular Man's *Spirit* with the *Spirit of God*. . . .

But now to conclude my Remarques upon this *Fourth Article*,
of *Repentance*; give me leave to offer these few Considerations
following, which may perhaps not be impertinent for the directing
of us in this difficult Point. *First*, That he that judgeth Man, is
his *Father*, and doth look on him as a frail Creature, obnoxious to Sin.
Secondly, That he generally finds Men sin rather out of this Frailty,
than out of any desire to offend his *Divine Majesty*. *Thirdly*, That if
Man had been made inwardly prone to sin, and yet destitute of all
inward Means to return to him again, he had been not onely remediless
in himself, but more miserable than it could be supposed an *Infinite
Goodness* did at first create, and doth still perpetuate Humane kind.
Fourthly, That *Man* can do no more on his part, for the satisfying of
Divine Justice, than to be *heartily sorry* and *repent* him of his *Sins*, as
well as to endeavour through his Grace to return to the Right way,
from which through his Transgression he had erred: Or if this did not
suffice for the making of his Peace, that the *Supreme God*, by inflicting
some Temporal Punishment in this Life, might satisfie his own *Justice*.
Fifthly, and lastly, That if Temporal Punishment in this Life were too
little for the Sin committed, he might yet inflict a greater Punishment
hereafter in the other Life, however, without giving *eternal Damnation*

to those, who (if not for the love of Goodness) yet at least upon sense of Punishment, would not sin eternally. Notwithstanding, since these things may again be controverted, I shall insist only upon this one *universally acknowledged Proposition. viz. That Repentance is the onely known and public Means which on our part is required for satisfying the Divine Justice, and returning to the Right way of serving God.*

Notes

1. Blount and Dryden, though friends, were undoubtedly at odds ideologically. Dryden, for example, argues forcefully in his *Religio Laici* for the doctrine of the Atonement (*ll.* 93-111), which Blount deems unnecessary (p. 122). There is certainly more than a possibility of ironic banter in the assertion in Blount's Epistle Dedicatory that he 'designed this Treatise . . . to be onely an *Addition*, or rather the *Consequence* of yours'.

2. See Ezekiel 11:19.

3. An heretical sect which held that Satan was co-eternal with God.

4. See 2 Corinthians 4:4; a tendentious scriptural quotation, since St Paul does not specifically identify the devil as the god of this world.

5. An Allusion to the legend that when Camillus (d. 365 BC), 'the Second Founder of Rome', wished to carry off the image of the goddess Juno to Rome from the citadel of the Veii, the image whispered its personal consent to the move.

6. See p. 42, n. 8.

7. The massacre of protestant settlers in Ireland (see Introduction, p. 6).

8. François Ravilliac (1578-1610), assassin of Henry IV of France.

9. See p. 72, n. 20.

10. Probably an illusion to the alleged poisoning of King John (reigned 1199-1216) by a monk of the abbey of Swineshead.

11. The Gunpowder Plot of 1605.

12. 'as much in war as in eloquence': Mars and Mercury were the gods of war and communication respectively.

13. Lord Herbert of Cherbury (1582-1648), soldier, poet and philosopher, the 'father of English deism' and brother of the poet, George Herbert. The Five Articles are to be found in Herbert's *De Religione Laici* (Hutcheson, 1944, 128, 129).

14. See n. 1 above.

15. 'We are cheated by appearances.'

16. 'It was certainly Divine Providence, but with me as its vehicle.'

8 From: *The Interest of Princes and States*

Slingsby Bethel, 1680

The Interest of England Stated.

Trade being the true and chief intrinsick Interest of *England*, without which it cannot subsist, . . . it is the undoubted Interest of his Majesty, to advance and promote Trade, by removing all obstructions, and giving it all manner of incouragement.

As First, By lessening the over great impositions upon Native Commodities, and upon such as are necessarily imported to be manufactured in *England*, or to be again transported.

Secondly, By causing the Native Commodities to be faithfully and truly made, and ordered.

Thirdly, By laying all Companies open,[1] or at least, by leaving them free, for all to come into them that please without fines, more than a small acknowledgement, tying them in such case, from burthening their own Manufactures with Taxes, as they usually do for the raising money to spend profusely and wantonly . . . .

Fourthly, By carefully protecting Merchants abroad, from the wrongs and injuries of other Nations.

Fifthly, By making the transferring Bills of debt good in Law, it being a great advantage to Traders (especially to young men of small Stocks) to be able to supply themselves with money, by the sale of their own Bills of debt.

Sixthly, By constituting a Court Merchant,[2] after the example of other Countries, to prevent tedious and chargeable Sutes in Law, taking men off from their business, and in making the advancement and protection of Trade, matter of State.

Seventhly, By having Registers of all Real Estates, as is profitably practised in other Countries, . . . which in a natural way, will abate the Interest of money, and make Purchases certain . . . for it is no little prejudice and blemish to *England*, that of all the Countries in *Europe*, there is none, where Purchasers, or Lenders of money upon Land, are upon such uncertainty in their dealings, as in *England*.

Eighthly, By taking away all priviledges (except of Parliament)

127

from persons and places, tending to the defrauding Creditors of their debts, and extending the Statute of Bankrupts against all persons not Trading, as well as Traders, it being but equal Justice, that all men should be alike liable to the payments of their debts.

Ninthly, Banks (not Bankers, but) such as are in use at *Venice, Amsterdam*, and *Hamburg*,[3] where the several States are security, keeping particular accounts of *Cash*, for all men, desiring it, are of great advantage to Merchants and Traders, in securing their monies from many casualities, and making receipts and payments, speedy and easie; besides, so certain, without the danger of losing acquittances, or by death, or otherwise to be in want of Witnesses, as takes away all occasions of suits about them, Bank accounts being allowed for undeniable testimonies in Law; but of these, I confess there are no thriving and flourishing examples, save under Republicks.

Tenthly, The making Free Ports (which *England* of all Countries in *Europe*, is most proper for) giving liberty to Strangers, as well as Natives, upon payment of a small duty, to keep Magazines of goods ready for transportation to other Countries, according to the encouragement of Markets abroad, are great increasers of Trade and Navigation, and so of riches. . . .

Eleventhly, Making business at the several Offices for Custom and Excise, and in all other places, as easie, and as little vexatious as may be, in employing such persons of honesty, integrity, and discretion, as will not abuse their trusts, no more in insolency than falseness, is a great encouragement to Traders; as also, making passing in and out of the Countrey by Strangers and Travellers, untroublesom, is a motive and inducement to them, to satisfie their curiosity in visiting the Kingdom, and spending their money in it. For to object, that the incivilities travellers meet with in going in, and coming out of *France*, hinders no resort thither, is more than can be proved; besides that, admit it is not, yet the like usage in any other Country, would be a prejudice to it, and would be surely so to *France*, were it not the humour at present of this giddy Age, to run a madding after them; and certainly, the facility that is in doing business in *Holland*, and the unmolested egress and regress that Strangers and Travellers meet with there, is a great benefit to them.

Twelfthly, Would the Trading Corporations, chuse after the example of *London*, and according to their own Interests, and reason of their institution, their members for Parliament out of themselves, the Interest of Trade would probably be better understood, and faithfullier prosecuted than it is, and it cannot but be a prejudice to Commerce, that they generally send Courtiers, Country-Gentlemen, or their Recorders, to Parliament, who will be sure to prefer their particular Interests before that of Trade, it being natural to all men, to seek their own profit, before that of others.

Thirteenthly, As *England* hath some beneficial Customs, which other Countries are strangers unto, so it hath others, as prejudicial, not known to Foreign Governments; as the great expences of Corporations,[4] undoing many Citizens and Townsmen; a Freeman of *York*, or *Southampton*, not being able to go through all their Offices, according to Custom and expectation, in the first, under seven or eight hundred pound; and the latter, six or seven hundred; which may well be judged one cause, why *York* is so poor, and the other thrives no better. . . .

But besides this, the administration of some of the fraternities in *London*, stand in more need of reformation . . . for whereas the Primitive Institution of most of them, was for regulating and improving mechanical Arts and Mysteries, now by mixing in the same Societies the more generous and free Trades and Callings; the original reason of their Incorporations is totally lost, many of the Trades, of which the Companies bear the name, not being looked after, nor indeed any thing else to speak of, besides managing their Revenues, and providing for eating and drinking: For the maintenance of which they are often very burthensom to men in years of mean Estates, as well as to young Traders of small beginnings, by imposing upon them greater Fines for their Liveries, (not allowing the Plea of inability, as their Charter obligeth) vain unnecessary Feasts, and not holding of Offices, than they are well able to bear, or indeed holds any proportion with the charge of the Offices, the Fines being in some Companies four times as much as the charge of the Offices comes to . . . For I am not of their opinion, who think popular Feastings and good Fellowship, called Hospitality, to be the Interest of the Nation, because it consumes the growth of the Country; but on the contrary, that it is altogether against it.[5] For, besides the provoking of the Judgments of God by such inordinate living, Excess weakens mens bodies, spends vainly their time, dulls their wits, and makes them unfit for action and business, which is the chief advancer of any Government, and to supply the want of people in any Land, by a riotous wasting the growth of it, is at best but a bad effect of a bad cause, and against that rule which forbids doing evil that good may come of it; and therefore, the true Interest of any Country is, by immunities, priviledges, and liberty of Conscience, so to encourage, and encrease the number of people, as they may rather be (in a sober way of living) too many, than too few for their professions. . . .

But, fourteenthly, imposing upon Conscience in matters of Religion, is a mischief unto Trade, transcending all others whatsoever; for if the Traders and Manufacturers be forced to fly their Countries, or withdraw their stocks, by vexatious prosecutions, the having Natural Commodities in a Country, or no gross impositions upon them, will signifie little to the Prince or People; and therefore Liberty of Conscience is not only the Common Interest of all the Nation, but especially of his Majesty, in that,

First, By it he obligeth all his Subjects equally to him, no man having just cause to be offended at another mans liberty, since he enjoys the same himself; and more particularly, he obligeth all the Non-Conformists to him, who can have no other Interest than his, that in grace and favour gives them Liberty; securing thereby, in an especial manner, all the several perswasions, from agreeing upon any thing to the prejudice of their common friend; whereas the Papists have, as others may have, other Interests. And were it in the power of man (as it is the Prerogative of God alone) to force a belief or disbelief in matters controversal, it were not (to speak politically) the moral interest of his Majesty to make all his Protestant Subjects (who own no other head than himself, and who differ only in Circumstantials) to be of one mind in Religion, but on the contrary, to keep them divided in opinions as checks upon each other. . . .

Secondly, It may be concluded to be the Interest of the King and Kingdom of *England*, to grant Liberty of Conscience, because by a general consent of Nations, liberty in Ceremonies, invented by men, seems to be accounted necessary for the good of humane Society. For I believe I may without boldness affirm, that *England* is singular in prosecuting them, who are one with them in Doctrine, for differing only in Ceremonies, no other Christian Church that I know of, doing the like. . . ; that the Church of *England*, who pretends not to infallibility, should to their civil prejudice, be rigid in imposing them upon those that agree with them, not only in Fundamentals, but in all material points of Faith, Worship, and Obedience, with punishment for denial, I cannot conceive the reason, except without Ceremonies to administer matter of employment in punishing tender Consciences, they think they should be without work in any kind adequate to their great Revenues, and that they dread the consequence of uselessness.

But if this be not the Case, and that they really design no more, than piously to bring the Non Conformists into their Churches, (as I will hope they do not) I shall (because the wrath of man will never accomplish the righteousness of Christ) humbly recommend unto them, as the most effectual remedy against separation:

First, Where the Parishes are so large, that the Churches cannot receive in some places half, in others not a third or fourth to an eighth part of the Parishioners, as the Churches of St. *Andrews*, *Sepulchres*, St. *Giles*, and St. *Martins in the Fields*, &c. they would be a means of procuring Acts of Parliament for dividing such Parishes, otherwise people cannot be justly blamed for going to other Churches rather than stay at home.

Secondly, To furnish the Parishes with Virtuous as well as able men, fit for the work of the Ministry, for that, where there is a defect in either qualification, hearers will think themselves obliged in duty to God, and excusable before man in seeking other Teachers. . . .

Thirdly, It is a good remedy against Non-Conformity, to follow the Apostles rule, in not imposing anything in the worship of God but what is necessary,[6] that so none may be kept out of the Church by offensive impositions, as by turning the Communion-Table Altar-wise (Churchmen bowing towards, if not to it;)[7] and exacting sitting bare all Sermon time, &c.

The first is directly against the Rubrick. . . . And as to that of sitting here bare all Sermon time, as it is without Authority, so it is against the practice of all Christian Churches, in antient as well as modern times, and never known in *England* until of late, except in the three last Years of Bishop Lauds[8] Dominion, when he was designing the reducement of Religion to Forms, Gestures, Habits and reverence to Persons and Stone-Walls: and this unwarrantable Ceremony keeps (upon several accounts) many out of the Church, as some from weakness of Constitution, no Caps being so good a fence against Cold, in a wide empty Church, as a broad brim'd Hat, others upon an account of Conscience, as thinking the Ceremony superstitious, and a third sort upon a political account, as not daring to trust the Church with an Arbitrary Power of imposing what Ceremonies they please, fearing that the Countenancing of one Innovation by complying with it, may usher in another (incroachments and breaking down of Fences, being always dangerous, but in some times more than in others) and so leave it uncertain where the Ecclesiastical Itch to Dominion will rest. . . . and if Church-men would according to the decrees of several Councils, apply themselves only to the affairs of the Church, they would find work enough there.

As first, in making strict Examination after mens parts, and inquiry after their Lives and Conversations before Ordination, which is so necessary for prevention of separation. . . .

Secondly, In procuring Acts of Parliament where it is needful, for securing our Religion against Popery, as for preventing Popish Mothers (according to the late if not present practice of the Reformed in *France*) in bringing up their Children (after the Death of their Protestant Fathers) to the Romish Religion as they often do. And also if their power for depriving scandalous Ministers guilty of most enormous crimes, be not sufficient, as some pretend it is not, to procure more, &c.

Thirdly, To promote the like for augmenting scandalous livings, and scandalous allowances by Incumbents of pluralities to their under Curates.

Fourthly, For providing (according to the Example of other Reformed Churches) maintenance for super annuated Ministers,[9] to the end that such as are qualified for the work of the Ministry, may be admitted to the places of those who from Age or other infirmities, either cannot Officiate, or are made so unfit for their Callings, that instead of instructing their Auditors, they administer nothing but matter of laughter, scorn, and contempt, even to the meanest Capacities of the people, of which I have sometimes been a witness.

Fifthly, For suppressing Popery in such places where Church Governours have most power, as where they are Lords of Mannors, and have Collegiate Churches with Deans, as at *Rippon* in *Yorkshire*, reducing that Parish, which (according to common fame) hath near two thousand Papists in it,[10] to the example of *Hallifax* and *Bradford,* two Parishes in the same County, remote and furthest from the eye of the Church, where the first hath not one Papist, though twenty thousand Communicants, and the latter but one (a silly old man) though it hath ten thousand in it. . . .

Thirdly, Liberty of Conscience to all Protestant Non-Conformists, is the true Interest of King and Kingdom, in that it is absolutely and indispensibly necessary, for raising the value of Land, which at present is miserably mean and low, and advancing the Trade and Wealth of the Kingdom.

First, Because imposition upon Conscience, hinders the resort of Strangers, and so the encreas of people, whereof England is greatly wanting. . . .

Secondly, Imposition upon Conscience, drives the soberest and most industrious sort of Natives into Corners, leaving Trade in too few hands, and to a kind of people that do but rarely mind it; amongst whom, though there are some that get large Estates, it is not the thriving of a small number, but diffusive wealth, that makes a Country rich. And, as most of the Corporations in *England* have declined in their flourishing condition, since many of the soberest and publick spirited Citizens and Townsmen, have, by the imposition of Oaths they could not comply with, been barred all share in Government, so the influence would have been the same upon the whole Nation, had not His Majesty wisely considered the good of his Kingdom, in expressing his sense for Liberty, and in some kind conniving at it. And if men, setting aside passion, would but seriously remember, how pernicious quarrels grounded upon differences in matters of Faith, have been to Mankind (of which History affords us plentiful Examples enough to make an honest heart tremble to relate) and ponder the sad consequence of Popish Persecutions in the Deaths (by several brutish ways and torments) of many Millions of Christians in *France, England, Netherlands, Germany,* the *Alpine Vallies; Italy, Spain,* and *Ireland,* besides the dreadful Wars, Confusions, Ruins, and desolations of Countries, that have been upon this account, producing no other effects than the depopulating of the three last, and increasing the number of Dissenters in all the rest, besides the irreparable damage of this Kingdom, in their former Bishops driving the Woollen Manufactures back into the *Netherlands,* (as the King of *Spain* had before driven them into *England*) by Persecution, where they have ever since increased, and where they now remain sad Monuments to this Nation, of the impolitick severity of those times, they could not but be convinced of the vanity and wickedness of such practices, as well as of the civil prejudice they bring to Nations, in destroying of their people, and therein depriving them of the benefit of Industry, thinking charitably of that saying, which was anciently in Vogue, and is still in some places remembred, that when a Bishop is Created, the Devil enters into him, and makes him his Executioner; which as it had its original in times of Popery, so it concerns their Bishops only.

And let no man believe, that because the Monarch of *Spain*, and Tyrant of *Rome*, by prohibiting the reading the Old and New Testament, exercising bloody and merciless Persecutions (thereby depopulating their several Countries) have cleared their Dominions of their Protestant Subjects, that therefore without using the like means, the Church of *England* may do the same by their Non-Conformists; for if the exercise of a coercive power over the Consciences of men in matters of Religion, causing poverty and the unpeopling of a Nation, were more to be desired than liberty of dissenting in the worship of God from Unscriptural Ceremonies, with populousness, and abounding in wealth and riches; yet with the Reformed Religion it is not feasible, because under the light that that brings with it, human inventions can never be imposed in the service of God without encountring opposition: for should the Nation be at once emptied of one whole Generation of Non-Conformists, so long as reading of the Bible is suffered, another will unavoidably (from the discovery it makes) immediately spring up. . . .

Thirdly, As it is the King and Kingdom of *England*'s Interest, to give Liberty of Conscience to all Protestant Dissenters, so it is not only to deny it to the Papists, after the Example of other Reformed Countries, as *Denmark, Sweden,* several Princes in *Germany*, and the reformed Cantons in *Switzerland,* but also to take care to prevent the growth of them, and that upon a civil score; as first, because they own a Foreign head upon the account of their Religion, in which they are carried on by such a blind zeal, as cannot render them less than Spies and Intelligencers for that Interest, and ready upon all occasions to appear for it. . . . I am not ignorant, that there are a sort of men, who, with the Author of that Book, Intituled *The State of England*,[11] seek to infuse a belief into the People, that the dispensing with the Laws against the Papists, is necessary for the prevention of persecution to Protestant Subjects, by their Popish Princes; but. . . it cannot but be of evil consequence, and a lessening unto Soveraignty, to own the having an eye to other Princes in the execution of their Laws, for nothing can be more dishonourable to a Prince, than to be under the awe of Foreign Potentates in his Administration, within his own Dominions; but this Gentleman doth not always ponder what he writes, for when I consider his sharpness against the Presbyterians, *&c.* in *England*, calling them Mushromes, Tares, and the Sons of *Belial*, insinuating the transplantation and extirpatron of them, I cannot but wonder he should have so much concern for the Reformed abroad, who are the same with the Presbyterians of *England*, and therefore must judge it to proceed from favour to the Papists, towards whom he so tenderly avoids all reflections and severity, as if he thought the revolt of a Presbyterian, *&c.* to Popery, to merit a pardon from transplantation or extirpation, and not from any kindness he can have for the Protestants in other Countreys. Nor do I know how to reconcile his boasting of the transcending Charity of the Church of *England* towards other Churches, with his accusing them of looking upon the Non-Conformists of *England* as Bastards, or making no account of any other Interest in them, than a man makes of the Vermin which breed out of his excrementitious sweat, or those *Ascarides*, which come sometimes in his most uncleanly parts,[12] but for such homely expressions, surely the

Church of *England*, will not think themselves beholding to him, no more than for rendring them so charitable so those that differ from them both in Doctrine and Discipline, as the Papists do, who are the Church he must mean, and so uncharitable to those that agree with them in all material points of Doctrine, and differ only from them in circumstantials, as the Non-Conformists do.

Secondly, The growth of Popery in *England* ought to be prevented, not only because the Principles of their Jesuits (who of all Orders bear the greatest sway) of good Intentions, Equivocations, Mental Reservations, Probability, and Necessity, &c. and of their Church, that there is no Faith to be kept with Hereticks, render them unfit for honest Conversation, especially for the Society of Protestants, there being no sence against such Principles. . . .

Thirdly, Because the vast sums of money that go out of *England*, sent by Papists to such uses as they call pious; for putting young Gentlewomen into Nunneries, and breeding Gentlemens Sons in Popish Schools and Universities, with the Popes Revenue gathered by his Penitentiaries and Missionaries, for Indulgences, Dispensations, Tolerations, Pardons and Commutations . . . and although this may peradventure be denied by Papists, who have no reason (though true) to own it, yet if their private and frugal manner and way of living, with their freedom from the charge of publick imployments be considered, it may rationally be concluded, that were they not under some great unknown expence, they could not but exceed their Neighbours abundantly in Wealth, whereas on the contrary, they do not generally increase so much in Estates, as Protestants do, who sometimes have less revenues, and always live more plentifully. . . .

And now upon the whole, though I believe the English Nation to be in the general the best conditioned people . . . and that therefore there may be some among them of the Romish Religion, who from a natural tenderness to Mankind, cannot bring up their natures to the exercise of the bloody and destroying Principles of their Church; yet as they in the general (and especially those in *Ireland*) are the most Bigots to *Rome*, so they want Bowels and good nature towards any of a contrary Religion to them. . . . And as their Priests working upon their blind zeal, do according to their own ambitious and restless Spirits, inflame their Disciples with desires of being uppermost, making them impatient of living under any other condition, so it is the Interest of the Protestants of *England* and *Ireland*, to be the more jealous of any Power in their Papists, as those whose faithless Principles are not to be trusted, and especially since in contemplation hereof were (I suppose) made those wise Statutes, Enacting that the Popish Recusants shall be restrained to their private Houses in the Country, and not at any time after to pass, or remove above five miles from thence, upon pain of forfeiture for life, of all Lands, Goods, and Chattels; That none of them, convicted, or to be convicted, shall remain within ten miles of *London*, nor come into the Court or House where his Majesty, or Heir Apparent shall be,[13] nor have in their own Houses, or in the hands or possession of any others, at their disposition, any Arms, Gun powder, or Ammunition whatsoever. . . .

And now upon the whole, since it appears that Trade depends much upon liberty of Conscience, the suggestions against it, either from unexperienced, or concerned persons, are not to be regarded; Gentlemen, bred only in the Country and brought up in a Religion which exacts little from them besides Conformity to humane Ceremonies, with opposition to every thing that is contrary, being tenacious of that which is so pleasing and grateful to frail Nature, are not generally competent Judges of this Interest, nor yet any sort of People, who, having spent their days in studying Books, more than Men or Things, employing themselves more in punishing tender Consciences for not obeying in the Worship of God the Commandments of men, than in the weightiest duties of their Callings, as in suppressing Papists, ignorant, debauched and scandalous Ministers, rendring their Actions thereby to proceed more from Self-Interest, than an enlightned and sincere Conscience; are not in this case against demonstrations to be harkened unto.

And indeed, it is a work most suitable unto Soveraignty, the Grand Child of *Henry* the Great of *France*,[14] and the large experience of his Majesty in Cases of Religion in other countries, to surmount all selfish opposition in his matter, for the advancement of his own Interest, and the good of his people, which whatsoever flatterers may suggest to the contrary, are bound up together. I know that the Enemies to Liberty of Conscience, do impose upon the World an apprehension of danger in it; but the position hath no Foundation in reason, presidents, or any thing else, save a confident running down of truth for their own advantage, it no where appearing, that ever Protestants dissenting from their National Church, having Liberty of Conscience given them, did rise up against their King, or disturbed the quiet of their Country, as those of the *Romish* Church have in all Ages and Nations done. . . . Did not the *Romish* Catholics in *France*, notwithstanding theirs was the National Religion, depose and degrade their lawful Soveraign *Henry* IV, the Parliament of *Tholouse*, in his absence, arraigning and condemning him to death, executing him in his Effigies by Harquebushes;[15] none of which Traiterous and Rebellious usage, did that great and excellent King (Grandfather of His Majesty of *England*) although he recovered all by force of Arms, in the least revenge; by which generous as well as politick carriage, he added to the Conquest of his Country, the Conquest of the hearts of all his people, reconciling at once all the animosities and factions, which had been the product of near forty years Civil Wars. . . . The present *French* Kings danger in 1650, &c. was from his Popish, and was delivered chiefly by his Reformed Subjects.[16] The Papists in *Ireland* had (as none can deny) liberty for exercise of their Religion, exceedingly above what the Non-Conformists had at that time, when they committed that not to be parallel'd bloody, and more than barbarous Massacre in the Year 1641.[17] Nay, the steady greatness and quiet of *Sweden*, is of no elder date than since they cast off Popery, pulled down their Bishops, and embraced *Protestantism*, the Church having been until then the occasion of much trouble unto that Kingdom. And none of these particulars being deniable, the Papists cannot without great impudence, boast (as many of them do) of their fidelity to their Princes, accusing the Protestants with want of it, and especially since if these instances were not enough to make good the assertion, that the Protestants are the best, and Papists the worst of Subjects, the like might be observed of every individual Country and Nation in the Christian part of *Europe*, in the times of Popery; but supposing these to be sufficient, I shall not give myself any farther trouble upon this point.

Notes

SLINGSBY BETHEL (1617-97) was the third son of a country gentleman. He was set on a business career by his father, in a manner he was later to praise. As an anti-Cromwellian republican, he was in opposition during the Protectorate, and retired to the country at the restoration. However he was elected Sheriff of London in 1680, but he refused to take the oaths required under the Corporation Act, though he eventually took the sacrament. Defeated in the election of 1681, he fled abroad until the revolution. Like so many others at this time his enemies accused him of being a papist. He appears as Shimei in *Absalom and Achitophel* (11.583-629).

1. A protest against the exclusiveness of the City Merchant Companies, and the restrictions which the expense of joining them and so of enjoying their

privileges placed on rising businessmen.

2. A separate body of law governing commercial activity, common in European countries subject to Roman Law, but unknown to English jurisprudence.

3. Traditional banking centres, ostensibly more advanced than London, even though the beginnings of the modern banking system were developing in the City with the deposit and credit facilities provided by London goldsmiths. The preference for cities with republican constitutions expressed here probably accounts for Dryden's jibe in *Absalom and Achitophel*, that Bethel thought that 'Kings were Useless, and a Clog to Trade' (*l*.615).

4. An expensive duty for provincial businessmen. In 1694, a non-conformist was nominated to be sheriff by the mayor and aldermen of Norwich, and was ordered by the courts to take the oaths and the sacrament whether he wanted to or not, the Toleration Act notwithstanding, since any 'exemption from an onerous office could be obtained only by letters patent or by Act of Parliament' (Ogg, 1969, 96).

5. A view of some significance in Bethel's case, as he did not own a house in London and while sheriff did no entertaining. This, with his dislike of City feasts, accounts for another of Dryden's jibes (*Absalom and Achitophel*, *ll*.617-21).

6. See 1 Corinthians 8: 4-13.

7. A matter of longstanding dispute in the Church of England. The Thirty-nine Articles explicitly deny that the Eucharist is a sacrifice, and implicitly deny the Real Presence in the bread and wine. Protestants argued, therefore, that it was wrong to treat the communion table as if it were an altar, and the consecrated bread and wine as if they were inherently sacred. In all versions of the Prayer Book, however, except the first, communicants were required to receive the sacrament kneeling, the 1662 Prayer Book adding the word 'meekly', and Laudian anglicans undoubtedly inclined to the catholic view in these matters. The argument that only questions of ceremony were at stake was therefore disingenuous. The tactic adopted by dissenting controvertialists was in fact designed to force their anglican opponents into admitting as much and so exposing their papist inclinations.

8. William Laud (1573-1645), who became Archbishop of Canterbury in 1645; he was not only closely implicated in Charles I's authoritarian government, but also strictly enforced Prayer Book ritual, the wearing of surplices, and the placing of the communion table at the east end of the chancel, in the position of the altar in catholic churches. He tried to enforce bowing at the name of Jesus and to limit the preaching of puritan divines. He was executed by Parliament in 1645.

9. A reference to the fact that church livings were mostly freeholds and so tenable for life, irrespective of an incumbent's age or fitness for office.

10. An exaggerated figure, though many catholics in Yorkshire and Lancashire lived under the protection of recusant nobility and gentry.

11. Edward Chamberlayne. See p. 65; see also Halifax's views on this topic (pp. 171-3).

12. See pp. 65-6.

13. An allusion to an Act of 1678 forbidding any catholic to come into the presence of the King or the Queen (who was herself a catholic) without permission from at least six privy councillors.

14. See p. 72, n. 20; see also Introduction, p. 10.

15. Portable firearms.

16. A reference to the Fronde, an opposition group which nearly brought down the French government during the minority of Louis XIV.

17. See p. 125, n. 7.

9 From: *Miscellania . . . An Essay upon the Original and Nature of Government*

Sir William Temple, 1680

Authority arises from the opinion of Wisdom, Goodness, and Valour in the persons who possess it.

Wisdom, As that which makes men judg what are the best ends, and what the best means to attain them; and gives a man advantage among the weak and the ignorant; as sight among the blind, which is that of Counsel and Direction. This gives Authority to Age among the younger, till these begin at certain years to change their opinion of the old, and of themselves. This gives it more absolute to a Pilot at Sea, whom all the passengers suffer to steer them as he pleases.

Goodness, As that which makes men prefer their Duty and their Promise, before their Passions, or their Interest; and is properly the object of Trust. In our Language, it goes rather by the name of Honesty; though what we call an honest man, the *Romans* called a good man; and honesty in their Language, as well as in *French*, rather signifies a composition of those qualities which generally acquire honour and esteem to those who possess them.

Valour, As it gives awe, and promises protection to those who want either heart or strength to defend themselves. This makes the Authority of Men among Women; and that of a Master-Buck in a numerous herd, though perhaps not strong enough for any two of them; but the impression of single fear holds when they are all together, by the ignorance of Uniting.

Eloquence, As it passes for a mark of Wisdom; Beauty of Goodness, And Nobility of Valour (which was its original) have likewise ever some effect upon the opinion of the People; but a very great one when they are really joined with the qualities they promise or resemble.

There is yet another source from which usually springs greater Authority than from all the rest, which is the opinion of Divine Favour, or designation of the persons, or of the races that Govern. This made the Kings among the Heathens ever derive themselves, or their Ancestors from some god; passing thereby for Heroes, that is, persons issued from the mixture of divine and humane race, and of a middle nature between gods and men: others joyned the Miter to the Crown,

139

and thereby the reverence of Divine, to the respect of Civil Power.

This made the *Caliphs*[1] of *Persia* and *Egypt*, and the great Emperors of *Arabia*, derive themselves by several branches from their great Prophet *Mahomet:* The *Yncas* in *Peru* from the Sun: And the *Ottoman* race to be adored among the *Turks*, as designed by Heaven for perpetual Empire. And the sacring of the Kings of *France* (as *Loysel*[2] says) is the sign of their Sovereign Priesthood, as well as Kingdom; and in the right thereof they are capable of holding all vacant Benefices of the Church.[3]

Piety, As it is thought a way to the favour of God, and Fortune as it looks like the effect either of that or at least of Prudence and Courage, beget Authority. As likewise splendor of living in great Palaces, with numerous attendance, much observance, and rich habits differering from common men: Both as it seems to be the reward of those Virtues already named, or the effect of Fortune; or as it is a mark of being obeyed by many.

From all these Authority arises, but is by nothing so much strengthned and confirmed as by custom. For no man easily distrusts the persons, or disputes the things which he and all men that he knows of, have been always bred up to observe, and believe; or if he does, he will hardly hope, or venture to introduce opinions wherein he knows none, or few of his mind, and thinks all others will defend those already received; so as no man, nor party can offer at the change of a Government establisht, without first gaining new Authority by the steps already traced out; and in some degree debasing the old, by appearance or impressions of contrary qualities in those who before enjoyed it. This induces a general change of opinion, concerning the person or party like to be obeyed, or followed by the greatest or strongest part of the people: according to which the power or weakness of each is to be measured. So as in effect all Government may be esteemed to grow strong or weak, as the general opinion of these qualities in those that Govern, is seen to lessen or increase.

And Power must be allowed to follow Authority in all Civil Bodies; as in Natural the motions of the body follow those of the mind, great numbers ever acting and pursuing what the few (whom they trust) begin or advise.

From this Principle, and from the discovery of some natural Authority, may perhaps be deduced a truer original of all Governments among men, than from any Contracts: though these be given us by the great Writers concerning Politicks and Laws. Some of them lay for their foundation, That men are sociable creatures, and naturally disposed to live in numbers and troops together.[4] Others, That they are naturally creatures of prey, and in a state of war one upon another[5]; so as to avoid confusion in the first case, and violence in the other, they found out the necessity of agreeing upon some Orders and Rules, by which every man gives up his common Right for some particular possession, and his power to hurt and spoil others, for the priviledg of not being hurt or spoiled himself. And the agreement upon such Orders, by mutual Contract, with the consent to execute them, by common strength and endeavours, They make to be the rise of all Civil Governments.

I know not whether they consider what it is that makes some creatures sociable, and others live and range more alone, or in smaller companies; but I suppose those creatures whose natural and necessary food is easie and plentiful, as Grass, or Plants, or Fruits (the common product of the earth) are the sociable creatures, because where-ever they go, they usually find what they want, and enough for them all without industry or contention. And those live more alone whose food (and therefore prey) is upon other sensitive creatures, and so not attained without pursuit and violence, and seldom in such quantities at once, as to satisfy the hunger of great numbers together. Yet this does not hold so far, but that Ravens are seen in flocks where a Carrion lies, and Wolves in herds to run down a Deer. Nay they feed quietly together while there is enough for them all: Quarrel only when it begins to fail, and when 'tis ended they scatter to seek out new encounters. Besides, those called sociable, quarrel in hunger and in lust, as well as the others; and the Bull and the Ram appear then as much in fury and war, as the Lyon and the Bear. So that if Mankind must be ranged to one of these sorts, I know not well to which it will be: and considering the great differences of customs and dispositions in several men, and even in the same men at several times, I very much doubt they must be divided into several forms. Nor do I know, if men are like sheep, why they need any Government: or if they are like Wolves, how they can suffer it. Nor have I read where the Orders of any State have been agreed on by mutual Contract among great numbers of men, meeting together in that natural state of War; where every man takes himself to have equal right to every thing. But often where such Orders have been invented by the Wisdom, and received by the Authority of some one man, under the name of a Lawgiver; And where this has not happened, the original of Government lives as undiscovered in story, as that of Time. All Nations appearing upon the first Records that are left us, under the Authority of Kings, or Princes, or some other Magistrates.

Besides, this principle of contract as the original of Government, seems calculated for the account, given by some of the old Poets of the original of man; whom they raise out of the ground by great numbers at a time in perfect Stature and Strength. Whereas if we deduce the several races of mankind in the several parts of the World from generation; we must imagine the first numbers of them who in any place agree upon any civil constitutions, to assemble not as so many single heads, but as so many heads of families, whom they represent, in the framing any Compact or common accord; and consequently as persons, who have already an Authority over such numbers as their families are composed of.

For if we consider a Man multiplying his Kind by the birth of many Children, and his Cares by providing even necessary food for them, till they are able to do it for themselves (which happens much later to the generations of men, and makes a much longer dependance of children upon Parents, than we can observe among any other creatures) If we consider not only the cares but the industry he is forced to, for the necessary sustenance of his helpless brood, either in gathering the natural fruits, or raising those which are purchased with labour and toil; if he be forced for supply of this stock to catch the tamer creatures, and hunt the wilder, sometimes to exercise his courage in defending his little Family, and fighting with the strong and Savage Beasts (that would prey upon him, as he does upon the weak and the mild) if we suppose him disposing with discretion and order, whatever he gets among his Children, according to each of their hunger or need, sometimes laying up for to morrow, what was more than enough for to day: at other times pinching himself rather than suffering any of them should want. And as each of them grows up, and able to share in the common support, teaching him both by lesson and example, what he is now to do as the Son of this family, and what hereafter as the Father of another; instructing them all, what qualities are good, and what are ill for their health and life, or common Society (which will certainly comprehend whatever is generally esteemed virtue or vice among men) cherishing and encouraging dispositions to the good; disfavouring and punishing those to the ill: And lastly, Among the various accidents of Life, lifting up his eyes to Heaven, when the earth affords him no relief; and having recourse to a higher and a greater nature, whenever he finds the frailty of his own: We must needs conclude, that the Children of this Man cannot fail of being bred up with a great opinion of his Wisdom, his Goodness, his Valour, and his Piety. And if they see constant plenty in the Family, they believe well of his fortune too.

And from all this must naturally arise a great paternal Authority, which disposes his Children (at least till the age when they grow Fathers themselves) to believe what he teaches, to follow what he advises, and obey what he commands.

Thus the Father, by a natural Right as well as Authority, becomes a Governour in this little State: and if his life be long, and his generations many (as well as those of his Children) He grows the Governour or King of a Nation, and is indeed a *Pater patriæ*,[6] as the best Kings are, and as all should be; and as those which are not, are yet content to be called. Thus the peculiar compellation of the Kings in *France*, is by the name of *Sire*, which in their ancient language is nothing else but Father, and denotes the Prince to be the Father of the Nation. For a Nation properly signifies a great number of Families, derived from the same Blood, born in the same Countrey, and living under the same Government and Civil Constitutions: As *Patria* does the land of our Father; and so the *Dutch*[7] by expressions of deerness, instead of our Countrey, say our *Father-land*. With such Nations we find in Scripture all the Lands of *Judea*, and the adjacent Territories, were planted of old. With such the many several Provinces of *Greece* and *Italy*, when they began first to appear upon the Records of Ancient Story or Tradition. And with such was the main Land of *Gaul* inhabited in the time of *Cæsar*,[8] and *Germany* in that of *Tacitus*.[9] Such were the many Branches of the old *British* Nation; the *Scepts*[10] among the *Irish*. And such the infinite variety and numbers of Nations in *Africa* and *America* upon the first discoveries, distinguisht by their several names, and living under their several Kings or Princes, till they came to be swallowed up by greater Empires.

These seem to have been the natural and original Governments of the World, springing from a tacite deference of many to the Authority of one single Person. Under Him (if the Father of the Family or Nation) the elder of his Children comes to acquire a degree of Authority among the younger by the same means the Father did among them; and to share with him in the consultation and conduct of their common affairs. And this, together with an opinion of Wisdom from experience, may have brought in the Authority of the Elders, so often mentioned among the *Jews*; and in general of aged men, not only in *Sparta* and *Rome*, but all other places in some degree, both civil and barbarous. For the names of Lord, *Signior*, *Seigneur*, *Senor*, in the *Italian; French*, and *Spanish* Languages, seem to have at first imported only elder men, who thereby were grown into Authority among the several Governments and Nations, which seated themselves in those Countreys upon the fall of the *Roman* Empire.

This perhaps brought in Vogue that which is called the Authority of the Ancients in matters of opinion, though by a mistaken sense: for I suppose Authority may be reasonably allowed to the opinions of ancient men in the present age; but I know not why it should be so to those of men in general that lived in ages long since past; nor why one age' of the World should be wiser than another; or if it be, why it should not be rather the latter than the former; as having the same advantage of the general experience of the World, that an old man has of the more particular experiments of life.

Thus a Family seems to become a little Kingdom, and a Kingdom to be but a great Family.

Nor is it unlikely that this Paternal Jurisdiction in its successions, and with the help of accidents, may have branched out into the several heads of Government commonly received in the Schools. For a Family Governed with order, will fall naturally to the several Trades of Husbandry, which are Tillage, Gardening, and Pasturage (the product whereof was the original riches). For the managing of these, and their encrease, and the assistance of one man, who perhaps is to feed twenty, it may be a hundred children (since it is not easily told how far Generations may extend, with the Arbitrary choice and numbers of women, practised anciently in most Countries) the use of servants comes to be necessary. These are gained by victory and captives, or by fugitives out of some worse governed Family, where either they cannot or like not to live, and so sell their liberty to be assured of what is necessary to life. Or else by the debased nature of some of the Children who seem born to drudgery, or who are content to encrease their pains that they may lessen their cares; and upon such terms become servants to some of their brothers, whom they most esteem or chuse soonest to live with.

The Family thus encreased, is still under the Fathers common, though not equal care; that what is due to the servants by Contract, or what is fit for them to enjoy, may be provided, as well as the portions of the Children: And that whatever they acquire by their industry or ingenuity (beyond what the Masters expect, or exact from them by the conditions of their servitude) should be as much their property, as any divisions of Land or of Stock that are made to the Sons; and the possession as secure, unless forfeited by any demerit or offence against the customs of the Family, which grow with time to be the orders of this little State.

Now the Father of a Family or Nation, that uses his Servants like

Children in point of Justice and Care; and advises with his Children in what concerns the Commonweal, and thereby is willingly followed and obeyed by them all: Is what I suppose the Schools mean by a Monarch. And he that by harshness of nature, wilfulness of humour, intemperance of passions, and arbitrariness of commands, uses his Children like Servants, is what they mean by a Tyrant. And whereas the first thought himself safe in the love and obedience of his Children, the other knowing that he is feared, and hated by them; thinks he cannot be safe among his children, but by putting arms into the hands of such of his Servants as he thinks most at his will; which is the original of Guards. For against a Forreign Enemy, and for defence of evident Interest, all that can bear Arms in a Nation are Soldiers. Their Cause is common safety; their Pay is Honour: And when they have purchased these, they return to their homes, and former conditions of peaceable lives. Such were all the Armies of *Greece*, and of *Rome*, in the first Ages of their States. Such were their *Gens d'ordonnance* in *France*, and the Train-bands[11] in *England:* but standing Troops, and in constant pay, are properly Servants armed, who use the Lance and the Sword, as other servants do the Sickle, or the Bill at the command and will of those who entertain them. And therefore Martial Law is of all other the most absolute, and not like the Government of a Father, but a Master.[12]

And this brings in another sort of Power, distinct from that already described, which follows Authority, and consists in the willing obedience of the people: But this in the command of Soldiers who as Servants are bound to execute the Will and Orders of those that Lead them. And as Authority follows the qualities before-mentioned; To this Power follows Riches, or the opinion of it; a multitude of Servants being his that is able to maintain them. And these kind of forces come to be used by good Princes only upon necessity of providing for their defence against great and armed neighbours or enemies; But by ill ones as a support of decayed Authority, or as they lose the force of that which is Natural and Paternal, and so grow to set up an Interest of those that Govern, different from that of those that are Governed, which ought ever to be the same.

Yet this seems a much weaker principle of Government than the other; for the number of Soldiers can never be great in proportion to that of People, no more than the number of those that are idle in a Country, to that of those who live by labour or industry: so as if the people come to unite by any strong passion, or general interest, or under the wise conduct of any Authority well rooted in their minds, They are Masters of Armies. Besides, the humour of the People, runs insensibly among the very Soldiers, so as it seems much alike to keep off by Guards, a general infection, or an universal sedition: for the distemper in both kinds is contagious, and seizes upon the defenders themselves. Besides, common pay is a faint principle of Courage and Action, in comparison of Religion, Liberty, Honour, Revenge, or Necessity; which make every Soldier have the quarrel as much at heart as their Leaders, and seem to have spirited all the great Actions, and Revolutions of the World. And lastly, without the force of Authority, this Power of Soldiers grows pernicious to their Master, who becomes their Servant, and is in danger of their mutinies, as much as any Government can be of the seditions of a people.

If the Father of our Family govern it with Prudence, Goodness, and Success; and his eldest Son appear Heir to the virtues and worth of his Father; He succeeds in the Government by a Natural Right, and by the Strength of an Authority both derived from his Father, and acquired by His own personal qualities: but if either the eldest Son by qualities degenerate and ill, happen to lose all trust and opinion, and thereby (Authority) in the Family, Or else to dye before his time, and leave a Child in his room; when the Father comes to fail, then the Children fall into Councils of Election, and either prefer the eldest of the Sons then living, or perhaps one later, and so remoter in birth, according as He may have acquired Authority by those qualities which naturally produce it, and promise the best conduct and protection to the common affairs of the Family.

Where the Father comes to lose his Authority, many of the elder, or wiser, or braver of the Sons increase in theirs by the same degree: and when both these arrive at a certain heighth, the Nature of the Government is ready for a change; and upon the Fathers death, or general defection of the Family, they succeed in his Authority, whilst the humour of the whole body runs against the succession, or election of any single person, which they are grown weary of by so late an example. And thus comes in what they call an *Aristocracy:* But Authority contracting it self (as it seems naturally to do till it ends in a point or single Person) this Government falls sometimes into the hands of a few who establish it in their Families: and that is called an *Oligarchy.* If the Authority come to be lost in either of these forms; while the children of the Family grow into the manners and qualities, and perhaps into the condition and poverty of Servants: and while many of the Servants by industry and virtue, arrive at riches and esteem, then the nature of the Government inclines to a *Democracy* or Popular State, which is nearest confusion, or *Anarchy*; and often runs into it, unless upheld or directed by the Authority of one, or of some few in the State; though perhaps without Titles or marks of any extra-ordinary Office or Dignity.

Governments founded upon Contract, may have succeeded those founded upon Authority: But the first of them should rather seem to have been agreed between Princes and Subjects, than between men of equal Rank and Power. For the original of Subjection was, I suppose, when one Nation warring against another (for things necessary to Life, or for Women, or for extent of Land) overcame their enemies: if they only won a Battel, and put their enemies to flight, those they took Prisoners became their Slaves, and continued so in their Generations, unless infranchized by their Masters; But if by great slaughter or fre-quent victories, they subdued the very courages of their enemies, while great numbers of them remained alive; then the vanquisht Nation became subject to the Conquerors by Agreement, and upon certain conditions of safety and protection; and perhaps equal enjoyment of liberties and customs, with the common Natives under the other Gover-Government: If by such frequent successes and additions, a Nation extended it self over vast Tracts of Land and numbers of People; it thereby arrived in time at the ancient name of Kingdom, or Modern of Empire.

After such a victory, the chiefest of the conquering Nations, become Rich and Great upon the divisions of Lands, of Spoils, and of Slaves: By all which they grow into Power, are Lords in their own Lands, and over those that inhabit them, with certain Rights or Jurisdictions, and upon certain homages reserved to the Prince. The custom of imploy-ing these great persons in all great Offices, and Councils, grows to pass for a Right; as all Custom does with length and force of time.

The Prince that Governs according to the conditions of subjection at first agreed upon (of which Use is the Authentique record) and according to the ancient Customs, which are the original Laws (and by which the Right of succession in the Crown, as well as private Inheritance and Common Justice is directed and establisht) is called a Lawful Sovereign: He that breaks and violates these ancient Constitu-tions (especially that of Succession) is termed an Usurper.

A Free Nation is that, which has never been conquered or thereby enter'd into any conditions of Subjection, as the *Romans* were, before they were subdued by the *Goths* and *Vandals:* and as the *Turks* seem to be at this time; who having been called from *Scythia* to assist the *Grecian* Empire against that of the *Saracens*, made themselves Masters of both.

In Countreys safer from Forreign Invasions either by Seas or Rivers, by Mountains and Passes, or great Tracts of rough barren and uninhabited Lands, People lived generally in scattered dwellings, or small Villages: But where Invasion is easie and passage open, and bordering Nations are great and valiant; men croud together and seek their safety from number better united, and from Walls and other Fortifications, the use whereof is to make the few a match for the many, so as they may Fight or Treat on equal terms. And this is the original of Cities; but the greatness and riches of them encrease according to the commodiousness of their scituation, in fertile Countries, or upon Rivers and Havens; which surpass the greatest fertility of any Soil, in furnishing plenty of all things necessary to Life or Luxury.

When Families meet together, surround themselves by Walls; fall into Order and Laws (either invented by the wisdom of some one, or some few men; and from the evidence of their publick utility received by all; or else introduced by experience and time) and these Cities preserve themselves in the enjoyment of their Possessions, and observance of their Institutions, against all Invasions; and never are forced to submit to the will of any Conqueror, or conditions of any absolute Subjection; They are called free Cities, and of such there were many of old, in *Greece* and *Sicily*, deducing their original from some one Founder or Lawgiver: And are many now in *Germany* subject to no Laws but their own, and those of the Empire, which is an Union of many Soveraign Powers, by whose general consent in their Dyets, all its Constitutions are framed and establisht.

Commonwealths[13] were nothing more in their original, but free Cities, though sometimes by force of orders, and discipline, or of a numerous and valiant people, they have extended themselves into mighty Dominions: and often by Scituation and Trade, grow to vast Riches, and thereby to great Power by force of mercenary Arms. And these seem to be the more artificial, as those of a single Person the more Natural Governments; being forced to supply the want of Authority by wise inventions, orders and institutions.

For Authority can never be so great in many as in one, because the opinion of those qualities which acquire it, cannot be equal in several persons.

These Governments seem to be introduced either by the wisdom and moderation of some one Lawgiver, who has Authority enough with the people to be followed and observed in all his orders and advices; and yet prefers that which he esteems publick utility, before any interest or greatness of his own (such were *Lycurgus*[14] in *Sparta*, and *Solon*[15] in *Athens*, and *Timoleon*[16] in *Syracuse*); Or else by the confluence of many Families out of some Countries exposed to some fierce or barbarous invasions, into places fortified by Nature, and secure from the fury and misery of such Conquests. Such were *Rhodes*[17] of old, and several small Islands upon the Coasts of *Ionia*; and such was *Venice* founded upon the Inundation of the barbarous Nations over *Italy:* Or lastly, by the suppression and extinction of some Tyranny, which being thrown off by the violent indignation of an oppressed people, makes way for a Popular Government, or at least some form very contrary to that which they lately execrated, and detested: Such were *Rome* upon the expulsion of the *Tarquins*;[18] and the *United Provinces* upon their revolt from *Spain*:[19] Yet are none of these forms to be raised or upheld without the influence of Authority, acquired by the force of opinion of those virtues above-mentioned, which concur'd in *Brutus* among the *Romans,* and in Prince *William* of *Orange* among those of the *Netherlands.*[20]

I will not enter into the Arguments or comparisons of the several forms of Government that have been, or are in the World; wherein that cause seems commonly the better, that has the better advocate, or is advantaged by fresher experience and impressions of good or evil from any of the Forms among those that judg: They have all their heighths and their falls, their strong and weak sides; are capable of great perfections, and subject to great corruptions: and though the preference seem already decided in what has been said of a single Persons being the original and natural Government; and that it is capable of the greatest Authority (which is the foundation of all ease, safety, and order, in the Governments of the World) yet it may perhaps be the most reasonably concluded, That those forms are best, which have been longest received and authorized in a Nation by custom and use; and into which the humours and manners of the people run with the most general and strongest current.

Or else, that those are the best Governments, where the best men Govern; and that the difference is not so great in the forms of Magistracy, as in the persons of Magistrates; which may be the sense of what was said of old (taking wise and good men, to be meant by Philosophers) that the best Governments were those, where Kings were Philosophers; or Philosophers Kings.

Notes

SIR WILLIAM TEMPLE (1628-99) was of an Irish settler family but was brought up on England. He went back to Ireland for a time after his marriage in 1655, returning to England in 1663 and entering the diplomatic service two years later. In 1668 he was instrumental in negotiating the 'Triple Alliance', the effects of which were undone by the Third Dutch War of 1672, which forced him into retirement. It was at this period that the *Essay* was composed. When the war ended, he resumed his diplomatic duties in the Netherlands, and was instrumental in arranging the marriage between William of Orange and the Duke of York's eldest daughter, the Princess Mary. He returned to public life yet again in 1680 but refused to become involved in the revolution of 1688, though he acquiesced in it. Swift became his secretary in 1689, and later wrote *The Battle of the Books* in his defence. At his death Swift wrote: 'with him [died] all that was good and amiable among men'.

1. A title used by the successors of the Prophet Mohamet – the word means 'successor'. Various later Islamic dynasties also used it – in Damascus, Baghdad and Cairo. The title was finally assumed by the Ottoman emperors.

2. Antoine Loisel (1536-1612), French jurist and author of *Institutes Coutumières*.

3. See Marvell's joke on this theme (pp. 77-8).

4. Notably Richard Hooker (1554-1600); see Keble, 1836, I, 239.53

5. Notably Hobbes (see Introduction, p. 8 and p. 112, n. 34).

6. 'the father of his country'.

7. Germans.

8. Julius Caesar (see p. 58, n. 5).

9. Cornelius Tacitus (AD 55?-117), Roman historian.

10. An Irish word for tribes.

11. Feudal armies in France and England, the modern form of which was the voluntary, locally raised militia.

12. See Chamberlayne's account of martial law, pp. 60-1; Swift was to share this characteristically tory dislike of a standing army. The Guards regiments in the British Army date from this period, and were formed in some cases on the flimsy excuse of imminent insurrection. The Royal Horse Guards, for example, were formed after a feeble rising by a London cooper called Venner in 1661.

13. Republics.

14. See p. 111, n. 5.

15. See p. 111, n. 6.

16. Timoleon (d. 337? BC), governor of Syracuse.

17. The three independent city states of which united into a single state in consequence of a war with-Athens (411-407 BC).

18. See p. 111, n. 4.

19. See pp. 73-4, n. 48.

20. William I ruled 1579-84), 'the Silent', Chief Stadholder of Holland, and leader of the revolt of the Netherlands against the rule of Spain.

10 From: *The History of the League . . . The Postscript of the Translator*

John Dryden, 1684

That Government generally consider'd, is of divine Authority, will admit of no dispute: For whoever will seriously consider, that no man has naturally a right over his own Life, so as to murder himself; will find by consequence, that he has no right to take away anothers Life; and that no pact betwixt man and man, or of Corporations and Individuals, or of Soveraigns and Subjects, can intitle them to this right. So that no Offender can lawfully, and without sin, be punish'd; unless that power be deriv'd from God. 'Tis He who has commission'd Magistrates, and authoriz'd them to prevent future Crimes by punishing Offenders, and to redress the injur'd by distributive Justice: Subjects therefore are accountable to Superiors, and the Superior to Him alone. For the Soveraign being once invested with lawful Authority, the Subject has irrevocably given up his power, and the dependance of a Monarch is alone on God. A King, at his Coronation, swears to govern his Subjects by the Laws of the Land, and to maintain the several Orders of Men under him, in their lawful priviledges; and those Orders swear Allegiance and Fidelity to him, but with this distinction, that the failure of the People is punishable by the King, that of the King is only punishable by the King of Kings. The People then are not Judges of good or ill administration in their King; for 'tis inconsistent with the Nature of Soveraignty, that they shou'd be so: And if at some times they suffer through the irregularities of a bad Prince, they enjoy more often the benefits and advantages of a good one, as God in his Providence shall dispose, either for their blessing or their punishment. The advantages and disadvantages of such subjection, are suppos'd to have been first consider'd, and upon this ballance they have given up their power without a capacity of resumption: So that it is in vain for a Common-wealth Party to plead, that men, for example, now in being, cannot bind their Posterity or give up their power: For if Subjects can swear only for themselves, when the Father dyes the subjection ends, and the Son who has not sworn can be no Traytor or Offender, either to the King or to the Laws. And at this rate a long-liv'd Prince may outlive his Soveraignty, and be no longer lawfully a King: But in the mean time, 'tis evident that the Son enjoys the benefit of the Laws and Government, which is an implicit acknowledgment of subjection. 'Tis endless to run through all the extravagancies of these men, and 'tis enough for us that we are settled under a Lawful Government of a Most Gracious Prince; that our Monarchy is Hereditary; that it is naturally poiz'd by our municipal Laws, with equal benefit of Prince and People; that he Governs as he has promis'd by explicit Laws; and what the Laws are silent in, I think I may conclude to be part of his Prerogative; for what the King has not granted away, is inherent in him. The point of Succession has sufficiently been discuss'd, both as to the Right of it, and to the interest of the People: One main Argument of the other side is, how often it has been remov'd from the Right Line? As in the case of King *Stephen*,[1] and of *Henry* the Fourth[2] and his Descendants of the house of Lancaster. But 'tis easie to answer them, that matter of Fact, and matter of Right are different Considerations: both those Kings were but Usurpers in effect, and the Providence of God restor'd the Posterities of those who were dispossess'd. By the same Argument they might as well justifie the Rebellion and Murder of the late King: For there was not only a Prince inhumanly put to death, but a Government overturn'd, and first an Arbitrary Common-wealth, then two Usurpers set up against the Lawful Soveraign; but to our happiness the same Providence has miraculously restor'd the Right Heir, and to their confusion, as miraculously preserv'd him. In this present History,[3] to go no further, we see *Henry* the Third, by a Decree of the *Sorbonne*, divested, what in them lay, of his Imperial Rights, a Parliament of *Paris*, such another as our first long Parliament, confirming their Decree, a Pope authorising all this by his Excommunication, and an Holy League and Covenant, prosecuting this Deposition by Arms: Yet an untimely death only hindred him from reseating himself in Glory on the Throne, after he was in manifest possession of the Victory. We see also the same *Sorbonists*, the same Pope, Parliament, and League, with greater force opposing the undoubted Right of King *Henry* the Fourth; and we see him, in the end, surmounting all these difficulties, and triumphing over all these dangers. God Almighty taking care of his own Anointed, and the True Succession: Neither the *Papist* nor *Presbyterian Association* prevailing at the last in their attempts, but both baffl'd and ruin'd, and the whole Rebellion ending either in the submission, or destruction of the Conspirators. . . .

How *Presbytery* was transplanted into *England*, I have formerly related out of good Authors.[4] The Persecution arising in Queen *Mary's*[5] Reign, forc'd many Protestants out of their Native Country into Foreign parts, where *Calvinism*,[6] having already taken root (as at *Francfort*, *Strasburg*, and *Geneva*) those Exiles grew tainted with that new Discipline; and returning in the beginning of Queen *Elizabeth*'s[7] Reign, spread the contagion of it both amongst the Clergy and Laity of this Nation.

Any man who will look into the Tenets of the first Sectaries, will find these to be more or less embued with them: Here they were supported underhand by Great Men for private interests: What trouble they gave that Queen, and how she curb'd them, is notoriously known to all who are conversant in the Histories of those times. How King *James*[8] was plagu'd with them is known as well, to any man who has read the Reverend and Sincere *Spotiswood:*[9] And how they were baffled by the Church of *England*, in a Disputation which he allowed them at *Hampton-Court*,[10] even to the Conversion of Dr. *Sparks*,[11] who was one of the two Disputants of their Party, and afterwards writ against them, any one who pleases may be satisfied.

The Agreement of their Principles with the fiercest Jesuits, is as easie to be demonstrated, and has already been done by several hands: I will only mention some few of them, to show how well prepar'd they came to that solemn Covenant[12] of theirs, which they borrowed first from the *Holy League* of *France*; and have lately copied out again in their intended Association[13] against his present Majesty.

Bellarmine,[14] as the Author of this History has told you, was himself a Preacher for the *League* in *Paris*, during the Rebellion there, in the Reign of King *Henry* the Fourth. Some of his Principles are these following.

In the Kingdoms of Men, the Power of the King is from the People, because the People make the King: Observing that he says, *In the Kingdoms of Men*, there is no doubt but he restrains this Principle to the subordination of the Pope: For his Holiness, in that Rebellion, as you have read, was declar'd *Protector of the League:* So that the Pope first Excommunicates (which is the Outlawry of the Church) and, by virtue of this Excommunication, the People are left to their own natural liberty, and may without farther Process from *Rome* depose him . . . .

Now consonant to this is *Buchanan's*[15] Principle, *That the People may confer the Government on whom they please.* . . .

'Tis the work of a Scavenger to rake together and carry off all these Dunghills; they are easie to be found at the Doors of all our Sects, and all our Atheistical Commonwealths men. . . .

What I have remark'd of them is no more than necessary, to show

how aptly their Principles are suited to their Practices: The History it self has sufficiently discover'd to the unbiass'd Reader, that both the last Rebellion, and this present Conspiracy,[16] (which is the mystery of Iniquity still working in the three Nations) were originally founded on the *French League:* that was their Model, according to which they built their *Babel.* You have seen how warily the first Association in *Picardy*[17] was worded: nothing was to be attempted but for the King's Service, and an Acknowledgement was formally made, that both the Right and Power of the Government was in him: but it was pretended, that by occasion of the true *Protestant* Rebels, the Crown was not any longer in condition, either of maintaining it self, or protecting them. And that therefore in the Name of God, and by the Power of the holy Ghost, they joyn'd together in their own Defence, and that of their Religion. But all this while, though they wou'd seem to act by the King's Authority, and under him, the Combination was kept as secret as possibly they cou'd, and even without the participation of the Soveraign; a sure Sign, that they intended him no good at the bottom. Nay, they had an Evasion ready too, against his Authority; for 'tis plain, they joyn'd *Humieres,*[18] the Governour of the Province, in Commission with him; and only nam'd the King for show; but engag'd themselves at the same time to his Lieutenant, to be obedient to all his Commands; levying Men and Money, without the King's Knowledge, or any Law, but what they made amongst themselves. So, that in effect, the Rebellion and Combination of the *Hugonots,*[19] was only a leading Card, and an example to the *Papists,* to rebel, on their side. And there was only this difference in the Cause, that the *Calvinists* set up for their Reformation, by the superior Power of Religion, and inherent Right of the People, against the King and Pope. The *Papists* pretended the same popular Right for their Rebellion against the King, and for the same end of Reformation, only they fac'd it, with Church and Pope.

Our Sectaries, and Long Parliament of 41, had certainly these *French* Precedents in their eye. They copy'd their Methods of Rebellion; at first with great professions of Duty and Affection to the King; all they did was in order to make him glorious; all that was done against him was pretended to be under his Authority and in his Name; and even the War they rais'd, was pretended for the King and Parliament. But these Proceedings are so notoriously known, and have imploy'd so many Pens, that it wou'd be a nauseous Work for me to dwell on them. To draw the likeness of the *French* Transactions and ours, were in effect to transcribe the History I have translated. . . . But for those Sectaries and Commonwealths-men of 41, before I leave them, I must crave leave to observe of them, that generally they were a sowr sort of thinking men, grim and surly Hypocrites; such as coud cover their Vices, with an appearance of great Devotion and austerity of Manners: neither Profaneness, nor Luxury, were encouragd by them, nor practisd publickly, which gave them a great opinion of Sanctity amongst the Multitude; and by that opinion principally they did their businesse. Though their Politicks were taken from the *Catholick League*, yet their Christianity much resembled those *Anabaptists*,[20] who were their Original in Doctrine; and these indeed were formidable Instruments of a religious Rebellion. But our new Conspirators of these seven last years, are men of quite another Make: I speak not of their non-Conformist Preachers, who pretend to *Enthusiasme*, and are as morose in their Worship, as were those first Sectaries, but of their Leading men, the Heads of their Faction, and the principal Members of it: what greater looseness of Life, more atheistical Discourse, more open Lewdness was ever seen, than generally was and is to be observ'd in those men? I am neither making a Satyr nor a Sermon here; but I wou'd remark a little the ridiculousness of their Management: The strictness of Religion is their pretence; and the men who are to set it up, have theirs to choose. The Long Parliament Rebels frequented Sermons, and observ'd Prayers and Fastings with all solemnity: but these new Reformers, who ought in prudence to have trodden in their steps, because their End was the same, to gull the People by an outside of Devotion, never us'd the means of insinuating themselves into the opinion of the Multitude. Swearing, Drunkenness, Blasphemies, and worse sins than Adultery are the Badges of the Party: nothing but Liberty in their mouths, nothing but License in their practice.

For which reason they were never esteem'd by the Zealots of their Faction, but as their Tools; and had they got uppermost, after the Royalists had been crush'd, they wou'd have been blown off, as too light for their Society: For my own part, when I had once observ'd this fundamental error in their Politiques, I was no longer afraid of their success: No Government was ever ruin'd by the open scandal of its opposers. This was just a *Catiline's*[21] Conspiracy, of profligate, debauch'd, and bankrupt men: The wealthy amongst them were the fools of the Party, drawn in by the rest whose Fortunes were desperate; and the Wits of the Cabal sought only their private advantages. They had either lost their Preferments, and consequently were piqu'd, or were in hope to raise themselves by the general disturbance. Upon which account, they never cou'd be true to one another: There was neither Honour nor Conscience in the Foundation of their *League*, but every man having an eye to his own particular advancement, was no longer a Friend, than while his Interest was carrying on: So that Treachery was at the bottom of their design, first against the Monarchy, and if that fail'd, against each other; in which, be it spoken to the honour of our Nation, the *English* are not behind any other Country. In few words, just as much fidelity might be expected from them in a common cause as there is amongst a Troop of honest murdering and ravishing Bandits; while the Booty is in prospect, they combine heartily and faithfully, but when a Proclamation of Pardon comes out, and a good reward into the bargain, for any one who brings in anothers Head, the Scene is chang'd, and they are in more danger of being betray'd every man by his Companion, than they were formerly by the joynt forces of their Enemies. 'Tis true, they are still to be accounted dangerous, because though they are dispers'd at present, and without an Head, yet time and lenity may furnish them again with a Commander: And all men are satisfied that the debauch'd Party of them, have no principle of Godliness to restrain them from Violence and Murders; nor the pretended Saints any principle of Charity, for 'tis an action of Piety in them to destroy their Enemies, having first pronounc'd them Enemies of God. What my Author says in general of the *Huguenots*, may justly be applyed to all our Sectaries: They are a malicious and bloody Generation, they bespatter honest Men with their Pens when they are not in power; and when they are uppermost, they hang them up like Dogs. To such kind of people all means of reclaiming, but only severity, are useless, while they continue obstinate in their designs against Church and Government: For tho' now their claws are par'd, they may grow again to be more sharp; they are still Lyons in their Nature, and may profit so much by their own errors in their late managements, that they may become more sanctify'd Traytors another time.

In the former part of our History, we see what *Henry* the Third gain'd from them by his remisness and concessions: Though our last King was not only incomparably more pious than that Prince, but also was far from being tax'd with any of his Vices; yet in this they may be compar'd, without the least manner of reflection, that extreme Indulgence and too great Concessions, were the ruin of them both.[22] And by how much the more, a King is subject by his Nature, to this frailty of too much mildness, which is so near resembling the God like Attribute of Mercy; by so much is he the more liable to be tax'd with Tyranny. A strange Paradox, but which was sadly verified in the Persons of those two Princes: For a Faction appearing zealous for the Publick Liberty, counts him a Tyrant who yields not up whatever they demand, even his most undoubted and just Prerogatives; all that distinguishes a Soveraign from a Subject, and the yielding up, or taking away of which, is the very Subversion of the Government.

Every point which a Monarch loses or relinquishes, but renders him the weaker to maintain the rest; and besides, they so construe it, as if what he gave up were the natural right of the people, which he or his Ancestors had usurp'd from them; which makes it the more dangerous for him to quit his hold, and is truly the reason why so many mild Princes have been branded with the names of Tyrants, by their incroaching Subjects. I have not room to enlarge upon this matter as I wou'd, neither dare I presume to press the Argument more closely: But passing by, as I promis'd, all the remarkable passages in the late Kings Reign, which resemble the Transactions of the *League*; I will briefly take notice of some few particulars, wherein our late Associators and Conspirators have made a Third Copy of the *League*. For the Original of their first Politiques was certainly no other than the *French*. This was first copied by the Rebels in Forty One, and since recopyed within these late years by some of those who are lately dead, and by too many others yet alive, and still drawing after the same design. In which, for want of time, many a fair blot shall be left unhit, neither do I promise to observe any method of times, or to take things in order as they happen'd.

As for the Persons who manag'd the two Associations, theirs and ours, 'tis most certain that in them is found the least resemblance: And 'tis well for us they were not like: For they had men of Subtilty and Valour to design and then to carry on their Conspiracy; ours were but bunglers in comparison of them, who having a Faction not made by them, but ready form'd and fashion'd to their hands, (thanks to their Fathers) yet fail'd in every one of their Projections, and manag'd their business with much less dexterity, though far more wickedness than the *French*. They had indeed at their Head an old Conspirator,[23] witty and turbulent, like the Cardinal of *Lorrain*,[24] and for courage in Execution much such another. But the good sense and conduct was clearly wanting on the *English* side; so that if we will allow him the contrivance of the Plot, or at least of the Conspiracy, which is an honour that no man will be willing to take from him; in all other circumstances he more resembled the old decrepit Cardinal of *Bourbon*,[25] who fed himself with imaginary hopes of power, dream'd of outliving a King and his Successor, much more young and vigorous than himself, and of governing the World after their decease: To dye in Prison, or in Banishment, I think will make no mighty difference, but this is a main one; th. t the one was the Dupe of all his Party, the other led after him, and made fools of all his Faction. As for a Duke of *Guise*, or even so much as a Duke of *Mayenne*,[26] I can find none in their whole Cabal. I cannot believe that any man now living cou'd have the vanity to pretend to it: 'Tis not every Age that can produce a Duke of *Guise*; a man who without the least shadow of a Title (unless we will believe the Memoires of the crack-brain'd Advocate *David*,[27] who gave him one from *Charlemaign*) durst make himself Head of a Party, and was not only so in his own conceit, but really; presum'd to beard a King, and was upon the point of being declar'd his Lieutenant General, and his Successor. None of these instances will hold in the Comparison, and therefore I leave it to be boasted, it may be, by one Party, but I am sure to be laugh'd at by another. ....

I begin aready to be tir'd with drawing after their deformities, as a Painter wou'd be, who had nothing before him in his Table but *Lazars*, Cripples, and hideous faces, which he was oblig'd to represent: Yet I must not omit some few of their most notorious Copyings. Take for example their *Council of Six*,[28] which was an imitation of the *League*, who set up their famous Council, commonly call'd *Of the Sixteen*.[29] And take notice, that on both sides they pick'd out the most heady and violent men of the whole Party; nay they consider'd not so much as their natural parts, but heavy Blockheads were thrown in for lumber, to make up the weight: Their Zeal for the Party, and their Ambition, atton'd for their want of Judgment, especially if they were thought to have any interest in the people. Loud roarers of *Ay* and *No* in the *Parliament*, without common sence in ordinary discourses, if they were favourites of the Multitude, were made Privy Counsellors of their Cabal; and Fools, who only wanted a parti-colour'd Coat, a Cap, and a Bawble, to pass for such amongst reasonable men, were to redress the imaginary Grievances of a Nation, by murdering, or at least seizing of the King. ....

I will trouble the Reader but with one Observation more, and that shall be to show how dully and pedantically they have copied, even the false steps of the *League*, in Politicks, and those very Maxims which ruin'd the Heads of it. The Duke of *Guise* was always ostentatious of his power in the States where he carried all things in opposition to the King: But by relying too much on the power he had there, and not using Arms when he had them in his hand, I mean by not prosecuting his Victory to the uttermost, when he had the King inclos'd in the *Louvre*, he miss'd his opportunity, and Fortune never gave it him again.

The late Earl of *Shaftesbury*, who was the undoubted Head and Soul of that Party, went upon the same maximes, being (as we may reasonably conclude) fearful of hazarding his Fortunes, and observing that the late Rebellion under the former King, though successful in War, yet ended in the Restauration of His Present Majesty, his aim was to have excluded His Royal Highness by an Act of Parliament; and to have forc'd such concessions from the King, by pressing the chymerical dangers of a Popish Plot, as wou'd not only have destroy'd the Succession, but have subverted the Monarchy. For he presum'd he ventur'd nothing, if he cou'd have executed his design by form of Law, and in a Parliamentary way. In the meantime, he made notorious mistakes: First, in imagining that his pretensions wou'd have pass'd in the House of Peers, and afterwards by the King. When the death of Sir *Edmondbury Godfrey*[30] had fermented the people, when the City had taken the alarm of a Popish Plot, and the Government of it was in Fanatique hands; when a Body of white Boys[31] was already appearing in the West, and many other Counties waited but the word to rise, then was the time to have push'd his business: But Almighty God, who had otherwise dispos'd of the Event, infatuated his Counsels, and made him slip his opportunity, which he himself observ'd too late, and would have redress'd by an Insurrection which was to have begun at *Wapping*, after the King had been murder'd at the *Rye*.

Notes

JOHN DRYDEN (1631-1700) was the greatest and most prolific writer of the age, distinguished as a dramatist and critic as well as a poet. A moderate Cromwellian, he supported the restoration and was appointed Poet Laureate in 1668 and Historiographer Royal in 1670. The latter office made him official propagandist for the government. In religion he moved from moderate anglicanism to roman catholicism, becoming a catholic in 1686. He remained loyal to his new church in 1688 when he was deprived of his offices. The writings of the closing years of his life are replete with coded and deftly expressed allusions to his jacobite principles, but he remained socially on good terms with supporters of the revolution, notably Halifax (see Introduction, pp. 19-20).

1. Stephen (reigned 1135-54), grandson of the Conqueror, who seized the throne of England from Matilda, only surviving child of Henry I (reigned

1100-35). On the death of his own son, Stephen was forced to recognise Matilda's son Henry as his heir. Dryden is mistaken in assuming that at this period the Crown of England was hereditary.

2. Henry IV (reigned 1399-1413) who seized the throne from Richard II (reigned 1377-99), establishing the Lancastrian dynasty. His grandson, Henry VI (reigned 1422-61; 1470-1), lost the throne to the Yorkist claimant, Edward IV (reigned 1461-70; 1471-83). The throne was subsequently seized from Edward V (reigned 1483) by his uncle, Richard III (reigned 1483-5), who lost it in his turn to the Lancastrian claimant, Henry VII (reigned 1484-1509). The latter's marriage to the eldest daughter of Edward IV gave his descendants undisputed rights to the English throne. Dryden was not alone in being fascinated by such 'providential' dynastic restorations, which provided a recurring theme for a number of his plays.

3. *The History of the League* by Louis Maimbourg (1610-86), historian and controversialist, who was expelled from the jesuit order for writing in defence of the independance of the French catholic church from Rome. He received a pension from Louis XIV. See pp. 72-3, n. 20 for a brief summary of the history of the League.

4. See Preface to *Religio Laici* (Kinsley, 1962, 279-80).

5. Mary I (reigned 1553-8), whose attempt to restore catholicism to England entailed the ruthless persecution of protestants.

6. Followers of John Calvin (1509-64), French protestant reformer, who established a theocratic dictatorship in Geneva in 1641, the source of presbyterian conceptions of church and state government (see p. 41, n. 4).

7. Elizabeth I (see p. 73, n. 25) restored the reformed religion to England.

8. See p. 72, n. 9.

9. John Spottiswoode (1565-1637), Archbishop of St Andrews and Scottish historian; originally a staunch presbyterian, he finally sided with the King against the kirk.

10. A debate between English bishops and puritan leaders presided over by James I and VI in 1603/4. It was on this occasion that he made his celebrated declaration 'no bishop, no king', thus firmly identifying the royalist and episcopalian causes.

11. Thomas Sparke (1548-1616), a puritan divine who was persuaded to conform at the Hampton Court conference.

12. See p. 42, n. 10.

13. See n. 23 below.

14. St Robert Bellarmine (1542-1621), jesuit controversialist, a man of moderate views on papal as well as royal authority.

15. George Buchanan (1506-82), Latin poet and historian; he was heavily involved in the campaign to discredit Mary Queen of Scots. He was tutor to the young James VI, and his book *De Juri Regum [On the Rule of Kings]* was published in 1579. It was suppressed in 1584, but had considerable influence among English radicals during and after the civil war.

16. The so-called Rye House plot of 1683, in which a group of whig extremists planned to assassinate Charles II. Their meetings were held at Rye House in Hertfordshire.

17. A league of French catholic nobles led by the Duke of Guise in 1576, which proposed to subordinate royal authority to that of the Estates (or parliament).

18. Jaques d'Humieres, the initiator of the League.

19. An allusion to an earlier plot by Huguenots to kidnap the King and

assassinate the Guises, who were then in the ascendant at court. The conspiracy was discovered in 1560 and the leaders executed at the castle of Amboise.

20. A particularly feared group (see pp. 41-2, n. 5); one group of anabaptists was associated with Thomas Munzer (1490-1525) who sympathised with the peasants' revolt in Germany and taught the doctrine of inward illumination later to be adopted by the Quakers. Between 1533 and 1535 an anabaptist kingdom of the saints was established in Munster, which became notorious for its acceptance of polygamy and other excesses.

21. Sergius Catilina (108-62 BC), whose conspiracy against the Republic of Rome was put down by Cicero (see p. 58, n. 3).

22. Charles I made numerous concessions to Parliament and reneged on them quite as frequently.

23. Anthony Ashley Cooper, first Earl of Shaftesbury (1621-83), Dryden's Achitophel; the leading exclusionist politician. Originally a Cromwellian, he was involved in numerous conspiracies at the end of the Commonwealth period, was a party to the restoration and Chancellor of the Exchequer from 1661 to 1672, when he became a notably principled Lord Chancellor. In opposition in the 1670s, he campaigned ruthlessly against the succession of the Duke of York. One of his most effective instruments in this campaign was the Protestant Association, to which Dryden makes frequent allusion. He was arrested in 1681, but acquitted by a whig jury. He fled abroad and died in exile. (See also n. 28 and headnote to Locke's *Essay . . . Of Civil Government*, p. 202.

24. See p. 72, n. 20.

25. See p. 72, n. 20.

26. Charles de Lorraine, Duke of Mayenne (1554-1611), leader of the League after the assassinations of his brothers, Henry Duke of Guise and the Cardinal of Lorraine; he submitted to Henry IV in 1595.

27. A lawyer whose papers were discovered after his death to contain purported proofs that the House of Lorraine were true heirs to the throne of France.

28. The informal grouping of politicians who took over the leadership of the opposition after Shaftesbury's flight abroad; they included the Duke of Monmouth. The extent of their involvement in treasonable conspiracy is uncertain.

29. A body established by the Duke of Guise and formed by representatives from the 16 districts of Paris.

30. Sir Edmund Bury Godfrey (1621-78), a magistrate who received the original revelations concerning the Popish Plot on 28 September 1678. He disappeared on the following 12 October and was found murdered a week later, an event which lent considerable credence to the allegations of a catholic conspiracy.

31. Literally 'choir boys' — a riotous mob.

11 From: *The Character of a Trimmer*

George Savile, Marquis of Halifax, 1704

Our Trimmer, as he has a great Veneration for Laws in general, so he has more particular for our own, he looks upon them as the Chains that tye up our unruly Passions, which else, like wild Beasts let loose, would reduce the world into its first State of Barbarism and Hostility; the good things we enjoy, we owe to them; and all the ill things we are freed from by their Protection.

God himself thought it not enough to be a Creator, without being a Lawgiver, and his goodness had been defective towards mankind in making them, if he had not prescribed Rules to make them happy too.

All Laws flow from that of Nature, and where that is not the Foundation, they may be legally impos'd, but they will be lamely obeyed: By this Nature, is not meant that which Fools and Madmen misquote to justifie their Excesses; it is innocent and uncorrupted Nature, that which disposes Men to chuse Vertue, without its being prescribed, and which is so far from inspiring ill thoughts into us, that we take pains to suppress the good ones it infuses. . . .

There would be no end of making a Panegyrick of Laws; let it be enough to add, that without Laws the World would become a Wilderness, and Men little less than Beasts; but with all this, the best things may come to be the worst, if they are not in good hands; and if it be true that the wisest Men generally make the Laws, it is as true, that the strongest do often Interpret them; And as Rivers belong as much to the Channel where they run, as to the Spring from whence they first rise, so the Laws depend as much upon the Pipes thro' which they are to pass, as upon the Fountain from whence they flow.

The Authority of a King who is Head of the Law, as well as the Dignity of Publick Justice, is debased, when the clear stream of the Law is puddled and disturbed by Bunglers, or convey'd by unclean Instruments to the People. . . .

A Judge has such power lodg'd in him, that the King will never be thought to have chosen well, where the Voice of Mankind has not before-hand recommended the Man to his Station; when Men are made Judges of what they do not understand, the World censures such a Choice, not out of ill will to the Men, but fear to themselves.

If the King had the sole Power of chusing Physicians, Men would tremble to see Bunglers preferred, yet the necessity of taking Physick from a Doctor, is generally not so great, as that of receiving Justice from a Judge: And yet the Inferences will be very severe in such cases; for either it will be thought, that such Men bought what they were not able to deserve; or which is as bad, that Obedience shall be look'd upon as a better Qualification in a Judge, than Skill or Integrity: When such sacred things as the Laws are not only touch'd, but guided by prophane Hands; Men will fear that out of the Tree of the Law, from whence we expect Shade and Shelter, such Workmen will make Cudgels to beat us with, or rather that they will turn the Canon upon our Properties, that were intrusted with them for their Defence.

To see the Laws Mangled, Disguised, Speak quite another Language than their own; to see them thrown from the Dignity of protecting Mankind, to the disgraceful Office of destroying them; and notwithstanding their Innocence in themselves, to be made the worst Instruments that the most refined Villany can make use of, will raise Mens Anger above the power of laying it down again, and tempt them to follow the Evil Examples given them of Judging without Hearing, when so provoked by their desire of Revenge. Our *Trimmer* therefore, as he thinks the Laws are Jewels, so he believes they are no better set, than in the constitution of our *English* Government, if rightly understood, and carefully preserved....

Our *Trimmer* thinks that the King and Kingdom ought to be one Creature, not to be separated in their Political Capacity; and when either of them undertake to act a-part, it is like the crawling of Worms after they are cut in pieces, which cannot be a lasting motion, the whole Creature not stirring at a time. If the Body has a dead Palsie, the Head cannot make it move; and God hath not yet delegated such a healing Power to Princes, as that they can in a Moment say to a Languishing People oppress'd and in despair, take up your Beds and walk.[1]

The Figure of a King, is so comprehensive and exalted a thing, that it is a kind of degrading him, to lodge that Power separately in his own natural Person, which can never be safely or naturally Great, but where the People are so united to him, as to be Flesh of his Flesh, and Bone of his Bone:[2] For when he is reduc'd to the single definition of a Man, he sinks into so low a Character, that it is a Temptation upon Mens Allegiance, and an impairing that Veneration which is necessary to preserve their Duty to him; whereas a Prince who is so joyned to his People, that they seem to be his Limbs rather than his Subjects, Cloathed with Mercy and Justice rightly apply'd in their several places, his Throne supported by Love as well as by Power, and the warm Wishes of his devoted Subjects, like never failing Incense, still ascending towards him, looks so like the best Image we can frame to our selves of God Almighty, that Men would have much ado not to fall down and worship him; and would be much more tempted to the Sin of Idolatry, than to that of Disobedience. . . .

Our *Trimmer* thinks it no advantage to a Government, to endeavour the suppressing all kind of Right which may remain in the Body of the People, or to employ small Authors in it, whose Officiousness or want of Money may encourage them to write, tho' it is very uneasie to have Abilities equal to such a Subject; they forget that in their too high strain'd Arguments for the Rights of Princes, they very often plead against humane Nature, which will always give a Biass to those Reasons which seem of her side: It is the People that Reads those Books, and it is the People that must judge of them; and therefore no Maxims should be laid down for the Right of Government, to which there can be any reasonable Objection; for the World has an Interest, and for that Reason is more than ordinary discerning to find out the weak sides of such Arguments as are intended to do them hurt; and it is a diminution to a Government, to Promote or Countenance such well affected mistakes which are turned upon it with disadvantage, whenever they are detected and expos'd; and Naturally the too earnest Endeavours to take from Men the Right they have, tempt them, by the Example, to claim that which they have not.

In Power, as in most other things, the way for Princes to keep it, is not to grasp more than their Arms can well hold; the nice and unnecessary enquiring into these things, or the Licensing some Books, and suppressing some others without sufficient Reason to Justifie the doing either, is so far from being an Advantage to a Government, that it exposes it to the Censure of being Partial, and to the suspicion of having some hidden designs to be carried on by these unusual Methods.

When all is said, there is a Natural Reason of State, an undefinable thing, grounded upon the common Good of Mankind, which is immortal, and in all Changes and Revolutions, still preserves its Original Right of saving a Nation, when the Letter of the Law perhaps would destroy it; and by whatsoever means it moves, carrieth a Power with it, that admits of no opposition, being supported by Nature, which inspires an immediate consent at some critical Times into every individual Member, to that which visibly tendeth to preservation of the whole; and this being so, a wise Prince instead of Controverting the right of this Reason of State, will by all means endeavour it may be of his side. . . .

Our *Trimmer* owns a Passion for Liberty, yet so restrained, that it does not in the least impair or taint his Allegiance; he thinks it hard for a Soul that does not love Liberty, ever to raise its self to another World; he takes it to be the foundation of all Vertue, and the only seasoning that gives a relish to Life; and tho' the laziness of a slavish subjection, has its Charm for the more gross and earthy part of Mankind, yet to Men made of a better sort of Clay, all that the World can give without Liberty has no taste: It is true, nothing is sold so cheap by unthinking Men, but that does no more lessen the real value of it, than a Country Fellow's Ignorance does that of a Diamond, in selling it for a Pot of Ale. Liberty is the Mistress of Mankind, she has powerful Charms which do so dazzle us, that we find Beauties in her which perhaps are not there, as we do in other Mistresses; yet if she was not a Beauty, the World would not run mad for her; therefore since the reasonable desire of it ought not to be restrain'd, and that even the unreasonable desire of it cannot be entirely suppress'd, those who would take it away from a People possess'd of it, are likely to fail in the attempting, or be very unquiet in the keeping of it.

Our *Trimmer* admires our blessed Constitution, in which Dominion and Liberty are so well reconciled; it gives to the Prince the glorious Power of commanding Free-men, and to the Subject, the satisfaction of seeing the Power so lodged, as that their Liberties are secure; it does not allow the Crown such a ruining Power, as that no Grass can grow where e're it treads, but a cherishing and protecting Power; such a one as hath a grim Aspect only to the offending Subjects, but is the Joy and the Pride of all the good ones; their own Interest being so bound up in it, as to engage them to defend and support it: and tho' in some instances the King is restrain'd, yet nothing in the Government can move without him: Our Laws make a distinction between Vassalage and Obedience, between devouring Prerogatives, and a licentious ungovernable Freedom; and as of all the Orders of Building, the Composite is the best, so ours, by a happy mixture and a wise choice of what is best in others, is brought into a Form that is our Felicity who live under it, and the Envy of our Neighbour that cannot imitate it.

The Crown has Power sufficient to protect our Liberties. The People have so much Liberty, as it necessary to make them useful to the Crown. . . .

Our *Trimmer* is a Friend to Parliaments, notwithstanding all their Faults and Excesses, which of late have given such matter of Objection to them; he thinks that tho' they may at sometimes be troublesome to Authority, yet they add the greatest strength to it under a wise Administration; he believes no Government is perfect except a kind of Omnipotence reside in it, to exercise upon great Occasions: Now this cannot be obtained by Force alone upon People, let it be never so great; there must be their consent too, or else a Nation moves only by being driven, a sluggish and constrained Motion, void of that Life and Vigour which is necessary to produce great things; whereas the virtual Consent of the whole being included in their Representatives, and the King giving the Sanction to the united Sense of the People, every Act done by such an Authority, seems to be an effect of their Choice, as well as a part of their Duty; and they do with an Eagerness, of which Men are uncapable whilst under a Force, execute whatsoever is so enjoyned, as their own Wills better explained by Parliament, rather than from the terrour of incurring the Penalty of the Law for omitting it; and by means of this Political Omnipotence, whatever Sap or Juice there is in a Nation, may be to the last drop produc'd, whilst it rises naturally from the Root: whereas all Power exercis'd without consent, is like the giving Wounds and Gashes, and tapping a Tree at unseasonable Times, for the present occasion, which in a very little time must needs destroy it.

Our *Trimmer* believes, that by the advantage of our Situation there can hardly any such sudden Disease come upon us, but that the King may have time enough left to consult with his Physicians in Parliament; Pretences indeed may be made, but a real necessity so pressing, that no delay is to be admitted, is hardly to be imagin'd: and it will be neither easie to give an instance of any such thing for the time past, or reasonable to Presume it will ever happen for the time to come: But if that strange thing should fall out, our *Trimmer* is not so streight-lac'd, as to let a Nation die or be stiffled, rather than it should be help'd by any but the proper Officers. The Cases themselves will bring the Remedies along with them; and he is not afraid to allow, That in order to its Preservation, there is a hidden Power in Government, which would be lost if it was designed, a certain Mystery, by Virtue of which a Nation may at some Critical times be secur'd from Ruine; but then it must be kept as a Mystery: it is rendred useless when touch'd by unskilful Hands: And no Government ever had, or deserv'd to have that Power, which was so unwary as to anticipate their Claim to it. Our *Trimmer* cannot help thinking it had been better, if the Triennial Act[3] had been observ'd, because 'tis the Law; and he would not have the Crown, by such an Example teach the Nation to break it: all irregularity is catching; it has a Contagion in it, especially in an Age, so much enclin'd to follow ill

Patterns than good ones.

He would have a Parliment, because 'tis an Essential part of the Constitution, even without the Law, it being the only Provision in extraordinary Cases, in which there would be otherwise no Remedy; and there can be no greater Solecism in Government, than a failure of Justice.

He would have had one, because nothing else can unite and heal us; all other Means are meer Shifts and Projects, Houses of Cards, to be blown down with the least Breath, and cannot resist the Difficulties which are ever presum'd in things of this kind; and he would have had one, because it might have done the King good, and could not possibly have done him hurt, without his consent, which in that Case is not to be supposed; and therefore for him to fear it, is so strange and so little to be comprehended, that the Reasons can never be presum'd to grow in our Soyl, or to thrive in it, when transplanted from any other Country; and no doubt there are such irresistible Arguments for calling a Parliament, and tho' it might be deny'd to the unmannerly mutinous Petitions of Men, that are malicious and disaffected, it will be granted to the soft and obsequious Murmurs of his Majesty's best Subjects; and there will be such Rhetorick in their silent Grief, that it will at last prevail against the Artifices of those, who either out of Guilt or Interest, are afraid to throw themselves upon their Country, knowing how scurvily they have used it; that day of Judgment will come, tho' we know neither the day nor the hour:[4] And our *Trimmer* would live so as to be prepared for it; with full Assurance in the mean time, that the lamenting Voice of a Nation cannot long be resisted, and that a Prince who could so easily forgive his People when they had been in the wrong, cannot fail to hear them when they are in the right.

The *Trimmer's* Opinion concerning the Protestant Religion.

Religion has such a Superiority above other things, and that indispensible Influence upon all Mankind, that it is as necessary to our Living Happy in this World, as it is to our being Sav'd in the next: without it man is an abandon'd Creature, one of the worst Beasts Nature hath produc'd, and fit only for the Society of Wolves and Bears; therefore in all Ages it has been the Foundation of Government: And tho' false Gods have been impos'd upon the Credulous part of the World, yet they were Gods still in their own Opinion; and the Awe and Reverence Men had to them and their Oracles, kept them within bounds towards one another, which the Laws with all their Authority could never have effected, without the help of Religion: the Laws would not be able to subdue the perverseness of Mens Wills, which are wild Beasts, and require a double Chain to keep them down. For this Reason 'tis said, That it is not a sufficient ground to make War upon a Neighbouring State, because they are of another Religion, let it be never so differing; yet if they Worship'd nor Acknowledg'd any Deity at all, they may be Invaded as publick Enemies of Mankind, because they reject the only thing that can bind them to live well with one another. The consideration of Religion is so twisted with that of Government, that it is never to be separated; and tho' the Foundations of it ought to be Eternal and Unchangeable, yet the Terms and Circumstances of Discipline, are to be suited to the several Climates and Constitutions, so that they may keep Men in a willing Acquiescence unto them, without discomposing the World by nice Disputes, which can never be of equal moment with the publick Peace.

Our Religion here in *England* seems to be distinguish'd by a peculiar Effect of God Almighty's Goodness, in permitting it to be introduc'd or rather restor'd, by a more regular Method, than the Circumstances of most other reformed Churches would allow them to do, in relation to the Government: and the Dignity with which it has supported it self since, and the great Men our Church has produced, ought to recommend it to the esteem of all Protestants at least: Our *Trimmer* is very partial to it, for these Reasons, and many more; and desires that it may preserve its due Jurisdiction and Authority; so far is he from wishing it oppressed, by the unreasonable and malicious Cavils of those who take pains to raise Objections against it.

The Questions will then be, how and by what Methods this Church shall best support itself (the present Circumstances consider'd) in relation to Dissenters of all sorts? I will first lay this for a ground, That as there can be no true Religion without Charity, so there can be no true humane Prudence without Bearing and Condescension. This Principle does not extend to oblige the Church always to yield to those who are disposed to Contest with her, the expediency of doing it is to be considered and determined according to the occasion; and this leads me to lay open the thoughts of our *Trimmer*, in reference first, to the Protestants, and then to the Popish Recusants.

What has lately hapned among us,[5] makes an Apology necessary for saying any thing, that looks like favour towards a sort of Men who have brought themselves under such a disadvantage. . . .

Our *Trimmer* therefore endeavours, to separate the detestation of those, who had either a hand or a thought in the late Plot, from the Principle of Prudential, as well as Christian Charity towards Mankind, and for that reason would fain use the means of reclaiming such of the Dissenters as are not incurable, and even bearing to a degree those that are as far as may consist with the Publick Interest and Security: he is far from justifying an affected Separation from the Communion of the Church; and even in those that mean well, and are mistaken, he looks upon it as a Disease that has seized upon their Minds, very troublesome as well as dangerous, by the Consequence it may produce. He does not go about to excuse their making it an indispensable Duty, to meet in numbers to say their Prayers, such Meetings may prove mischievous to the State at least; the Laws which are the best Judges, have determined that there is a danger in them: He has good nature enough to lament that the Perverseness of a Part, should have drawn Rigorous Laws upon the whole Body of the Dissenters; but when they are once made, no private Opinion must stand in Opposition to them: if they are in themselves reasonable, they are in that respect to be regarded, even without being enjoyned; and if by the Change of Time and Circumstances, they should become less reasonable than when they were first made, even then they are to be obeyed too, because they are Laws till they are mended or repealed by the same Authority that enacted them.

He has too much deference to the Constitution of our Government, to wish for more Pre[r]ogative Declarations[6] in favour of scrupulous Men, or to dispence with Penal Laws in such manner, or to such an end, that suspecting Men might with some reason pretend, that so hated a thing as Persecution could never make way for it self with any hopes of Success, otherwise than by preparing the deluded World by a false prospect of Liberty and Indulgence. The inward Springs and Wheels whereby the Engine moved, are now so fully laid open and expos'd, that it is not supposable that such a baffled Experiment should ever be tryed again; the effect it had at the time, and the Spirit it raised, will not easily be forgotten; and it may be presum'd the remembrance of it, may secure us from any more attempts of that Nature for the future: We must no more break a Law to give Men ease, than we are to riffle an House with a devout Intention of giving the Plunder to the Poor; in this case, our Compassion would be as ill directed, as our Charity in the other.

In short, the Veneration due to the Laws is never to be thrown off, let the Pretences be never so specious: Yet with all this he cannot bring himself to think, that an extraordinary diligence to take the uttermost penalty of Laws upon the poor offending Neighbour, is of it self such an all sufficient Vertue, that without any thing else to recommend Men, it should Entitle them to all kinds of Preferments and Rewards: he would not detract from the merits of those who execute the Laws, yet he cannot think such a piece of service as this, can entirely change the Man, and either make him a better Divine, or a more knowing Magistrate than he was before; especially if it be done with a partial and unequal hand in Reference to greater and more dangerous Offenders. . . .

Our *Trimmer* would have the Clergy supported in their Lawful Rights, and in all the Power and Dignity that belongs to them, and yet he thinks that possibly there may be in some of them a too great eagerness to extend the Ecclesiastical Jurisdiction; which tho' it may be well intended, yet the straining of it too high, has an appearance of Ambition that raises Men's Objections to it: and is far unlike the Apostolick Zeal, which was quite otherwise employ'd, that the World draws inferences from it, which do the Church no service. . . .

Our *Trimmer* approves the Principles of our Church, that Dominion is not founded in Grace, and that our Obedience is to be given to a Popish King in other things, at the same time that our Compliance with him in his Religion is to be deny'd; yet he cannot but think it a very extraordinary thing, if a Protestant Church should by a voluntary Election, chuse a Papist for their Guardian, and receive Directions for supporting their Religion, from one who must believe it a Mortal Sin not to endeavour to destroy it; such a refined piece of Breeding would not seem to be very well plac'd in the Clergy, who will hardly find Precedents to justifie such an extravagant piece of Courtship, and which is so unlike the Primitive Methods, which ought to be our Pattern; he hath no such unreasonable tenderness for any sorts of Men, as to expect their faults should not be impartially laid open as often as they give occasion for it; and yet he cannot but smile to see, that the same Man, who sets up all the Sails of his Rhetorick to fall upon Dissenters, when Popery is to be handled, he does it so gingerly, that he looks like an Ass mumbling of Thistles, so afraid he is of letting himself loose, where he may be in danger of letting his Duty get the better of his Discretion.[7]

Our *Trimmer* is far from relishing the impertinent wandrings of those, who pour out long Prayers upon the Congregation, and all from their own Stock, which God knows, for the most part is a barren Soil, which produces weeds instead of Flowers, and by this means they expose Religion it self, rather than promote Men's Devotions: On the other side, there may be too great Restraint put upon Men, whom God

and Nature hath distinguished from their Fellow Labourers, by blessing
them with a happier Talent, and by giving them not only good Sense,
but a powerful Utterance too; has enabled them to gush out upon the
attentive Auditory, with a mighty stream of devout and unaffected
Eloquence; when a Man so qualified, endued with Learning too, and
above all, adorned with a good Life, breaks out into a warm and well
deliver'd Prayer before his Sermon, it has the appearance of a Divine
Rapture, he raises and leads the Hearts of the Assembly in another
manner, than the most Compos'd or best Studied Form of set Words
can ever do, and the Pray-wees,[8] who serve up all their Sermons with
the same Garnishing, would look like so many Statues, or Men of Straw
in the Pulpit, compar'd with those who speak with such a powerful Zeal,
that men are tempted at the moment to believe Heaven it self has
dictated their words to 'em.

Our *Trimmer* is not so unreasonably indulgent to the Dissenters, as
to excuse the Irregularities of their Complaints, and to approve their
threatning Stiles, which are so ill-suited to their Circumstances as well
as their Duty; he would have them to shew their Grief, and not their
Anger to the Government, and by such a Submission to Authority, as
becomes them, if they cannot acquiesce in what is imposed: let them
deserve a Legislative Remedy to their Sufferings, there being no other
way to give them perfect Redress; and either to seek it, or pretend to
give it by any other Method, would not only be vain, but Criminal too
in those that go about it; yet with all this, there may in the mean time
be a prudential Latitude left, as to the manner of preventing the Laws
now in force against them: The Government is in some degree answer-
able for such an Administration of them, as may be free from the
Censure of Impartial Judges; and in order to that, it would be necessary
that one of these methods be pursued, either to let loose the Laws to
their utmost extent, without any Moderation or Restraint, in which at
least the Equality of the Government would be without Objection, the
Penalties being exacted, without Remission from the Dissenters of all
kinds; or if that will not be done (and indeed there is no Reason it
should) there is a necessity of some Connivance to the Protestant
Dissenters to execute that which in Humanity must be allowed to the
Papists, even without any leaning towards them, which must be supposed in those who are or shall be in the administration of Publick
Business; and it will follow, that, according to our Circumstances, the
distribution of such Connivance must be made in such a manner, that
the greatest part of it may fall on the Protestant side, or else the Objections will be so strong, and the Inferences so clear, that the Friends, as

well as the Enemies of the Crown, will be sure to take hold of them.

It will not be sufficient to say that the Papists may be conniv'd at, because they are good Subjects, and that the Protestant Dissenters must suffer because they are ill ones; these general Maxims will not convince discerning Men, neither will any late Instances make them forget what passed at other times in the World; both sides have had their Turns in being good and ill Subjects; and therefore 'tis easie to imagine what suspicions would arise in the present conjecture, if such a partial Argument as this should be impos'd upon us: the truth is, this Matter speaks so much of it self, that it is not only unnecessary, but it may be unmannerly to say any more of it.

Our *Trimmer* therefore could wish, that since, notwithstanding the Laws which deny Churches to say mass in, even not only the Exercise, but also the Ostentation of Popery is as well or better performed in the Chappels of so many Foreign Ministers, where the *English* openly resort in spight of Proclamations and Orders of Council, which are grown to be as harmless things to them, as the Popes Bulls, and Excommunications are to Hereticks who are out of his reach; I say, he could wish that by a seasonable as well as an equal piece of Justice, there might be so much consideration had of the Protestant Dissenters, as that there might be at some times, and at some places, a Veil thrown over an innocent and retired Conventicle, and that such an Indulgence might be practis'd with less prejudice to the Church, or diminution to the Laws, it might be done so as to look rather like a kind Omission to enquire more strictly, than an allowed Toleration of that which is against the Rule established.

Such a skilful hand as this, is very necessary in our Circumstances, and the Government by making no sort of Men entirely desperate, does not only secure it self from Villainous attempts, but lay such a Foundation for healing and uniting Laws, when ever a Parliament shall meet, that the Seeds of Differences and Animosities between the several contending sides may (Heaven consenting) be for ever destroyed.

Notes

GEORGE SAVILLE, MARQUIS OF HALIFAX (1633-95) became involved in public life during the 1660s. Charles II 'bought' his services in 1668 by ennobling him. He became a privy counsellor in 1672. He was a tolerationist, opposing the Test Act of 1673, but he also tried to legislate against future heirs to the throne marrying catholics. He was dismissed from office in 1676, but was reinstated in 1679 and began to exercise considerable influence, speaking impressively against the Exclusion Bill, though he disliked the Duke of York. He is represented in *Absalom and Achitophel* as '*Jotham* of piercing wit and pregnant thought' (*ll*.882-7). In 1681 he temporarily withdrew from public life, and exercised great influence for a while on his return to it. However, he was deeply opposed to the persecution of both catholics and whigs, and in particular to the executions of Stafford on the one hand and Russell and Sidney on the other (see Introduction, pp. 15 and 20 and p. 160, n. 16). He also opposed the extremism of the Six (see p. 161, n. 28), and tried to keep Monmouth from involvement with them. He seemed to be regaining his influence in 1685, when copies of *The Character of a Trimmer* began to circulate in private, but lost all influence on the death of Charles II. He published *A Letter to a Dissenter* anonymously in 1687, in which he warned dissenters against the blandishments of the court. He was not among those who supported the revolution from the beginning and at first he tried to negotiate on behalf of the King, but the task was a hopeless one and it was he who in the end formally requested William to assume the provisional government of the country and was instrumental in securing the offer of the throne to William and Mary. Thereafter he took little part in public life. *The Character of a Trimmer* was first published pseudonymously in 1688.

1. See Matthew 9:6; Mark 2:9.
2. See Genesis 2:23; Halifax here implies a 'marriage' between king and kingdom.
3. An Act of 1664 requiring that Parliament be summoned 'once in three years at the least'. It was ignored by Charles II in April 1684, three years after the dissolution of the Parliament of 1681. James II observed the Act.
4. See Matthew 24:36; Mark 13:32.
5. The Rye House Plot (see p. 160, n. 16).
6. See p. 86, n. 16.
7. A topic on which Bethel also had views (see p. 134).
8. A form of 'Let us pray': i.e. clergy who rely mechanically on liturgical formulae.

12 From: *Miscellanies . . . I. The Lady's New-Years-Gift: or, Advice to a Daughter*[1]

George Savile, Marquis of Halifax, 1688

That which challengeth the place in your Thoughts, is how to live with a *Husband*. And though that is so large a Word, that few *Rules* can be fix'd to it which are unchangeable, the *Methods* being as various as the several *Tempers* of *Men* to which they must be suited: yet I cannot omit some *General Observations*, which, with the help of your own may the better direct you in the part of your Life upon which your *Happiness* most dependeth.

It is one of the *Disadvantages* belonging to your *Sex*, that young Women are seldom permitted to make their own *Choice*; their Friends Care and Experience are thought safer Guides to them, than their own *Fancies*; and their *Modesty* often forbiddeth them to refuse when their Parents recommend, though their *inward Consent* may not entirely go along with it. In this case there remaineth nothing for them to do but to endeavour to make that easie which falleth to their *Lot*, and by a wise use of every thing they may dislike in a *Husband*, turn that by degrees to be very supportable, which, if neglected, might in time beget an *Aversion*.

You must first lay it down for a Foundation in general, That there is *Inequality* in the *Sexes*, and that for better Oeconomy of the World, the *Men*, who were to be the Law givers, had the larger share of *Reason* bestow'd upon them; by which means your Sex is the better prepar'd for the *Compliance* that is necessary for the better performance of those *Duties* which seem to be most properly assign'd to it. This looks a little uncourtly at the first appearance; but upon Examination it will be found, that *Nature* is so far from being unjust to you, that she is partial on our side. She hath made you such large *Amends* by other Advantages, for the seeming *Injustice* of the first Distribution, that the Right of Complaining is come over to our Sex. You have it in your power not only to free your selves, but to subdue your Masters, and without violence throw both their *Natural* and *Legal Authority* at your Feet. We are made of differing *Tempers*, that our *Defects* may the better be mutually supplied: Your *Sex* wanteth our *reason* for your *Conduct*, and our *Strength* for your *Protection: Ours* wanteth your *Gentleness* to

175

soften, and to entertain us. The first part of our Life is a good deal
subjected to you in the *Nursery*, where you Reign without Competition, and by that means have the advantage of giving the first *Impres-*
sions. Afterwards you have stronger Influences, which, well manag'd,
have more force in your behalf, than all our *Privileges* and *Jurisdictions*
can pretend to have against you. You have more strength in your
Looks, than we have in our *Laws*, and more power by your *Tears*, than
we have by our *Arguments*.

It is true, that the *Laws* of *Marriage* run in a harsher stile towards
your *Sex*, *Obey* is an ungenteel word, and less easie to be digested, by
making such an unkind distinction in the words of the Contract, and so
very unsuitable to the excess of *Good Manners*, which generally goes
before it. Besides the *universality* of the Rule seemeth to be a *Griev-*
ance, and it appeareth reasonable, that there might be an *Exemption*
for extraordinary Women, from ordinary Rules, to take away the just
Exception that Lieth against the false measure of *general Equality*.

It may be alledged by the *Counsel* retained by your Sex, that as
there is in all other Laws, an appeal from the *Letter* to the *Equity*, in
Cases that require it: It is as reasonable, that some *Court* of a larger
Jurisdiction might be erected, where some *Wives* might resort and
plead *specially*. And in such instances where Nature is so kind, as to
raise them above the *level* of their own *Sex*, they might have *Relief*,
and obtain a *Mitigation* in their own particular, of a *Sentence* which was
given generally against *Woman-kind*. The causes of *Separation*[2] are now
so very course, that few are *confident* enough to buy their *Liberty* at
the price of having their Modesty so expos'd. And for *disparity of*
Minds, which above all others things requireth a *Remedy*, the *Laws*
have made no *provision*; so little refin'd are numbers of Men, by whom
they are compil'd. This and a great deal more might be said to give a
colour to the Complaint.

But the Answer to it, in short is, That the *Institution* of *Marriage* is
too sacred to admit a *Liberty* of *objecting* to it; That the supposition of
yours being the weaker *Sex*, having without all doubt a good Foundation, maketh it reasonable to subject it to the *Masculine Dominion*; That
no *Rule* can be so *perfect*, as not to admit some *Exceptions*; But the
Law presumeth there would be so few found in this Case, who would
have a sufficient Right to such a Privilege, that it is safer some *Injustice*
should be *conniv'd* at in a very few Instances, than to break into an
Establishment, upon which the Order of Humane Society doth so much
depend.

You are therefore to make your best of what is *settled* by *Law* and

Custom, and not vainly imagine, that it will be *changed* for your sake. But that you may not be discouraged, as if you lay under the weight of an *incurable Grievance*, you are to know, that by a *wise* and *dexterous* Conduct, it will be in your power to *relieve* your self from any thing that looketh like a disadvantage in it. For your better direction, I will give a hint of the most ordinary *Causes* of *Dissatisfaction* between Man and Wife, that you may be able by such a *Warning* to live so upon your *Guard*, that when you shall be married, you may know how to *cure* your Husband's *Mistakes*, and to *prevent* your own.

First then, you are to consider, you live in a time which hath rendred some kind of Frailties so habitual, that they lay claim to large *Grains* of *Allowance*. The world in this is somewhat unequal, and our Sex seemeth to play the *Tyrant* in distinguishing *partially* for our selves, by making that in the utmost degree *Criminal* in the *Woman*, which in a *Man* passeth under a much *gentler Censure*. The Root and the excuse of this Injustice is the *Preservation* of Families from any *Mixture* which may bring a Blemish to them: And whilst the *Point* of *Honour* continues to be so plac'd it seems unavoidable to give your *Sex*, the greater share of the penalty. But if in this it lieth under any *Disadvantage*, you are more than recompens'd, by having the *Honour* of *Families* in your keeping. The Consideration so great a Trust must give you, maketh full amends; and this Power the World hath lodged in you, can hardly fail to restrain the Severity of an *ill* Husband, and to improve the Kindness and Esteem of a *good* one. This being so, remember, That next to the danger of *committing* the fault your self, the greatest is that of *seeing* it in your *Husband*. Do not seem to look or hear that way: If he is a Man of Sense, he will reclaim himself; the Folly of it, is of it self sufficient to cure him; if he is not so, he will be provok'd, but not reform'd. To expostulate in these Cases, looketh like declaring War, and preparing Reprisals; which to a *thinking Husband* would be a dangerous Reflection. Besides, it is so course a reason which will be assign'd for a Lady's too great warmth upon such an occasion, that Modesty no less than Prudence ought to restrain her; since such an undecent Complaint makes a Wife much more ridiculous, than the Injury that provoketh her to it. But it is yet worse and more unskilful, to *blaze* it in the World, expecting it should rise up in Arms to take her part: Whereas she will find, it can have no other Effect, than that she will be served up in all Companies, as the *reigning Jest* at that time; and will continue to be the common Entertainment, till she is rescu'd by some *newer Folly* that cometh upon the Stage, and driveth her away from it. The Impertinence of such Methods is so plain, that it doth not deserve the pains of being laid open. Be assur'd, that in these Cases your *Discretion* and *Silence* will be the most *prevailing Reproof*, An *affected Ignorance*, which is seldom a *Vertue*, is a great one here: And when your *Husband* seeth how unwilling you are to be uneasie, there is no stronger Argument to perswade him not to be unjust to you. Besides, it will naturally make him more *yielding* in other things: And whether it be to *cover* or redeem his *Offence*, you may have the good Effects of it whilst it lasteth, and all that while have the most reasonable Ground that can be, of presuming, such a behaviour will at last entirely convert him. There is nothing so glorious to a *Wife*, as a Victory so gain'd: A Man so reclaim'd, is for ever after subjected to her *Vertue*; and her *bearing* for a time, is more than rewarded by a Triumph that will continue as long as her life.

The next thing I will suppose, is that your *Husband* may love *Wine* more than is convenient. It will be granted, That though there are Vices of a deeper dye, there are none that have greater *Deformity* than this, when it is not restrain'd: But with all this, the same Custom which is the more to be lamented for its being so general, should make it less uneasie to every one in particular who is to suffer by the Effects of it: So that in the first place, it will be no new thing if you should have a *Drunkard* for your *Husband*; and there is by too frequent Examples evidence enough, that such a thing may happen, and yet a *Wife* may live too without being miserable. *Self love* dictateth aggravating words to every thing we feel; *Ruine* and *Misery* are the Terms we apply to whatever we do not like, forgetting the Mixture allotted to us by the Condition of Human Life, by which it is not intended we should be quite exempt from trouble. It is fair if we can escape such a degree of it as would oppress us, and enjoy so much of the pleasant part as may lessen the ill taste of such things as are unwelcome to us. Every thing hath two Sides, and for our own ease we ought to direct our Thoughts to that which may be least liable to exception. To fall upon the *worst side* of a *Drunkard*, giveth so unpleasant a prospect, that it is not possible to dwell upon it. Let us pass then to the more *favourable part*, as far as a *Wife* is concern'd in it.

I am tempted to say (if the Irregularity of the Expression could in strictness be justified) That a *Wife* is to thank God her *Husband* hath *Faults*. Mark the seeming Paradox my Dear, for your own Instruction, it being intended no further. A *Husband* without *Faults* is a dangerous observer; he hath an Eye so piercing, and seeth every thing so plain, that it is expos'd to his full Censure. And though I will not doubt but that your *Vertue* will disappoint the sharpest Enquiries; yet few Women can bear the having all they say or do *represented* in the clear Glass of an Understanding without *Faults*. Nothing softneth the *Arrogance* of our *Nature*, like a Mixture of some *Frailties*. It is by them we are best told, that we must not strike too hard upon others, because we our selves do so often deserve Blows: they pull our Rage by the Sleeve, and whisper Gentleness to us in our Censures, even when they are rightly applied. The *Faults* and *Passions* of *Husbands* bring them down to you, and make them content to live upon less unequal Terms, than Faultless Men would be willing to stoop to; so haughty is Mankind till humbled by common Weakness and Defects, which in our corrupted State contribute more towards the reconciling us one to another, than all the *Precepts* of the *Philosophers* and *Divines*. So that where the *Errors* of our *Nature* make amends for the *Disadvantages* of yours, it is more your part to make use of the *Benefit*, than to quarrel at the *Fault*.

Thus in case a *Drunken Husband* should fall to your share, if you will be *wise* and *patient*, his *Wine* shall be of your side; it will throw a *Veil* over your Mistakes, and will set out and improve every thing you do, that he is pleased with. Others will like him less, and by that means he may perhaps like you the more. When after having dined too well, he is receiv'd at home without a *Storm*, or so much as a *reproaching Look*, the *Wine* will naturally work out all in Kindness, which a *Wife* must encourage, let it be wrapped up in never so much Impertinence. On the other side it would boil up into *Rage*, if the mistaken *Wife* should treat him roughly, like a certain thing called a *kind Shrew*, than which the World, with all its Plenty, cannot shew a more senseless, ill-bred, forbidding Creature. Consider that where the Man will give such frequent Intermissions of the use of his *Reason*, the *Wife* insensibly getteth a Right of *Governing* in the Vacancy, and that raiseth her *Character* and *Credit* in the Family, to a higher pitch than perhaps could be done under a *sober Husband*, who never putteth himself into an Incapacity of holding the *Reins*. If these are not intire *Consolations*, at least they are *Remedies* to some Degree. They cannot make *Drunkenness* a *Vertue*, nor a *Husband* given to it a *Felicity*; but you will do your self no ill office in the endeavouring, by these means, to make the best of such a *Lot*, in case it should happen to be yours, and by the help of a wise Observation, to make that very supportable, which would otherwise be a *Load* that would oppress you.

The next Case I will put is that your *Husband* may be *Chollerick* or *Ill-humour'd*. To this it may be said, That *passionate* Men generally make amends at the Foot of the Account. Such a Man, if he is angry one day without any *Sense*, will the next day be as kind without any

Reason So that by marking how the *Wheels* of such a Man's Head are used to move, you may easily bring over all his *Passion* to your Party. Instead of being struck down by his Thunder, you shall direct it where and upon whom you shall think it best applied. Thus are the *strongest Poisons* turn'd to the *best Remedies*; but then there must be *Art* in it, and a *skilful Hand*, else the least *bungling* maketh it mortal. There is a great deal of nice Care requisite to deal with a Man of this Complexion. *Choler* proceedeth from *Pride*, and maketh a Man so partial to himself that he swelleth against Contradiction; and thinketh he is lessened if he is opposed. You must in this Case take heed of *increasing the Storm* by an *unwary Word*, or *kindling the Fire* whilst the Wind is in a Corner which may blow it in your Face: You are dextrously to yield every thing till he beginneth to cool, and then by slow degrees you may rise and gain upon him: Your *Gentleness* well timed, will, like a Charm, dispel his Anger ill placed; a *kind Smile* will *reclaim*, when a *shrill pettish Answer* would *provoke* him; rather than fail upon such occasions, when other *Remedies* are too weak, a little *Flattery* may be admitted, which by being necessary, will cease to be Criminal.

If *Ill-Humour and Sullenness*, and not open and sudden Heat is his Disease, there is a way of treating that too, so as to make it a Grievance to be endured. In order to it, you are first to know, that naturally *good Sense* hath a mixture of *surly* in it: and there being so much *Folly* in the World, and for the most part so triumphant, it giveth frequent Temptations to raise the *Spleen* of Men who think right. Therefore that which may generally be call'd *Ill-Humour*, is not always a Fault; it becometh one when either it is wrong applied, or that it is continued too long, when it is not so: For this Reason you must not too hastily fix an ill name upon that which may perhaps not deserve it; and though the Case should be, that your *Husband* might too sowerly resent any thing he disliketh, it may so happen, that more Blame shall belong to your *Mistake*, than to his *Ill-Humour*. If a *Husband* behaveth himself sometimes with an *Indifference* that a *Wife* may think offensive, she is in the wrong to put the worst sence upon it; if by any means it will admit a better. Some *Wives* will call it *Ill-Humour* if their Husbands change their *Style* from that which they used whilst they made their Addresses to them: Others will allow no *Intermission* or *Abatement* in the Expressions of Kindness to them, not enough distinguishing times, and forgetting that it is impossible for Men to keep themselves up all their Lives to the height of some *extravagant Moments*. A Man may at some times be less careful in little things, without any cold or dis-obliging Reason for it; as a *Wife* may be too expecting in smaller matters, without drawing upon her-self the inference of being *unkind*. And if your *Husband* should be really sullen, and have such frequent Fits, as might take away the excuse of it, it concerneth you to have an Eye prepared to discern the first Appearances of Cloudy Weather, and to watch when the Fit goeth off, which seldom lasteth long if it is let alone. But whilst the Mind is sore, every thing galleth it, and that maketh it necessary to let the *Black Humour* begin to spend it self, before you come in and venture to undertake it.

If in the Lottery of the World you should draw a *Covetous Husband*, I confess it will not make you proud of your good Luck; yet even such a one may be endured too, though there are few Passions more untractable than that of *Avarice*. You must first take care that your *Definition* of *Avarice* may not be a Mistake. You are to examine every Circumstance of your *Husbands* Fortune and weigh the Reason of every thing you expect from him before you have right to pronounce that sentence. The Complaint is now so general against all *Husbands*, that it giveth great suspicion of its being often ill-grounded; it is impossible they should all deserve that Censure, and therefore it is certain, that it is many times misapplied. He that *spareth* in every thing is an *inexcusable Niggard*; he that *spareth* in nothing is as *inexecusable a Madman*. The *mean* is, to spare in what is least necessary, to lay out more liberally in what is most required in our several circumstances. Yet this will not always satisfie. There are *Wives* who are impatient of the Rules of Oeconomy, and are apt to call their *Husband*'s Kindness in question, if any other measure is put to their expence than that of their own Fancy. Be sure to avoid this dangerous Error, such a partiality to your Self, which is so offensive to an understanding Man, that he will very ill bear a *Wife*'s giving her self such an injurious preference to all the *Family*, and whatever belongeth to it.

But to admit the worst, and that your *Husband* is really a *Close-handed Wretch*, you must in this, as in other Cases, endeavour to make it less afflicting to you; and first you must observe *seasonable Hours* of speaking. When you offer any thing in opposition to this reigning Humour, a *third hand* and a *wise Friend*, may often prevail more than you will be allowed to do in your own Cause. Sometimes you are dexterously to go along with him in things, where you see that the niggardly part of his Mind is most predominant, by which you will have the better opportunity of persuading him in things where he may be more indifferent. Our *Passions* are very unequal, and are apt to be raised or lessened according as they work upon different Objects; they are not to be *stopped* or *restrained* in those things where our Mind is more particularly engaged. In other matters they are more tractable, and will sometimes give Reason a hearing, and admit a fair dispute. More than that, there are few Men, even in this instance of *Avarice*, so entirely abandoned to it, that at some hours, and upon some occasions, will not forget their natures, and for that time turn Prodigal. The same Man who will *grudge* himself what is *necessary*, let his *Pride* be raised and he shall be *profuse*; at another time his *Anger* shall have the same effect; a fit of *Vanity, Ambition*, and sometimes of *Kindness*, shall open and inlarge his *narrow Mind*; a Dose of Wine will work upon this tough humour, and for the time dissolve it. Your business must be, if this Case happeneth, to watch these *critical Moments*, and not let one of them slip without making your advantage of it; and a *Wife* may be said to want *skill* if by this means she is not able to secure her self in a good measure against the Inconveniences this scurvy quality in a *Husband* might bring upon her, except he should be such an incurable *Monster*, as I hope will never fall to your share.

The last supposition I will make, is That your *Husband* should be *weak* and *incompetent* to make use of the Privileges that belong to him. It will be yeilded, that such a one leaveth room for a great many Objections. But God Almighty seldom sendeth a *Grievance* without a *Remedy*, or at least such a Mitigation as taketh away a great part of the sting, and the smart of it. To make such a *Misfortune* less heavy, you are first to bring to your Observation, That a *Wife* very often maketh better Figure, for her *Husband*'s making no great one: And there seemeth to be little reason, why the same *Lady* that chuseth a *Waiting-Woman* with *worse Looks*, may not be content with a *Husband* with *less Wit*; the Argument being equal from the advantage of the Comparison. If you will be more ashamed in some Cases, of such a *Husband*, you will be less afraid than you would perhaps be of a wise one. His *Unseasonable Weakness* may no doubt sometimes grieve you, but then set against this, that it giveth you the *Dominion*, if you will make the right use of it. It is next to his being dead, in which Case the *Wife* hath right to Administer;[3] therefore be sure, if you have an Idiot, that none, except your self, may have the benefit of the forfeiture; Such a Fool is a dangerous Beast, if others have the keeping of him; and you must be very undexterous if when your *Husband* shall resolve to be an *Ass*, you do not take care he may be *your Ass*. But you must go skilfully about it; and above all things, take heed of distinguishing in publick, what kind of *Husband* he is: Your inward thoughts must not hinder the outward payment of the consideration that is due to him: Your *slighting* him in *Company*, besides that it would, to a discerning By-stander, give too great encouragement for the making nearer applications to you, is in itself such an undecent way of assuming, that it may provoke the tame Creature to break loose, and to shew his *Dominion* for his Credit, which he was content to forget for his Ease. In short, the surest and the most approved method will be to do like a wise *Minister* to an easie *Prince*; first give him the Orders you afterwards receive from him.

With all this, that which you are to pray for, is a *Wise Husband*, one that by knowing how to be a *Master*, for that very reason will not let you feel the weight of it; one whose Authority is so soften'd by his Kindness, that it giveth you ease without abridging your *Liberty*; one that will return so much tenderness for your *Just Esteem* of him, that you will never want *power*, though you will seldom care to use it. Such a *Husband* is as much above all the other Kinds of them, as a *rational subjection* to a Prince, great in himself, is to be preferr'd before the disquiet and uneasiness of *Unlimited Liberty*.

Before I leave this Head, I must add a little concerning your *Behaviour* to your *Husband's Friends*,[4] which requireth the most refined part of your Understanding to acquit yourself well of it. You are to study how to live with them with more care than you are to apply to any other part of your Life; especially at first, that you may not stumble at the first setting out. The *Family* into which you are grafted will generally be apt to expect, that like a Stranger in a Foreign Country, you should conform to their Methods, and not bring in a new Model by your own Authority. The *Friends* in such a Case are tempted to rise up in Arms as against an unlawful Invasion, so that you are with the utmost Caution to avoid the least appearances of anything of this Kind. And that you may with less difficulty afterwards give your Directions, be sure at first to receive them from your *Husband's* Friends. Gain them to you by early applying to them, and they will be so satisfied, that as nothing is more thankful than Pride, when it is complied with, they will strive which of them shall most recommend you; and when they have helped you to take Root in your *Husband's* good Opinion, you will have less dependence upon theirs, though you must not neglect any reasonable means of preserving it. You are to consider, that a Man govern'd by his *Friends*, is very easily inflamed by them; and that one who is not so, will yet for his own sake expect to have them consider'd. It is easily improved to a point of Honour in a *Husband*, not to have his *Relations* neglected; and nothing is more dangerous, than to raise an Objection, which is grounded upon *Pride*: It is the most stubborn and lasting Passion we are subject to, and where it is the first cause of the *War*, it is very hard to make a secure *Peace*. Your *Caution* in this is of the last importance to you.

And that you may the better succeed in it, carry a strict Eye upon the *Impertinence* of your *Servants*; take heed that their *Ill-humour* may not engage you to take Exceptions, or their too much assuming in small matters, raise Consequences which may bring you under great Disadvantage. Remember that in the case of a *Royal Bride*, those about her are generally so far suspected to bring in a Foreign Interest, that in most Countries they are insensibly reduced to a very small number, and those of so low a Figure, that it does not admit the being *Jealous* of them. In little and in the Proportion, this may be the Case of every *New married Woman*, and therefore it may be more adviseable for you, to gain the *Servants* you find in a Family, than to tie yourself too fast to those you carry into it.

You are not to overlook these small Reflections, because they may appear low and inconsiderable; for it may be said, that as the *greater streams* are made up of the *small drops* at the head of the Springs from whence they are derived, so the *greater circumstances* of your Life, will be in some degree directed by these seeming *trifles*, which having the advantage of being the first acts of it, have a greater effect than singly in their own nature they could pretend to.

I will conclude this Article with my Advice, That you would as much as Nature will give you leave, endeavour to forget the great *Indulgence* you have found at home. After such a gentle Discipline as you have been under, every thing you dislike will seem the harsher to you. The tenderness we have had for you, *My Dear*, is of another nature peculiar to kind Parents, and differing from that which you will meet with first in any Family into which you shall be transplanted; and yet they may be very kind too, and afford no justifiable reason to you to complain. You must not be frighted with the first Appearances of a *differing Scene*; for when you are used to it, you may like the House you go to, better than that you left; and your *Husbands* Kindness will have so much advantage of ours, that we shall yeild up all *Competition*, and as well as we love you, be very well contented to Surrender to such a *Rival*.

Notes

1. Elizabeth, the only child of Halifax's second marriage. She married Philip Stanhope, later third Earl of Chesterfield, in 1692, at the age of 20. Her son, the fourth Earl, wrote the celebrated *Letters to his Son*.
2. Suits for divorce, a singularly humilating and expensive business at this

time; see Mrs Marwood's speech to Lady Wishfort on this theme in *The Way of the World* (1700) by William Congreve.

3. I.e. control her own property; married women had no legal existence and could not sue or be sued in their own name; widows, however, were legally persons. (See, for example, *The Plain Dealer* (1674) by William Wycherley.)

4. His relations and members of his household.

13 From: *An Essay Concerning the True Original Extent, and End of Civil Government*

John Locke, 1713

II. Of the State of Nature.

4. To understand political Power, right, and derive it from its Original, we must consider, what State all Men are naturally in, and that is, a *State of perfect Freedom* to order their Actions, and dispose of their Possessions, and Persons as they think fit, within the bounds of the Law of Nature, without asking leave, or depending upon the Will of any other Man.

A *State* also *of Equality*, wherein all the Power and Jurisdiction is Reciprocal, no one having more than another; there being nothing more evident, than that Creatures of the same species and rank, promiscuously born to all the same advantages of Nature, and the use of the same Faculties, should also be equal one amongst another without Subordination or Subjection. . . .

6. But though this be *a State of Liberty*, yet *it is not a State of Licence*; though Man in that State have an uncontrolable Liberty, to dispose of his Person or Possessions, yet he has not Liberty to destroy himself, or so much as any Creature in his Possession, but where some nobler Use, than its bare Preservation calls for it. The *State of Nature* has a Law of Nature to govern it, which obliges every one: And Reason, which is that Law, teaches all Mankind, who will but consult it, that being all *equal and independent*, no one ought to harm another in his Life, Health, Liberty, or Possessions. For Men being all the Workmanship of one Omnipotent, and infinitely wise Maker: All the Servants of one Sovereign Master, sent into the World by his Order, and about his Business, they are his Property, whose Workmanship they are, made to last during his, not one anothers Pleasure: And being furnished with like Faculties, sharing all in one Community of Nature, there cannot be supposed any such *Subordination* among us, that may authorize us to destroy one another, as if we were made for one another's Uses, as the inferior ranks of Creatures are for ours. Every one as he is *bound*

to preserve himself, and not to quit his Station wilfully, so by the like reason, when his own Preservation comes not in Competition, ought he, as much as he can, *to preserve the rest of Mankind*, and may not unless it be to do Justice on an Offender, take away, or impair the Life, or what tends to the Preservation of the Life, the Liberty, Health, Limb, or Goods of another.

7. And that all Men may be restrained from invading others Rights, and from doing hurt to one another, and the Law of Nature be observed, which willeth the Peace and *Preservation of all Mankind*, the *Execution* of the Law of Nature is in that State, put into every Man's Hands, whereby every one has a Right to punish the Trangressors of that Law to such a Degree, as may hinder its Violation. For the *Law of Nature* would, as all other Laws, that concern Men in this World, be in vain, if there were no Body that in the State of Nature, had a *Power to execute* that Law, and thereby preserve the Innocent and restrain Offenders. And if any one in the State of Nature may punish another, for any evil he has done, every one may do so. For in that *State of perfect Equality*, where naturally there is no Superiority or Jurisdiction of one, over another, what any may do in Prosecution of that Law, every one must needs have a Right to do . . . .

. . . And thus it is, that every Man in the State of Nature, has a Power to kill a Murderer, both *to deter* others from doing the like Injury, which no Reparation can compensate, by the Example of the Punishment that attends it from every body, and also to secure Men from the attempts of a Criminal, who having renounced Reason, the common Rule and Measure, God hath given to Mankind, hath by the unjust Violence and Slaughter he hath committed upon one, declared War against all Mankind, and therefore may be destroyed as a *Lyon* or a *Tyger*, one of those wild savage Beasts, with whom Men can have no Society nor Security: . . .

12. By the same reason, may a Man in the State of Nature *punish the lesser Breaches* of that Law. It will perhaps be demanded with Death? I answer, each Transgression may be *punished* to that *Degree*, and with so much *Severity*, as will suffice to make it an ill Bargain to the Offender, give him Cause to repent, and terrifie others from doing the like. Every Offence that can be committed in the State of Nature, may in the State of Nature be also punished equally, and as far forth as it may, in a Commonwealth. For though it would be besides my present Purpose, to enter here into the particulars of the Law of Nature, or its *measures of Punishment*; yet, it is certain there is such a Law, and that

too, as intelligible and plain to a rational Creature, and a Studier of that Law, as the positive Laws of Commonwealths; nay possibly plainer . . . .

III. Of the State of War

16. The *State of War* is a state of *Enmity* and *Destruction*: And therefore declaring by Word or Action, not a passionate and hasty, but a sedate settled Design, upon another Man's Life, *puts him in a State of War* with him against whom he has declared such an Intention, and so has exposed his Life to the others Power to be taken away by him, or any one that joyns with him in his Defence, and espouses his Quarrel; it being reasonable and just I should have a Right to destroy that, which threatens me with Destruction. For *by the fundamental Law of Nature, Men being to be preserved*, as much as possible, when all cannot be preserved, the safety of the Innocent is to be preferred: And one may destroy a Man who makes War upon him, or has discovered an Enmity to his being, for the same Reason, that he may kill a *Woolf* or a *Lion*; because such Men are not under the ties of the Common-Law of Reason, have no other Rule, but that of Force and Violence, and so may be treated as Beasts of Prey, those dangerous and noxious Creatures, that will be sure to destroy him, whenever he falls into their Power. . . . ,

18. This makes it lawful for a Man to *kill a Thief*, who has not in the least hurt him, nor declared any Design upon his Life, any farther, than by the use of Force, so to get him in his Power, as to take away his Money, or what he pleases from him; because using Force, where he has no Right, to get me into his Power, let his Pretence be what it will, I have no reason to suppose, that he, who would *take away my Liberty* would not, when he had me in his Power, take away every thing else. And therefore it is lawful for me to treat him, as one who has *put himself into a state of War* with me, *i.e.* kill him if I can; for to that Hazard does he justly expose himself, whoever introduces a State of War, and is aggressor in it.

19. And here we have the plain *Difference between the state of Nature, and the state of War*, which however some Men have confounded, are as far distant, as a state of Peace, good Will, mutual Assurance and Preservation; and a state of Enmity, Malice, Violence and mutual Destruction are one from another. Men living together according to Reason, without a common superior on Earth, with Authority to judge between them, is *properly the state of Nature*. But force, or a declared design of Force upon the Person of another,

where there is no common Superior on Earth to appeal to for Relief, *is the state of War*: And 'tis the want of such an Appeal gives a Man the right of War even against an *Aggressor*, though he be in Society and a fellow Subject. Thus a *Thief*, whom I cannot harm, but by Appeal to the Law, for having stolen all that I am worth, I may kill, when he sets on me to rob me but of my Horse or Coat; because the Law, which was made for my preservation where it cannot interpose to secure my Life from present Force, which if lost, is capable of no Reparation, permits me my own Defence, and the right of War, a Liberty to kill the Aggressor, because the Aggressor allows not time to appeal to our common Judge, nor the decision of the Law, for Remedy in a Case, where the Mischief may be irreparable. *Want of a common Judge with Authority, puts all Men in a state of Nature: Force without Right, upon a Man's Person, makes a state of War*, both where there is, and is not, a common Judge. . . .

V. Of Property.

25. Whether we consider natural *Reason*, which tells us, that Men, being once born, have a right to their Preservation, and consequently to Meat and Drink, and such other things, as Nature affords for their Subsistence; or *Revelation*, which gives us an account of those Grants God made of the World to *Adam*, and to *Noah*, and his Sons, 'tis very clear, that God, as *K. David* says, *Psal.* CXV. xvj. *has given the Earth to the Children of Men*; given it to Mankind in common. But this being supposed, it seems to some a very great Difficulty, how any one should ever come to have a *Property* in any thing: . . .

27. Though the Earth, and all inferior Creatures be common to all Men, yet every Man has a *Property* in his own *Person*: This no Body has any right to but himself. The *Labour* of his Body, and the *Work* of his Hands, we may say, are properly his. Whatsoever then he removes out of the State that Nature hath provided, and left it in, he hath mixed his *Labour* with, and joyned to it something that is his own, and thereby makes it his *Property*. It being by him removed from the common State Nature hath placed it in, it hath by this *Labour* something annexed to it, that excludes the common Right of other Men. For this *Labour* being the unquestionable Property of the Labourer, no Man but he can have a Right to what that is once joyned to, at least where there is enough, and as good left in common for others. . . .

31. It will perhaps be objected to this, That if gathering the Acorns, or other Fruits of the Earth, *&c.* makes a Right to them, then any one may *ingross* as much as he will. To which I answer, Not so. The same Law of Nature, that does by this means give us Property, does also *bound* that *Property* too. *God has given us all things richly*, I Tim. vi. 12. is the Voice of Reason confirmed by Inspiration. But how far has he given it us? *To enjoy.* As much as any one can make use of to any Advantage of Life before it spoils; so much he may by his Labour fix a Property in: Whatever is beyond this, is more than his Share, and belongs to others. Nothing was made by God for Man to spoil or destroy. And thus considering the Plenty of natural Provisions there was a long time in the World, and the few Spenders; and to how small a Part of that Provision the Industry of one Man could extend itself, and ingross it to the Prejudice of others; especially keeping within the *Bounds*, set by Reason, *of* what might serve for his *Use*; there could be then little room for Quarrels or Contentions about Property so establish'd.

32. But the *chief Matter of Property* being now not the Fruits of the Earth, and the Beasts that subsist on it, but *the Earth it self*, as that which takes in and carries with it all the rest: I think it is plain, that *Property* in that too is acquir'd as the former. *As much Land* as a Man Tills, Plants, Improves, Cultivates, and can use the Product of, so much is his *Property*. . . .

40. Nor is it so strange, as perhaps before consideration it may appear, that the *Property of Labour* should be able to over-balance the Community of Land. For 'tis *labour* indeed that *puts the difference of value* on every thing; and let any one consider what the difference is between an Acre of Land planted with Tabacco or Sugar, sown with Wheat or Barley; and an Acre of the same Land lying in common, without any Husbandry upon it, and he will find, that the improvement of *labour makes* the far greater part of the Value. I think it will be but a very modest Computation to say, that of the *Products* of the Earth useful to the Life of Man $\frac{9}{10}$ are the *effects of labour*: Nay, if we will rightly estimate things as they come to our Use, and cast up the several expences about them, what in them is purely owing to *Nature*, and what to *Labour*, we shall find, that in most of them $\frac{99}{100}$ are wholly to be put on the account of *Labour*.

41. There cannot be a clearer demonstration of any thing, than several Nations of the *Americans* are of this, who are rich in Land, and poor in all the Comforts of Life; whom Nature having furnished as liberally as any other People, with the materials of Plenty, *i.e.* a fruitful Soil, apt to produce in abundance, what might serve for Food, Ray-

ment, and Delight; yet for *want of improving it by Labour*, have not one hundredth part of the Conveniences we enjoy: And a King of a large and fruitful Territory there Feeds, Lodges, and is clad worse than a day Labourer in *England*. . . .

46. The greatest part of *things really useful* to the life of Man, and such as the necessity of subsisting made the first Commoners of the World look after, as it doth the *Americans* now, *are* generally things of *short Duration*; such as, if they are not consumed by use, will decay and perish of themselves: Gold, Silver and Diamonds, are things, that Fancy or Agreement hath put the Value on, more than real Use, and the necessary support of Life. Now of those good things which Nature hath provided in common, every one had a Right [as hath been said] to as much as he could use, and *Property* in all he could affect with his Labour; all that his *Industry* could extend to, to alter from the state Nature had put it in, was his. He that *gathered* a hundred Bushels of Acorns or Apples, had thereby a *Property* in them, they were his Goods as soon as gathered. He was only to look, that he used them before they spoiled, else he took more than his share, and robb'd others. And indeed it was a foolish thing, as well as dishonest, to hoard up more, than he could make use of. If he gave away a part to any body else, so that it perished not uselesly in his Possession, these he also made use of. And if he also bartred away Plumbs, that would have rotted in a Week, for Nuts that would last good for his eating a whole Year he did no injury; he wasted not the common Stock; destroyed no part of the portion of Goods that belonged to others, so long as nothing perished uselesly in his hands. Again, If he would give his Nuts for a piece of Metal, pleased with its Colour; or exchange his Sheep for Shells, or Wooll for a sparkling Peble or a Diamond, and keep these by him all his Life, he invaded not the Right of others, he might heap up as much of these durable things as he pleased; the *exceeding of the bounds of* his *just Property* not lying in the largeness of his Possession, but the perishing of any thing uselesly in it.

47. And thus *came in the use of Money*, some lasting thing that Men might keep without spoiling, and that by mutual Consent Men would take in exchange for the truly useful, but perishable supports of Life. . . .

49. Thus in the Beginning all the World was *America*, and more so than that is now; for no such thing as *Money* was any where known. Find out something that hath the *Use and Value of Money* amongst his Neighbours, you shall see the same Man will begin presently to *enlarge* his Possessions.

50. But since Gold and Silver, being little useful to the Life of Man in proportion to Food, Rayment, and Carriage, has its *Value* only from the consent of Men, whereof *Labour* yet *makes*, in great part, *the Measure*, it is plain, that Men have agreed to a disproportionate and unequal *Possession of the Earth*, they having by a tacit and voluntary Consent, found out a Way how a Man may fairly possess more Land, than he himself can use the Product of, by receiving in Exchange for the overplus Gold and Silver, which may be hoarded up without Injury to any one; these Metals not spoiling or decaying in the hands of the Possessor. This Partage of things in an inequality of private Possessions, Men have made practicable out of the bounds of Society, and without Compact only by putting a Value on Gold and Silver, and tacitly agreeing in the use of Money. For in Governments, the Laws regulate the right of Property, and the possession of Land is determined by positive Constitutions.

51. And thus, I think, it is very easie to conceive without any Difficulty, *how Labour could at first begin a title of Property* in the common things of Nature, and how the spending it upon our uses bounded it. So that there could then be no reason of quarreling about Title, nor any doubt about the largeness of Possession it gave. Right and Conveniency went together; for as a Man had a Right to all he could imploy his Labour upon, so he had no Temptation to labour for more than he could make use of. This left no room for Controversie about the Title, nor for Incroachment on the right of others; what Portion a Man carved to himself, was easily seen; and it was useless as well as dishonest to carve himself too much, or take more than he needed.

VI. Of Paternal Power.

52. It may perhaps be censured as an impertinent Criticism in a discourse of this Nature to find fault with Words and Names that have obtained in the World: And yet possibly it may not be amiss to offer new ones, when the old are apt to lead Men into Mistakes as this of *paternal Power* probably has done, which seems so to place the power of Parents over their Children wholly in the *Father*, as if the *Mother* had no share in it, whereas, if we consult Reason or Revelation, we shall find, she hath an equal Title. This may give one reason to ask, whether this might not be more properly called *parental Power*. For whatever obligation Nature and the right of Generation lays on Children, it must certainly bind them equal to both the concurrent Causes of it. And accordingly we

see the positive Law of God every where joyns them together, without Distinction when it commands the Obedience of Children, *Honour thy Father and thy Mother*, Exod. 20. 12. *Whosoever curseth his Father or his Mother*, Lev. 20. 9. *Ye shall fear every Man his Mother and his Father*, Lev. 19. 3. *Children obey your Parents*, &c. Eph. 6. 1. is the stile of the Old and New Testament.

53. Had but this one thing been well consider'd, without looking any deeper into the Matter, it might perhaps have kept Men from running into those gross Mistakes, they have made, about this power of Parents; which however it might, without any great Harshness, bear the name of absolute Dominion, and regal Authority, when under the Title of *paternal Power* it seem'd appropriated to the Father, would yet have sounded but odly, and in the very Name shewn the Absurdity, if this supposed absolute Power over Children had been called *Parental*; and thereby have discover'd, that it belong'd to the *Mother* too; for it will but very ill serve the turn of those Men, who contend so much for the absolute power and authority of the *Fatherhood*, as they call it, that the Mother should have any Share in it. And it would have but ill supported the *Monarchy* they contend for, when by the very Name it appeared, that that fundamental Authority, from whence they would derive their Government of a single Person only, was not plac'd in one, but two Persons joyntly. But to let this of Names pass....

58. The *Power . . . that Parents have* over their Children, arises from that Duty which is incumbent on them, to take care of their Off-spring, during the imperfect state of Childhood. To inform the Mind, and govern the Actions of their yet ignorant Nonage, till Reason shall take its Place, and ease them of that Trouble, is what the Children want, and the Parents are bound to. For God having given Man an Understanding to direct his Actions, has allowed him a freedom of Will, and liberty of Acting, as properly belonging thereunto, within the bounds of that Law he is under. But whilst he is in an Estate, wherein he has not *Understanding* of his own to direct his *Will*, he is not to have any *Will* of his own to follow: He that *understands* for him, must *will* for him too; he must prescribe to his Will, and regulate his Actions....

64. But what reason can hence advance this care of the *Parents* due to their Offspring into an *absolute Arbitrary Dominion* of the Father, whose Power reaches no farther, than by such a Discipline, as he finds most effectual, to give such Strength and Health to their Bodies, such vigour and rectitude to their Minds, as may best fit his Children to be

most useful to themselves and others; and, if it be necessary to his Condition, to make them Work, when they are able, for their own Subsistence. But in this Power the *Mother* too has her share with the *Father*.

65. Nay this *Power* so little belongs to the *Father* by any peculiar right of Nature, but only as he is Guardian of his Children, that when he quits his care of them, he loses his Power over them, which goes along with their Nourishment and Education, to which it is inseparably annexed; and it belongs as much to the *Foster-Father* of an exposed Child, as to the Natural Father of another. So little Power does the bare *act of begetting* give a Man over his Issue, if all his Care ends there, and this be all the Title he hath to the Name and Authority of a Father. And what will become of this *Paternal Power* in that part of the World, where one Woman hath more than one Husband at a Time? Or in those parts of *America*, where, when the Husband and Wife part, which happens frequently, the Children are all left to the Mother, follow her, and are wholly under her Care and Provision? If the Father die whilst the Children are young, do they not naturally every where owe the same Obedience to their *Mother*, during their Minority, as to their Father were he alive? And will any one say, that the Mother hath a Legislative Power over her Children? that she can make standing Rules, which shall be of perpetual Obligation, by which they ought to regulate all the concerns of their Property, and bound their Liberty all the course of their Lives? Or can she inforce the Observation of them with Capital Punishments? For this is the proper *Power of the Magistrate*, of which the Father hath not so much as the shadow. His Command over his Children is but Temporary, and reaches not their Life or Property: It is but a help to the weakness and imperfection of their Nonage, a Discipline necessary to their Education: And though a *Father* may dispose of his own Possessions as he pleases, when his Children are out of danger of perishing for Want, yet *his Power* extends not to the Lives or Goods, which either their own Industry, or anothers bounty has made theirs; nor to their Liberty neither, when they are once arrived to the infranchisement of the Years of Discretion. The *Father's Empire* then ceases, and he can from thence forwards no more dispose of the liberty of his Son, than that of any other Man: . . .

72. Though the Obligation on the Parents to *bring up* their Children, and the Obligation on Children to *honour* their Parents, contain all the Power on the one Hand, and Submission on the other, which are proper to this Relation, yet there is *another Power* ordinarily *in the Father*, whereby he has a tie on the Obedience of his Children; which though

it be common to him with other Men, yet the Occasions of shewing it, almost constantly happening to Fathers in their private Families, and the Instances of it elsewhere being rare, and less taken notice of, it passes in the World for a part of *Paternal Jurisdiction.* And this is the Power Men generally have to *bestow their Estates* on those who please them best. The Possession of the Father being the Expectation and Inheritance of the Children, ordinarily in certain Proportions, according to the Law and Custom of each Country; yet it is commonly in the Father's Power to bestow it with a more sparing or liberal Hand, according as the Behaviour of this or that Child hath comported with his Will and Humour.

73. This is no small Tie on the Obedience of Children: And there being always annexed to the Enjoyment of Land, a Submission to the Government of the Country, of which that land is a part; it has been commonly suppos'd, That a *Father* could *oblige his Posterity to that Government,* of which he himself was a Subject, and that his Compact held them; whereas, it being only a necessary Condition annexed to the Land, and the Inheritance of an Estate which is under that Government, reaches only those who will take it on that Condition, and so is no natural Tie or Engagement, but a voluntary Submission. For *every Man's Children* being by Nature as *free* as himself, or any of his Ancestors ever were, may, whilst they are in that Freedom choose what Society they will join themselves to, what Common-wealth they will put themselves under. But if they will enjoy the *Inheritance* of their Ancestors, they must take it on the same Terms their Ancestors had it and submit to all the Conditions annex'd to such a Possession. . . .

VII. Of Political or Civil Society.

77. God having made Man such a Creature, that, in his own Judgment, it was not good for him to be alone, put him under strong Obligations of Necessity, Convenience, and Inclination to drive him into *Society*, as well as fitted him with Understanding and Language to continue and enjoy it. The *first Society* was between Man and Wife, which gave beginning to that between Parents and Children; to which, in time, that between Master and Servant came to be added: And though all these might, and commonly did meet together, and make up but one Family, wherein the Master or Mistress of it had some sort of Rule proper to a Family; each of these, or all together, came short of *political Society*, as we shall see, if we consider the different Ends, Ties, and Bounds of each of these.

78. *Conjugal Society* is made by a voluntary Compact between Man and Woman; and tho' it consist chiefly in such a Communion and Right in one anothers Bodies as is necessary to its chief End, Procreation; yet it draws with it mutual Support and Assistance, and a Communion of Interests too, as necessary not only to unite their Care and Affection, but also necessary to their common Off-spring, who have a Right to be nourished, and maintained by them, till they are able to provide for themselves. . . .

82. But the Husband and Wife, though they have but one common Concern, yet having different Understandings, will unavoidably some-times have different Wills too; it therefore being necessary that the last Determination, *i.e.* the Rule, should be placed somewhere; it naturally falls to the Man's Share, as the abler and the stronger. But this reaching but to the things of their common Interest and Property, leaves the Wife in the full and free Possession of what by Contract is her peculiar Right, and gives the Husband no more Power over her Life than she has over his. The *Power of the Husband* being so far from that of an absolute Monarch, that the *Wife* has in many Cases a Liberty to separate from him; where natural Right or their Contract allows it, whether that Contract be made by themselves in the State of Nature, or by the Customs or Laws of the Country they live in; and the Children upon such Separation fall to the Father or Mother's lot, as such Contract does determine. . . .

85. *Master* and *Servant* are Names as old as History, but given to those of far different Condition; for a Freeman makes himself a Servant to another, by selling him for a certain time, the Service he undertakes to do, in exchange for Wages he is to receive: And though this com-monly puts him into the Family of his Master, and under the ordinary Discipline thereof; yet it gives the Master but a temporary Power over him, and no greater, than what is contained in the *Contract* between 'em. But there is another sort of Servants, which by a peculiar Name we call *Slaves*, who being Captives taken in a just War, are by the Right of Nature subjected to the absolute Dominion and arbitrary Power of their Masters. These Men having, as I say, forfeited their Lives, and with it their Liberties, and lost their Estates; and being in the *State of Slavery*, not capable of any Property, cannot in that State be considered as any part of *Civil Society*; the chief End whereof is the Preservation of Property. . . .

VIII. Of the Beginning of Political Societies.

95. Men being, as has been said, by Nature, all free, equal, and independent, no one can be put out of this Estate, and subjected to the political Power of another, without his own Consent. The only Way whereby any one devests himself of his natural Liberty, and puts on the *Bonds of civil Society* is by agreeing with other Men to joyn and unite into a Community, for their comfortable, safe, and peaceable Living one amongst another, in a secure Enjoyment of their Properties, and a greater Security against any, that are not of it. This any number of Men may do, because it injures not the Freedom of the rest; they are left as they were in the Liberty of the state of Nature. When any number of Men have so *consented to make one Community or Government*, they are thereby presently incorporated, and make *one Body politick*, wherein the *Majority* have a Right to act and conclude the rest. . . .

100. To this I find two Objections made.

First, *That there are no Instances to be found in Story, of a Company of Men Independent, and equal one amongst another, that met together, and in this way began and set up a Government.*

Secondly, *'Tis impossible of Right, that Men should do so, because all Men being born under Government, they are to submit to that, and are not at liberty to begin a new one.*

101. To the first there is this to answer, That it is not at all to be wonder'd, that *History* gives us but a very little account of *Men, that lived together in the State of Nature*. The Inconveniences of that Condition, and the Love, and want of Society no sooner brought any number of them together, but they presently united, and incorporated, if they designed to continue together. . . .

105. I will not deny, that if we look back as far as History will direct us, towards the *Original of Commonwealths*, we shall generally find them under the Government and Administration of one Man. And I am also apt to believe, that where a Family was numerous enough to subsist by itself, and continued entire together, without mixing with others, as it often happens, where there is much Land, and few People, the Government commonly began in the Father. For the Father having, by the Law of Nature, the same Power with every Man else to punish, as he thought fit, any Offences against that Law, might thereby punish his transgressing Children, even when they were Men, and out of their Pupilage; and they were very likely to submit to his Punishment, and all

joyn with him against the Offender, in their turns, giving him thereby Power to Execute his Sentence against any transgression, and so in effect make him the Law-Maker, and Governor over all, that remained in Conjunction with his Family. He was fittest to be trusted; Paternal affection secured their Property, and Interest under his Care; and the Custom of obeying him, in their Childhood, made it easier to submit to him, rather than to any other. If therefore they must have one to rule them, as Government is hardly to be avoided amongst Men that live together; who so likely to be the Man, as he that was their common Father; unless Negligence, Cruelty, or any other defect of Mind, or Body made him unfit for it? But when either the Father died, and left his next Heir, for want of Age, Wisdom, Courage, or any other Qualities, less fit for Rule; or where several Famil[i]es met, and consented to continue together; There 'tis not to be doubted, but they used their natural Freedom, to set up him, whom they judged the ablest, and most likely, to Rule well over them. Conformable hereunto we find the People of *America*, who (living out of the reach of the Conquering Swords, and spreading domination of the two great Empires of *Peru* and *Mexico*) enjoy'd their own natural Freedom, though, *cæteris paribus*,[1] they commonly prefer the Heir of their deceased King; yet if they find him any way weak, or uncapable, they pass him by, and set up the stoutest, and bravest Man for their Ruler....

112. . . . *The other Objection I find urged against the beginning of Politics, in the way I have mentioned, is this*, viz.

113. *That all Men being born under Government, some or other, it is impossible any of them should ever be free, and at liberty to unite together, and begin a new one, or ever be able to erect a lawful Government.*

If this Argument be good; I ask, how came so many lawful Monarchies into the World? . . .

115. For there are no Examples so frequent in History, both sacred and prophane, as those of Men withdrawing themselves, and their Obedience, from the Jurisdiction they were born under, and the Family or Community they were bred up in, and *setting up new Governments* in other Places; from whence sprang all that number of petty Commonwealths in the Beginning of Ages, and which always multiplied, as long as there was room enough, till the stronger, or more fortunate, swallowed the weaker; and those great ones again breaking to Pieces, dissolved into lesser Dominions. All which are so many Testimonies against paternal

Sovereignty, and plainly prove, That it was not the natural right of the *Father* descending to his Heirs, that made Governments in the Beginning, since it was impossible, upon that Ground, there should have been so many little Kingdoms; all must have been but only one universal Monarchy, if Men had not been at *Liberty to separate* themselves from their Families, and the Government, be it what it will, that was set up in it, and go and make distinct Commonwealths and other Governments, as they thought fit.

116. This has been the practice of the World from its first beginning to this day; Nor is it now any more Hindrance to the freedom of Mankind, that they are *born under constituted and ancient Polities*, that have established Laws, and set Forms of Government, than if they were born in the Woods, amongst the unconfined Inhabitants, that run loose in them. For those, who would persuade us, that *by being born under any Government, we are naturally Subjects to it*, and have no more any Title or Pretence to the freedom of the state of Nature, have no other reason (bating that of paternal Power, which we have already answer'd) to produce for it, but only, because our Fathers or Progenitors passed away their natural Liberty, and thereby bound up themselves and their Posterity to a perpetual Subjection to the Government, which they themselves submitted to. 'Tis true, that whatever Engagements or Promises any one has made for himself, he is under the Obligation of them, but *cannot* by any *Compact* whatsoever, *bind his Children or Posterity*. For his Son, when a Man, being altogether as free as the Father, any *Act of the Father can no more give away the liberty of the Son*, than it can of any Body else: He may indeed annex such Conditions to the Land, he enjoyed as a Subject of any Commonwealth, as may oblige his Son to be of that Community, if he will enjoy those Possessions which were his Father's; because that Estate being his Father's Property, he may dispose, or settle it, as he pleases.

117. And this has generally given the occasion to mistake in this Matter; because Commonwealths not permitting any part of their Dominions to be dismembred, nor to be enjoyed by any but those of their Community, the Son cannot ordinarily enjoy the Possession of his Father, but under the same Terms his Father did; by becoming a member of the Society; whereby he puts himself presently under the Government, he finds there established, as much as any other Subject of that Commonwealth. And thus *the Consent of Freemen, born under Government*, which only *makes them Members of it*, being given separately in their Turns, as each comes to be of Age, and not in a Multitude together; People take no Notice of it, and thinking it not done at all, or

not necessary, conclude they are naturally Subjects as they are Men. . . .

IX. Of the End of Political Society and Government.

123. If Man in the state of Nature be so free, as has been said; if he be absolute Lord of his own Person and Possessions, equal to the greatest and subject to no Body, why will he part with his Freedom? Why will he give up this Empire, and subject himself to the Dominion and Controul of any other Power? To which 'tis obvious to answer, that though in the state of Nature he hath such a Right, yet the Enjoyment of it is very uncertain, and constantly exposed to the Invasion of others. For all being Kings as much as he, every Man his Equal and the greater Part no strict Observers of Equity and Justice, the enjoyment of the Property he has in this State, is very unsafe, very unsecure. This makes him willing to quit this Condition, which however free, is full of Fears and continual Dangers: And 'tis not without Reason, that he seeks out, and is willing to joyn in Society with others, who are already united, or have a Mind to unite, for the mutual *Preservation* of their Lives, Liberties and Estates, which I call by the general Name, *Property*.

124. The great and *chief End* therefore, of Mens uniting into Commonwealths, and putting themselves under Government, *is the Preservation of their Property*.

XI. Of the Extent of the Legislative Power.

134. The great end of Mens entring into Society, being the Enjoyment of their Properties in Peace and Safety, and the great instrument and means of that being the Laws establish'd in that Society . . . ,

139. . . . *Government* . . . the Prince, or Senate, however it may have Power to make Laws, for the regulating of *Property*, between the Subjects one amongst another, yet can never have a Power to take to themselves the whole, or any part of the Subjects *Property*, without their own Consent. For this would be in effect to leave them no *Property* at all. And to let us see, that even *absolute Power*, where it is necessary, is *not Arbitrary* by being absolute, but is still limited by that Reason, and confined to those Ends, which required it in some Cases to be absolute, we need look no farther than the common practice of Martial Discipline. For the preservation of the Army, and in it of the whole

Commonwealth, requires an *absolute Obedience* to the Command of every superior Officer, and it is justly Death to disobey or dispute the most dangerous or unreasonable of them; but yet we see, that neither the Serjeant, that could Command a Soldier to march up to the mouth of a Cannon, or stand in a Breach, where he is almost sure to perish, can command that Soldier to give him one Penny of his Money; nor the *General*, that can condemn him to Death for deserting his Post, or for not obeying the most desperate Orders, can yet with all his *absolute Power* of Life and Death, dispose of one Farthing of that Soldier's Estate, or seize one jot of his Goods; whom yet he can command any Thing, and hang for the least Disobedience. Because such a blind Obedience is necessary to that end, for which the Commander has his Power, *viz.* the preservation of the rest; but the disposing of his Goods has nothing to do with it.

Notes

JOHN LOCKE (1632-1704), physician and philosopher, like most radicals of the period was anti-clerical. For this reason he avoided taking orders as a young man. He was a tolerationist for all but catholics and atheists. Though he devoted himself to medical studies and was elected to the Royal Society in 1668, he never qualified. By 1667 he had become a close friend of Sir Anthony Ashley Cooper, later Earl of Shaftesbury (see p. 161, n. 23), on whom he performed a celebrated surgical operation for an internal abcess. He gave Shaftesbury advice about the education of his grandson, and drew up a constitution for the colony of Carolina which was anti-democratic and permitted negro slavery. He was Shaftesbury's secretary while he was Lord Chancellor and was at his side from 1677 during the exclusionist campaign. He probably framed his answer to Filmer at this time. He was subsequently involved in the plans of the Council of Six (see p. 161, n. 28) and went into exile in 1684, being deprived of his studentship at Christchurch College, Oxford at this time. After the revolution he became a commissioner of appeal and began publishing the works for which he is celebrated, notably his *Epistola de Tolerantia [Letter concerning Toleration]* (1689), the *Two Treatises of Government* (1690), of which *Of Civil Government* is the second, *An Essay concerning Humane Understanding* (1690) and *A Second Letter concerning Toleration* (1690). This extract from *Of Civil Government* is taken from the edition of 1713.

1. 'other things being equal'.

14 From: *Some Thoughts concerning Education*

John Locke, 1693

127. That which every Gentleman (that takes any care of his Education) desires for his Son, besides the Estate he leaves him, is contain'd, I suppose, in these four Things, *Virtue, Wisdom, Breeding* and *Learning*. . . .

128. I place *Vertue* as the first and most necessary of those Endowments, that belong to a Man or a Gentleman, as absolutely requisite to make him valued and beloved by others, acceptable or tolerable to himself; without that, I think, he will neither be happy in this, nor the other World.

129. As the Foundation of this, there ought very early to be imprinted on his Mind a true Notion of *God*, as of the independent Supreme Being, Author and Maker of all Things, from whom we receive all our Good, that loves us, and gives us all Things; and consequent to it a Love and Reverence of him. . . .

132. Having laid the Foundations of Vertue in a true Notion of a God, such as the Creed wisely teaches, as far as his Age is capable, and by accustoming him to pray to him. The next thing to be taken Care of, is to keep him exactly to speaking of *Truth*, and by all the ways imaginable, inclining him to be *good natur'd*. Let him know that Twenty Faults are sooner to be forgiven than the *straining of Truth* to cover any one *by an Excuse*. And to teach him betimes to love, and be *good natur'd* to others, is to lay early the true Foundation of an honest Man: All Injustice generally springing from too great Love of our selves, and too little of others. . . .

133. *Wisdom*, I take in the popular acceptation, for a Man's managing his Business ably, and with fore-sight in this World. This is the product of a good natural Temper, application of Mind, and Experience together, and not to be taught Children. The greatest Thing that in them can be done towards it, is to hinder them, as much as may be, from being *Cunning*, which being the ape of *Wisdom*, is the most distant from it that can be, and as an Ape, for the likeness it has to a Man, wanting what really should make him so, is by so much the uglier. *Cunning* is only the want of Understanding, which, because it cannot compass its ends by direct ways, would do it by a Trick and Circumvention; and

the Mischief of it is, a *cunning* Trick helps but once, but hinders, ever after. No cover was ever made either so big or so fine as to hide its self. No Body was ever so *cunning* as to conceal their being so; and when they are once discovered, every body is shie, every Body distrustful of *crafty* Men, and all the World forwardly joyn to oppose and defeat them. Whilst the open, fair, *wise* Man has every Body to make way for him, and goes directly to his business. . . .

134. The next good Quality belonging to a Gentleman, is *good Breeding*. There are Two Sorts of *ill Breeding*, The one a *sheepish Bashfulness*, and the other a *mis-becoming Negligence and Disrespect* in our Carriage, both which are avoided by duly observing this one Rule, *Not to think meanly of our selves, and not to think meanly of others*. . . .

138. Though the managing our selves well, in this part of our Behaviour, has the name of *Good-Breeding*, as if peculiarly the effect of Education; yet, . . . young Children should not be much perplexed about it; I mean about putting off their Hats, and making Legs modishly. . . .

If you can teach them to love and respect other People, they will, as their Age requires it, find ways to express it acceptably to every one, according to the Fashions they have been used to. And as to their Motions and Carriage of their Bodies, a Dancing-Master, as has been said, when it is fit, will teach them what is most becoming. In the mean time, when they are young, People expect not that Children should be over-mindful of these Ceremonies; Carelessness is allow'd to that Age, and becomes them as well as Complements do grown People: Or at least, if some very nice People will think it a fault, I am sure it is a fault, that should be over-look'd and left to Time and Conversation only to cure. . . .

140. You will wonder, perhaps, that I put *Learning* last, especially if I tell you I think it the least part. This will seem strange in the mouth of a bookish Man; and this making usually the chief, if not only bustle and stir about Children, this being almost that alone, which is thought on, when People talk of Education, makes it the greater Paradox. When I consider what a-do is made about a little *Latin* and *Greek*, how many Years are spent in it, and what a noise and business it makes to no purpose, I can hardly forbear thinking, that the Parents of Children still live in fear of the School-masters Rod, which they look on as the only Instrument of Education, as a Language or two to be its whole Business. How else is it possible that a Child should be chain'd to the Oar, Seven, Eight, or Ten of the best Years of his Life to get a Language or Two, which I think, might be had at a great deal cheaper rate of Pains and Time, and be learn'd almost in playing.

Forgive me therefore, if I say, I can not with Patience think, that a young Gentleman should be put into the Herd, and be driven with Whip and Scourge, as if he were to run the Gantlet through the several Classes, *ad capiendum ingenii cultum*.[1] What then, say you, would you not have him Write and Read? Shall he be more ignorant than the Clerk of our Parish, who takes *Hopkins* and *Sternhold*[2] for the best Poets in the World, whom yet he makes worse, than they are, by his ill Reading? Not so, not so fast, I beseech you. Reading, and Writing, and Learning, I allow to be necessary, but yet not the chiefest Business. I imagine you would think him a very foolish Fellow, that should not value a Vertuous or a Wise Man, infinitely before a great Scholar: Not but that I think Learning a great help to both in well dispos'd Minds; but yet it must be confess'd also, that in others not so dispos'd, it helps them only to be the more foolish or worse Men. I say this, that when you consider of the Breeding of your Son, and are looking out for a School-Master, or a Tutor, you would not have (as is usual) *Latin* and *Logick* only in your Thoughts. Learning must be had, but in the second place, as subservient only to greater Qualities: Seek out some-body, that may know how discreetly to frame his Manners: Place him in Hands, where you may, as much as possible, secure his Innocence, cherish and nurse up the Good, and gently correct and weed out any Bad Inclinations, and settle in him good Habits. This is the main Point, and this being provided for, *Learning*, may be had into the Bargain, and that, as I think, at a very easie rate, by Methods that may be thought on.

141. When he can talk; 'tis time he should begin to *learn to read*. But as to this, give me leave here to inculcate again, what is very apt to be forgotten, *viz*. That a great Care is to be taken, that it be never made as a Business to him, nor he look on it as a Task. We naturally, as I said, even from our Cradles, love Liberty, and have therefore an aversion to many Things, for no other Reason, but because they are enjoyn'd us. I have always had a Fancy, that *Learning* might be made a Play and Recreation to Children; and that they might be brought to desire to be taught, if it were propos'd to them as a thing of Honour, Credit, Delight and Recreation, or as a Reward for doing something else; and if they were never chid or corrected for the neglect of it. . . . I remember that being at a Friend's House, whose younger Son, a Child in Coats, was not easily *brought* to his Book (being taught *to Read* at home by his Mother) I advised to try another way, then requiring it of him as his Duty; we therefore, in a Discourse on purpose amongst our selves, in his hearing, but without taking any notice of him, declared, That it was the Privilege and Advantage of Heirs and Elder Brothers, to be

Scholars; that this made them fine Gentlemen, and beloved by every body: And that for Younger Brothers, 'twas a Favour to admit them to Breeding; to be taught to *Read* and Write, was more than came to their share; they might be ignorant Bumpkins and Clowns, if they pleased. This so wrought upon the Child, that afterwards he desired to be taught; would come himself to his Mother to *learn*, and would not let his Maid be quiet till she heard him his Lesson. . . .

148. When by these gentle ways he begins to be able to *read*, some easy pleasant Book suited to his Capacity, should be put into his Hands, wherein the entertainment, that he finds, might draw him on, and reward his Pains in Reading, and yet not such as should fill his Head with perfectly useless trumpery, or lay the principles of Vice and Folly. To this purpose, I think, *Aesop's Fables* the best, which being Stories apt to delight and entertain a Child, may yet afford useful Reflections to a grown Man. . . . *Raynard the Fox*,[3] is another Book, I think, may be made use of to the same purpose. And if those about him will talk to him often about the Stories he has read, and hear him tell them, it will, besides other Advantages, add Incouragement, and delight *to* his *Reading*, when he finds there is some use and pleasure in it, which in the ordinary Method, I think Learners do not till late; and so take Books only for fashionable amuzements or impertinent troubles good for nothing.

149. The Lord's Prayer, the Creeds, and Ten Commandments, 'tis necessary he should learn perfectly by heart, but I think, not by reading them himself in his Primer, but by some body's repeating them to him, even before he can read. But learning by heart, and *learning to read*, should not I think be mixed, and so one made to clog the other. But his *learning to read* should be made as little trouble or business to him as might be. . . .

152. When he can read English well, it will be seasonable to enter him in *Writing*: . . .

153. When he can Write well, and quick, I think it may be convenient, not only to continue the exercise of his Hand in Writing, but also to improve the use of it farther in *Drawing*, a thing very useful to a Gentleman in several occasions; but especially if he travel, as that which helps a Man often to express, in a few Lines well put together, what a whole Sheet of Paper in Writing, would not be able to represent, and make intelligible. How many Buildings may a Man see, how many Machines and Habits meet with, the Idea's whereof would be easily retain'd and communicated, by a little Skill in *Drawing*; which being committed to Words, are in danger to be lost, or at best but ill retained in the most

exact Descriptions? I do not mean, that I would have your Son a *perfect Painter*; to be that to any tolerable degree, will require more time than a young Gentleman can spare from his other Improvements of greater importance: But so much insight into *Perspective*, and skill in *Drawing*, as will enable him to represent tolerably on Paper any thing he sees, except Faces, may, I think, be got in a little time, especially if he have a Genius to it: ...

154. As soon as he can speak *English*, 'tis time for him to learn some other Language: This no body doubts of, when *French* is proposed. And the Reason is, because People are accustomed to the right way of teaching that Language: which is by talking it into Children in constant Conversation, and not by Grammatical Rules. ...

156. *Latin*, I look upon as absolutely necessary to a Gentleman, and indeed, Custom, which prevails over every thing, has made it so much a Part of Education, that even those Children are whipp'd to it, and made spend many Hours of their precious time uneasily in *Latin*, who, after they are once gone from School, are never to have more to do with it as long as they live. Can there be any thing more ridiculous, than that a Father should waste his own Money, and his Son's time, in setting him to learn the *Roman Language*, when at the same time he designs him for a Trade, wherein he having no use of *Latin*, fails not to forget that little, which he brought from School, and which 'tis Ten to One he abhorrs, for the ill usage it procur'd him? Could it be believ'd, unless we had every where amongst us Examples of it, that a Child should be forced to learn the Rudiments of a Language, which he is never to use in the course of Life, he is designed to, and neglect all the while the writing a good Hand, and casting Account, which are of great Advantage in all Conditions of Life, and to most Trades indispensibly necessary? But though these Qualifications, requisite to Trade and Commerce, and the Business of the World, are seldom or never to be had at Grammar Schools, yet thither, not only Gentlemen send their younger Sons, intended for Trades; but even Tradesmen and Farmers fail not to send their Children, though they have neither Intention nor Ability to make them Scholars. ...

157. But how necessary soever *Latin* be to some, and is Thought to be to others, to whom it is of no manner of Use or Service; yet the ordinary way of learning it in a Grammar School is that, which having had thoughts about I cannot be forward to encourage. ... If ... a Man could be got, who himself speaks good *Latin*, who would always be about your Son, and talk constantly to him, and make him read *Latin*, that would be the true Genuine, and easy way of teaching him *Latin*,

and that that I could wish, since besides teaching him a Language, without Pains or Chiding (which Children are wont to be whipp'd for at School Six or Seven Years together) he might at the same time, not only form his Mind and Manners, but instruct him also in several Sciences, such as are a good Part of *Geography*, *Astronomy*, *Chronology*, *Anatomy*, besides some Parts of *History*, and all other Parts of Knowledge of Things, that fall under the Senses, and require little more than Memory: For there, if we would take the true way, our Knowledge should begin, and in those Things be laid the Foundation; and not in the abstract Notions of *Logick* and *Metaphysicks*, which are fitter to amuze, than inform the Understanding, in its first setting out towards Knowledge: . . .

161. But if, after all, his Fate be to go to School to get the *Latin Tongue*, 'tis in vain to talk to you concerning the method I think best to be observed in Schools; you must submit to that you find there; nor expect to have it changed for your Son: But yet by all means obtain, if you can, that he be not employ'd in making *Latin Themes* and *Declamations*, and least of all *Verses* of any kind. You may insist on it if it will do any good, that you have no design to make him either a *Latin* Orator, or a Poet; but barely would have him understand perfectly a *Latin* Author; and that you observe, that those, who teach any of the modern Languages, and that with success, never amuse their Scholars, to make Speeches, or Verses, either in *French* or *Italian*, their Business being *Language barely*, and not Invention. . . .

164. But, perhaps, we shall be told,'Tis to improve and perfect them in the *Latin* Tongue. 'Tis true, that is their proper Business at School; but the making of *Themes* is not the way to it: That perplexes their Brains about invention of things to be said, not about the signification of Words to be learn'd: And when they are making a *Theme*, 'tis Thoughts they search and sweat for, and not Language. But the Learning and Mastery of a Tongue, being uneasie and unpleasant enough in it self, should not be cumbred with any other Difficulties, as is done in this way of proceeding. In fine, if boys invention be to be quickn'd by such Exercise, let them make *Themes* in *English*; where they have facility, and a command of Words, and will better use what kind of Thoughts they have, when put into their own Language: And if the *Latin* Tongue be to be learn'd, let it be done the easiest way, without toiling and disgusting the mind, by so uneasie an imployment, as that of making Speeches join'd to it.

165. If these may be any Reasons against Children's making *Latin Themes* at School, I have much more to say, and of more weight, against

their making *Verses*; *Verses* of any sort: For if he has no *Genius* to *Poetry*, 'tis the most unreasonable thing in the World, to torment a Child, and waste his time about that which can never succeed: And if he have a Poetick Vein, 'tis to me the strangest thing in the World, that the Father should desire, or suffer it to be cherished, or improved. Methinks the Parents should labour to have it stifled, and suppressed, as much as may be; and I know not what reason a Father can have, to wish his son a Poet, who does not desire to have him bid defiance to all other Callings, and Business, which is not yet the worst of the case; for if he proves a successful Rhymer, and get once the reputation of a Wit, I desire it may be consider'd what Company and Places he is Like to spend his Time in, nay, and Estate too. For it is very seldom seen that any one discovers Mines of Gold or Silver in *Parnassus*.[4] 'Tis a pleasant Air, but a barren Soil; and there are very few instances of those, who have added to their Patrimony by any thing they have reaped from thence. Poetry and Gaming, which usually go together, are alike in this too, That they seldom bring any advantage, but to those who have nothing else to live on. Men of Estates almost constantly go away losers; and 'tis well if they escape at a cheaper rate than their whole Estates, or the greatest part of them. If therefore you would not have your Son the Fiddle to every jovial Company, without whom the Sparks could not relish their Wine, nor know how to pass an Afternoon idly; if you would not have him waste his Time and Estate, to divert others, and contemn the dirty Acres left him by his Ancestors, I do not think you will much care he should be a *Poet*, or that his School-master should enter him in Versifying. But yet, if any one will think Poetry a desirable Quality in his Son, and that the study of it would raise his Fancy and Parts, he must needs yet confess, that to that end reading the excellent *Greek* and *Roman* Poets is of more use, than making bad Verses of his own, in a Language that is not his own. And he, whose design it is to excell in *English* Poetry, would not, I guess, think the way to it were to make his first Essays in *Latin* Verses. . . .

168. At the same time that he is learning *French* and *Latin*, a Child, as has been said, may also be enter'd in *Arithmetick*, *Geography*, *Chronology*, *History*, and *Geometry* too. For if these be taught him in *French* or *Latin*, when he begins once to understand either of these Tongues, he will get a knowledge in these Sciences, and the Language to boot. . . .

176. It would be strange to suppose an *English* Gentleman should be ignorant of the *Law* of his Country. This, whatever station he is in, is so requisite, that from a Justice of the Peace, to a Minister of State, I

know no Place he can well fill without it. I do not mean the chicane or wrangling and captious part of the *Law*; a Gentleman, whose Business it is to seek the true measures of Right and Wrong, and not the Arts how to avoid doing the one, and secure himself in doing the other, ought to be as far from such a study of the *Law*, as he is concerned diligently to apply himself to that, wherein he may be serviceable to his Country. And to that purpose, I think the right way for a Gentleman to study *Our Law*, which he does not design for his Calling, is to take a view of our *English* Constitution and Government, in the ancient Books of the *Common Law*; and some more modern Writers, who out of them have given an account of this Government. And having got a true Idea of that, then to read our History, and with it join in every King's Reign the *Laws* then made. This will give an insight into the reason of our *Statutes*, and shew the true ground upon which they came to be made, and what weight they ought to have.

177. *Rhetorick* and *Logick* being the Arts that in the ordinary method usually follow immediately after Grammar, it may perhaps be wondered that I have said so little of them: The reason is, because of the little advantage young People receive by them: For I have seldom or never observed any one to get the Skill of reasoning well, or speaking handsomly by studying those Rules, which pretend to teach it: And therefore I would have a young Gentleman take a view of them in the shortest Systems could be found, without dwelling long on the contemplation and study of those Formalities.

178. *Natural Philosophy*, as a speculative Science, I think we have none, and perhaps, I may think I have reason to say we never shall. The Works of Nature are contrived by a Wisdom, and operate by ways too far surpassing our Faculties to discover, or Capacities to conceive, for us ever to be able to reduce them into a Science. *Natural Philosophy* being the Knowledge of the Principles, Properties and Operations of Things, as they are in themselves, I imagine there are Two Parts of it, one comprehending Spirits with their Nature and Qualities; and the other *Bodies*. The first of these is usually referr'd to *Metaphysicks*, but under what Title soever the consideration of *Spirits* comes, I think it ought to go before the study of Matter, and Body, not as a Science that can be methodized into a System, and treated of upon Principles of Knowledge; but as an enlargement of our Minds towards a truer and fuller comprehension of the intellectual World to which we are led both by Reason and Revelation. And since the clearest and largest Discoveries we have of other *Spirits* besides God and our own Souls is imparted to us from Heaven by Revelation, I think the information, that at least

young People should have of them, should be taken from that Revelation. To this purpose, I think, it would be well if there were made a good History of the Bible for young People to read, wherein every thing, that is fit to be put into it, being laid down in its due Order of Time, and several things omitted, which were suited only to riper Age, that Confusion, which is usually produced by promiscuous reading of the Scripture, as it lies now bound up in our Bibles, would be avoided. . . .

181. But to return to the study of *Natural Philosophy*, though the World be full of Systems of it, yet I cannot say, I know any one which can be taught a young Man as a Science, wherein he may be sure to find truth and certainty, which is what all Sciences give an expectation of. I do not hence conclude that none of them are to be read: It is necessary for a Gentleman in this learned Age to look into some of them, to fit himself for Conversation. But whether that of *Des Cartes*[5] be put into his Hands, as that which is most in Fashion; or it be thought fit to give him a short view of that and several other also. I think the Systems of *Natural Philosophy* that have obtained in this part of the World, are to be read, more to know the *Hypotheses*, and to understand the Terms and Ways of Talking of the several Sects, than with hopes to gain thereby a comprehensive scientifical and satisfactory Knowledge of the Works of Nature: Only this may be said, that the Modern *Corpuscularians*[6] talk in most Things more intelligibly than the *Peripateticks*,[7] who possessed the Schools immediately before them. . . .

182. Though the Systems of *Physick*, that I have met with, afford little encouragement to look for Certainty or Science in any Treatise, which shall pretend to give us a body of *Natural Philosophy* from the first Principles of Bodies in general, yet the incomparable Mr. *Newton*,[8] has shewn how far Mathematicks, applied to some Parts of Nature, may, upon Principles that matter of fact justifie, carry us in the knowledge of some, as I may so call them, particular Provinces of the incomprehensible Universe. And if others could give us so good and clear an account of other parts of *Nature*, as he has of this our Planetary World, and the most considerable *Phoenomena* observable in it, in his admirable Book, *Philosophiæ naturalis principia Mathematica*,[9] we might in time hope to be furnished with more true and certain Knowledge in several Parts of this stupendious Machin, than hitherto we could have expected. And though there are very few, that have Mathematicks enough to understand his Demonstrations, yet the most accurate Mathematicians, who have examined them, allowing them to be such, his Book will deserve to be read, and give no small light and pleasure to those, who willing to understand the Motions, Properties, and Operations of the great

Masses of Matter, in this our Solar System, will but carefully mind his
Conclusions, which may be depended on as Propositions well proved.

183. This is, in short, what I have thought concerning a young
Gentleman's Studies; wherein it will possibly be wondred, that I should
omit *Greek*, since amongst the *Grecians* is to be found the Original, as
it were, and Foundation of all that Learning which we have in this part
of the World. I grant it so; and will add, That no Man can pass for a
Scholar, that is ignorant of the *Greek* Tongue. But I am not here considering of the Education of a profess'd Scholar, but of a Gentleman,
to whom *Latin* and *French*, as the World now goes, is by every one
acknowledged to be necessary. When he comes to be a Man, if he has
a mind to carry his Studies farther, and look into the *Greek* Learning,
he will then easily get that Tongue himself: And if he has not that Inclination, his learning of it under a Tutor will be but lost Labour, and
much of his Time and Pains spent in that, which will be neglected and
thrown away, as soon as he is at liberty. For how many are there of
an hundred, even amongst Scholars themselves, who retain the *Greek*
they carried from School; or ever improve it to a familiar reading, and
perfect understanding of *Greek* Authors?

184. Besides what is to be had from Study and Books, there are other
Accomplishments necessary to a Gentleman, to be got by exercise, and
to which time is to be allowed, and for which Masters must be had.

Dancing being that which gives *graceful Motions* all the life, and
above all things Manliness, and a becoming Confidence to young Children, I think it cannot be learn'd too early, after they are once of an Age
and Strength capable of it. . . .

185. *Musick* is thought to have some affinity with Dancing, and a
good Hand, upon some Instruments, is by many People mightily valued;
but it wastes so much of a young Man's time, to gain but a moderate
Skill in it, and engages often in such odd Company, that many think it
much better spared: And I have, amongst Men of Parts and Business, so
seldom heard any one commended, or esteemed for having an Excel-
lency in *Musick*, that amongst all those things that ever came into the
List of Accomplishments, I think I may give it the last place. . . .

186. *Fencing* and *Riding* the *Great Horse*, are look'd upon as so
necessary parts of Breeding, that it would be thought a great *omission*
to neglect them: The latter of the two being for the most part to be
learn'd only in Great Towns, is one of the best Exercises for Health
which is to be had in those Places of Ease and Luxury; and upon that
account makes a fit part of a young Gentleman's Employment during his
abode there. And as far as it conduces to give a Man a firm and graceful

Seat on Horseback, and to make him able to teach his Horse to stop and turn quick, and to rest on his Haunches, is of use to a Gentleman both in Peace and War. . . .

187. As for *Fencing*, it seems to me a good Exercise for Health, but dangerous to the Life. The confidence of it being apt to engage in Quarrels, those that think they have some Skill, and to make them more touchy than needs, on Points of Honour, and slight Occasions. Young Men in their warm Blood are forward to think, they have in vain learned to Fence, if they never shew their Skill and Courage in a Duel, and they seem to have Reason. But how many sad Tragedies that Reason has been the Occasion of, the Tears of many a Mother can witness. . . .

189. I have one Thing more to add, which as soon as I mention, I shall run the danger to be suspected to have forgot what I am about, and what I have above written concerning Education, which has all tended towards a Gentleman's Calling, with which a *Trade* seems wholly to be inconsistent. And yet, I cannot forbear to say, I would have him *learn a Trade, a Manual Trade*; nay, two or three, but one more particularly.

190. The busy Inclination of Children being always to be directed to some thing, that may be useful to them. The Advantage may be considered of two Kinds; 1. Where the Skill it self, that is got by exercise, is worth the having. Thus Skill not only in Languages, and learned Sciences, but in Painting, Turning, Gardening, Tempering, and Working in Iron, and all other useful Arts is worth the having. 2. Where the Exercise it self, without any other Consideration, is necessary, or useful for Health. Knowledge in some Things is so necessary to be got by Children whilst they are young, that some part of their time is to be allotted to their improvement in them, though those Imployments contribute nothing at all to their Health: Such are Reading and Writing and all other sedentary Studies, for the improvement of the Mind, and are the unavoidable Business of Gentlemen quite from their Cradles. Other *Manual Arts*, which are both got and exercised by Labour, do many of them by their Exercise contribute to our Health too, especially, such as imploy us in the open Air. In these, then, Health and Improvement may be joyn'd together, and of these should some fit ones be chosen, to be made the Recreations of one, whose chief Business is with Books and Study. In this Choice, the Age and Inclination of the Person is to be considered, and Constraint always to be avoided in bringing him to it. For Command and Force may often create, but can never cure an Aversion. And whatever any one is brought to by compulsion, he will leave as soon as he can, and be little profited, and less recreated by, whilst he is at it. . . .

197. But if his mistaken Parents, frighted with the disgraceful Names of *Mechanick* and *Trade*, shall have an aversion to any thing of this kind in their Children; yet there is one thing relating to Trade, which when they consider, they will think absolutely necessary for their Sons to learn.

Merchants Accompts, though a Science not likely to help a Gentleman to get an Estate, yet possibly there is not any thing of more use and efficacy, to make him preserve the Estate he has. 'Tis seldom observed, that he who keeps an Accompt of his Income and Expences, and thereby has constantly under view the course of his domestick Affairs, lets them run to ruine: And I doubt not but many a Man gets behind-hand, before he is aware, or runs further on, when he is once in, for want of this Care, or the Skill to do it. I would therefore advice all Gentlemen to learn perfectly *Merchants Accounts*, and not think it is a Skill, that belongs not to them, because it has received its Name, and has been chiefly practised by Men of Traffick. . . .

199. The last Part usually in Education is *Travel*, which is commonly thought to finish the Work, and compleat the Gentleman. I confess *Travel* into Foreign Countries has great Advantages but the time usually chosen to send young Men abroad is, I think, of all other, that which renders them least capable of reaping those Advantages. Those which are propos'd, as to the main of them, may be reduced to these Two, first Language, secondly an Improvement in Wisdom and Prudence, by seeing Men, and conversing with People of Tempers, Customs, and Ways of living, different from one another, and especially from those of his Parish and Neighbourhood. But from Sixteen to One and Twenty, which is the ordinary *time of Travel*, Men are of all their Lives, the least suited to these Improvements. The first Season to get Foreign Languages, and from their Tongue to their true Accents, I should think, should be from Seven to Fourteen or Sixteen; and then too a Tutor with them is useful and necessary, who may with those Languages teach them other things. But to put them out of their Parents view at a great distance, under a Governour, when they think themselves too much Men to be governed by others, and yet have not Prudence and Experience enough to govern themselves, what is it, but to expose them to all the greatest Dangers of their whole Life, when they have the least Fence and Guard against them? . . .

201. This, how true soever it be, will not, I fear alter the Custom, which has cast the time of Travel upon the worst part of a Man's Life; but for Reasons not taken from their Improvement. The young Lad must not be ventured abroad at Eight or Ten, for fear what may happen

to the tender Child, though he then runs ten times less risque than at Sixteen or Eighteen. Nor must he stay at home till that dangerous heady Age be over, because he must be back again by One and twenty to marry and propagate. The Father cannot stay any longer for the Portion, nor the Mother for a new Sett of Babies to play with; and so my young Master, whatever comes on't must have a Wife look'd out for him, by that time he is of Age; though it would be no prejudice to his Strength, his Parts, nor his Issue, if it were respited for some time, and he had leave to get, in Years and Knowledge, the start a little of his Children, who are often found to tread too near upon the heels of their Fathers, to the no great Satisfaction either of Son or Father. But the young Gentleman being got within view of Matrimony, 'tis time to leave him to his Mistress.

202. Though I am now come to a Conclusion of what obvious Remarks have suggested to me concerning Education, I would not have it thought that I look on it as a just Treatise on this Subject: There are a thousand other things that may need consideration, especially if one should take in the various Tempers, different Inclinations, and particular Defaults, that are to be found in Children, and prescribe proper Remedies: The variety is so great, that it would require a Volume; nor would that reach it. Each Man's Mind has some peculiarity, as well as his Face, that distinguishes him from all others; and there are possibly scarce two Children, who can be conducted by exactly the same method. Besides, that I think a Prince, a Nobleman, and an ordinary Gentleman's Son, should have different ways of Breeding. But having had here only some general Views, in reference to the main End and Aims in Education, and those designed for a Gentleman's Son, who being then very little, I considered only as white Paper, or Wax, to be moulded and fashioned as one pleases; I have touch'd little more than those Heads, which I judged necessary for the Breeding of a young Gentleman of his Condition in general; and have now published these my occasional Thoughts with this Hope, That though this be far from being a compleat Treatise on this Subject, or such, as that every one may find what will just fit his Child in it, yet it may give some small light to those, whose Concern for their dear Little Ones, makes them so irregularly bold, that they dare venture to consult their own Reason, in the Education of their Children, rather than wholly to rely upon Old Custom.

Notes

1. 'in order to acquire the cultivation of talent'.

2. John Hopkins (d. 1570) and Thomas Sternhold (d. 1549), translators of the Psalms into rudimentary verse though their use in church services was very popular.

3. French medieval beast epic. In 1641 Caxton printed a translated Flemish version, *The Historye of Reynart the Fox*.

4. A mountain near Delphi in Greece, sacred to Apollo and the Muses and so the seat of music and poetry.

5. René Descartes (1596-1650), French mathematician and philosopher, whose radical distinction between mind and body highlighted the problem of their relationship. His rigorously mechanistic view of the physical world makes him a key figure in the development of modern philosophy.

6. Philosophers working in the traditions of Democritus, a Greek philosopher of the 5th century BC, who had taught that the universe was made up of minute corpuscules, and of Descartes (see n. 5), who had more recently developed atomic theory on complex mathematical principles. Classical atomism was frequently regarded as atheistical and materialist. Locke here expresses his preference for it over traditional Aristotelian or peripatetic philosophical traditions (see Introduction, p. 00).

7. See p. 58, n. 21.

8. Sir Isaac Newton (1642-1727), the great mathematician and founder of modern physicis, a close associate of Locke's in the 1690s.

9. *The Mathematical Principles of Natural Philosophy*.

15 From: *Of National Churches. Their Description, Institution, Use, Preservation, Danger, Maladie, and Cure: Partly applied to England*

Richard Baxter, 1691

Chap. II. That Christ instituted such a Church-Form.

I. That Christ instituted such a Kingdom or National Church. I prove as followeth.

1. He was by the Prophets still described as such before his coming, as was to be the King of *Israel*, and *Israel* under him a National Church....

2. Christ is proclaimed the King of the Jews, and claimed that title and their subjection to him. *Matth.* 2. 2. & 27.11. *Mark* 15.2. He was of the Line of *David*, and had right to his Kingdom. He was scorned and crucified for that claim, *Mat.* 27.29, 37. *Mark* 15.9, 12, 18, 26. *Luke* 23. 37. *John* 19.21. The People acknowledged him King by their *Hosanna*. He destroyeth them as Enemies that would not he should Reign over them, *Luke* 19. 14, 27.

3. He laid the Foundation of his offered National Kingdom among them: He owned the Title and chose twelve Apostles in relation to the twelve Tribes; and the seventy Disciples[1] related to their great Council: He would Preach to none but *Israel*, till they rejected him: He would have gathered all *Jerusalem* and her Children as the Hen gathereth her Chickens; but they would not, *Mat.* 23. 37. He destroyed them for refusing him.

4. He commissioned his Apostles to stay at *Jerusalem* till they rejected them. They made up the broken number of twelve as related to the twelve Tribes by *Matthias*, though *Joses* and others had also followed Christ.[2]

5. He appointed them to Preach the Gospel to Nations, and to disciple Nations, *Mat.* 28. *Mark* 16.

6. He planted the Gentiles into the same Olive tree that the Jews were broken off from, *Rom.* 11.

7. The Jews had not been broken off from their National Church-state, but for unbelief, *Rom.* 11.

8. He translated the Kingdom from them, to a Nation that would bring forth the fruits of it.

9. In due time the Kingdoms of the World were made the Kingdoms of the Lord and of his Christ, *Rev.* 11. & 19.

10. Kings are to be the Churches Nursing Fathers.

11. All Power in Heaven and Earth is given to Christ, *Mat.* 28. and by him Kings Reign. He is King of Kings[3] and not of single persons[4] only.

12. But what need there any other proof, while all Christians confess that All Kings are bound to be Christian Kings, and to promote Christianity to their Power; and all Magistrates and Subjects to be Christians: And are not they then bound to be Christian Kingdoms; and that is National Churches.

2. When he had prepared them to be voluntary Subjects, by the Preaching of the Gospel, and the Church came to maturity, Christ actually set up National Kingdom-Churches; and Ruled by *Constantine*[5] & successive Christian Princes: And Heaven and Earth rejoyced that he had taken to him his great Power and Reigned, and that the Kingdoms of the World were become his Kingdoms, *Rev.* 17. & 18 & 19. Infancy is fitter for Instruction than to Govern. Man is made to use Reason; but he useth little in Infancy, or till maturity. That which was first in intention, is last in execution. Mature Reason in Man, and Princely Government in Kingdom-Churches, was first in intention, tho' not in execution. Who would wish that Pagans had still Reigned? What Christian wisheth not that the *Persians, Indians, Turks, Tartars,* &c. were all Christian Kingdoms? Why else do the Millennies hope for such a state of holy Government?

3. *Obj.* But tho' there be no doubt of the command, institution and duty, what hope have we of the constitution and event that Kingdoms should become Christian?

Ans. Our Question is of the Institution and Duty: confess that, and let us do our endeavour.

2. Is not this a Christian Kingdom, while King and Subjects are baptized professed Christians? Are we a Protestant Kingdom, and not a Christian Kingdom? And are not others such?

Obj. But these be mostly but nominal Hypocrite Christians.

Ans. They are visible professed Christians. The Corn is not without Straw and Chaff. Do you look for Kingdoms that consist only of the sincere?

Obj. But Churches must consist only of those that seem sincere.

Ans. All seem sincere that profess sincerity, till it be by tryal and witness publickly disproved. There are several degrees of seeming;

some by fuller evidences than others; but all that Vow it, and stand to that Vow, do seem and profess it till disproved.

Obj. But how prove you that a Christian Kingdom is a Church?

Ans. Doth your Question mean *de Re*, or *de Nomine?*[6] I told you what I mean by a Church, no other than a Christian Kingdom consisting of a Christian Soveraign, and Christian Subjects, worshiping God in confederate particular Churches (ordinarily) will you deny the Being or the Duty of such?

If it be the *Name*, 1. The word *Ecclesia* is used for even common Assemblies, and therefore much more for Christian Societies.

2. The Israelites were called *The Church* in the Wilderness;[7] much more when more fully stablished.

3. If you have any reason against the Name, disprove it.

4. If the *Name* be all the difference, call it as you please.

But make it not your pretence that only Priests are persons Holy enough to be Heads of Churches, and not Kings; and therefore that it is no National Church that hath not a Clergy Head, Monarchical or Aristocratical; for that's the Popish Doctrine which I have confuted. . . .

Chap VII: What is the Confederacy or Concord needful to a National Church.

1. Affirmatively. 1. A Baptismal Confederacy, to be all the true Subjects of one God, one Christ and Holy Ghost, against the Devil, World and Flesh.[8]

2. 2. A Consent to live as Christians in Love to one another; and to addict ourselves to the good of one another, specially to the welfare of the whole Body, and to do as we would (justly) be done by.

3. 3. To be all the Loyal subjects of one Christian Soveraigns Power.

4. 4. To be all for the publick Worshiping of God and our Redeemer in Christian Assemblies, guided and ruled by Christian Pastors (or Bishops)[9] qualified and described by Christ in his Word the instituter of the Pastoral Office, and not of any new sort of humane Ministry, or uncapable persons that are wanting in any thing essential to the Office.

5. 5. To take the Sacred Scripture for the Word of God, and the sufficient Rule of Divine Faith and Holy living, And to profess an explicite Belief of the Creed as it was transmitted to us from the Apostolick Churches, and to take the Lords Prayer for the summary rule of our desires and hopes; and the Decalogue[10] as owned and expounded by Christ, for the summary rule of our Obedience, with the Sacraments instituted by him.

6. 6. To profess Obedience to true Authority in Parents, Magistrates and Pastors and all true Governours, so far as they are empowered by God, and to obey God above all, and no men against him and his Laws. And Rulers to profess to obey God, and Rule as his Ministers for the Common welfare and to promote the obedience of Gods Laws.

7. 7. For Magistrates, Pastors and Parents, to profess their endeavour to promote the true Preaching of the Gospel, and the transmitting of it in Purity to Posterity, and to encourage and not unjustly forbid or hinder the publication and practice of it.

8. Negatively, 1. It is not meet that this confederacy so appropriate the Body of the National Church, to any one Party or Sect though it should be (or thought to be) sounder or better than the rest, excluding any that have all the necessaries before named, though they have many tolerable errors and imperfections.

9. It is not lawful to make things unnecessary to be taken or used as necessary to the National Church Unity. Nor to make snares and impose them by such needless Laws, to silence or eject any true and tolerable Ministers; much less the soundest; imposing things sinful or needless, or that are unfit to be the Conditions of Unity, and so unavoidably excluding capable Conscionable worthy men for want of complying with those terms, is the commonest cause of Schism in the Christian World, and the effect of Ignorance, Pride and Tyranny, none being more worthy to be excluded than such Schismatical excluders, that make the Laws that should be the bonds of Concord, to be the greatest Engines of Division.

10. The present Orthodox Protestant Nonconformists, are as truely Members of the Church of *England*, justly so called, as any Diocesans or Conformists in the Land, and if they be not better confuted than hitherto they have been, they may truely be said to be the soundest, most judicious, and most conscionable, and the most peaceable Members of this Church. And to deny such Nonconformists to be true and honourable parts of the Church of *England*, is but such an effect of Ignorant Arrogance and Slanders as is the shame of the speaker, and implieth some dishonourable definition of the said Church. And they that make their mutable Forms and Ceremonies essential to the Church, make a Ceremony of the Church it self, and cannot answer the Papists that challenge us to prove its antiquity: Our Liturgy is not so old as *Luthers*[11] time.

As *Rome* but claiming to be the *whole* Church, hath made many think that it is not so much as a part; so Conformists calling themselves the *whole* Church of *England*, hath tempted many to take them for no part.

11. But yet unsound and hurtful Members may be restrained and corrected, when they are not silenced, or cast out: And proving them true parts doth not prove them to be sound parts, or such as must not be rebuked. But tender avoiding sin, by preferring Gods Law before Mans, and founding our Concord on Christs instituted capable terms, and not on the Sand of ensnaring humane Impositions, is far from being the mark of unsound Members. Yet meerly to tolerate them to Preach in deep Poverty that deserve most encouragement, is not free from Injury and Schism.

Notes

RICHARD BAXTER (1615-91) was born in poor circumstances and denied an adequate education. He was drawn to non-conformist piety as a young man. In 1638 he became a schoolmaster, and in 1641 pastor in Kidderminster (he was not an ordained priest). Never a radical, he was upset by the sacrilegious use of the sacrament by open sinners. He also refused to wear the surplice and make the sign of the cross. In the civil war he was a monarchist who sided with Parliament and ministered to the parliamentary armies. He returned to Kidderminster in 1647, where he wrote his most celebrated work, *The Saint's Everlasting Rest* (1650). In 1660 he hoped for a tolerant religious settlement and was appointed a royal chaplain. He participated in the unsuccessful Savoy House conference and refused a bishopric. He was subsequently imprisoned for six months for irregular preaching, and suffered regular harassment for the rest of Charles II's reign. Under James II he was grossly abused by Judge Jeffreys and again imprisoned. He rejected government advances when policy towards dissenters changed, and naturally welcomed the revolution, but his hopes for a National Church were not fulfilled. He was among the most gifted and deeply religious men of his generation.

1. Luke 10:1. There were 71 members of the Sanhedrin.
2. Acts 1:15-26.
3. Revelation 19:16.
4. Private individuals.
5. See p. 112, n. 38.
6. 'Are you inquiring about the thing itself or about the name of the thing?'
7. Acts 7:38.
8. A union of all baptised persons; at baptism the person being baptised (or the godparent of an infant) renounces the world, the flesh and the devil.

9. An indication of the gulf between Baxter and orthodox anglicans. He rejected as unpastoral the division of the church into large dioceses; he was prepared to accept episcopy if the powers of the bishop were in effect vested in each individual pastor.

10. The ten commandments.

11. Martin Luther (1483-1546), the first of the protestant reformers.

16 From: *The Poor Husbandman's Advocate to Rich Racking Landlords, Written in compassion especially of their* sowls *and of the* land

Gildas Salvianus[1] (Richard Baxter), [1691]

To the Lords Knights and Gentlemen of England, the Legacy of a Dying lover of Soules and of Charity, who would fain persuade them not to come to Divese's place of torment[2] : and to believe Christ who assureth them that by what they faithfully give to the poore they give incomparably more to themselves, as giving it to him that will reward them.

A Request to the subdescribed Readers.

It is a great edifice that is to be built and therefore requireth many hands: Lords, Knights and other Rich country Landlords must be the Master builders. I have here prepared some materials but we want carrying Labourers to reach them up. I am too low and feeble to climb high. Without such Conveyance all is lost. As for the wise Godly temperate Gentlemen, I hope they have not much need of such exhortations: they are taught of God to love their poore Brethren, and to feed, cloath and relieve Christ in the least of his servants, whom he disdaineth not to call his Brethren (and the greatest Lord should not disdain it). But those that most need it I have no access to: and if they chance to see this little book they will not read it: they have other work to spend the day in; at their tables with Dives his five Brethren, and at the Tavern and the Play House and the Gaming House and such like: the very Title of it will provoke them to cast it by with scorn. But I hope there is not a Lord, Knight, or Esq. in England, that hath not some men of Conscience and Clemency that have access to them, and some freedom with them, and interest in them; it is such that I intreate for the sake of the Kingdom, and of their poor neighbours, and these Rich men's Souls, to put this book, or such another, into these Landlords hands, and to intreate them seriously to read it: especially the Parish Ministers whose case doth doubly oblige them to take care of the Poor. Those Ministers that have not sufficient to relieve the poor themselves, may thus helpe them by the hands of those that can. And pious servants that dwell with such men may find some opportunity to offer them such a book. But sure no Lord or Knight that is of the Church of England can be offended with his Pastor or Chaplaine for such charitable motions. . . .

Octob. 18. 1691. Moriturus[3] G. Salvianus.

Chap. 1. The matter of fact described.

1. The Body of this Kingdom consisteth of Land-Proprietors, of Hand-Labourers, of Tradesmen and Merchants, and of the Literate Professions of divers sorts. The Land-proprietors are such as use their land by *themselves* and *servants*, or by *Tenants*. These Tenants are they whose case I am now to open and plead. The Husbandmen are the *Stamen*[4] of the Commonwealth. All the rest do live by them. It is the fruits of the earth and of their labours (with a little addition of fishing) that maintaineth all. And yet whose case is so hard as theirs? Gentleman say, Oure Land is our owne and therefore we may make the best of it for our owne commodity, and he that will give most for it shall be our Tenant.

2. The old custome was to let lands by Lease for Lives or for a long term of years, and to take a fine at first and a small yearly rent afterward, and so, when a man, with his marriage portion, had taken a Lease he lived comfortably afterward and got somewhat for his children. But now in most countrys[5] the custom is changed into yearly rack-rents:[6] or, if a man takes a Lease for many years it is yearly to pay as much as the tenement is worth and that is as much as any man will give for it, and in all counties the small Livings are the farre greatest number: where there is one of 80£ or 70£ or 60£. yea or 50£ value, there are many of 30£ or 20£ or 10£ or 5£. And what will one of 10£ or 20£ do towards the charge of stocking and manuring it, and the maintaining of himselfe, wife, and children with food and cloathing, and paying them for their labour: And how hard will it be after all this, to pay for it 20£ rent? And Greater Livings must have a greater stock and more servants and labourers to manage them. But usually such have the better advantage, having much to sell besides what maintaineth them. But few have so good a bargaine as to lay up anything considerable for their children. Its well if all their care and toil will serve to pay their rent.

3. The Labor of these men is great, and circular or endless: insomuch that their bodyes are allmost in constant wearyness and their minds in constant care or trouble. Yet for all this I pitty not their bodyes much because their Labour is usually recompensed with health. Nor do I

much pitty them for their coarse fare, so they have but fire and cloathing to keepe them warme, and food that is not an enemy to health. For
by the advantage of their labour and health, their browne bread and
milk and butter and cheese and cabbages and turnips and parsnips and
carrots and onions and potatoes and whey and buttermilk and pease
pies and apple pies and puddings and pancakes and gruel and
flummery[7] and furmety,[8] yea dry bread, and small drinke, do afford
their appetites a pleasanter relish and their bodyes more strength and
longer life than all the varieties and fullness of flesh and wines and strong
drinkes do, to the idle gluttonous and voluptuous rich men: and usually
now it is the Diveses that lie ulcerated by sores and tormented with the
Gowt, and the tongues of their flatterers cannot lick them into ease.
The worst of the poore mans case as to health, is that they are put to
goe through raine and wett, through thick and thin, through heat and
cold and oft want that which nature needeth.

4. But alas it is a greater cause of pitty that they usually want those
helpes for knowledge and a godly and heavenly life, and comfortable
preparation for, and prospect of, death that others more ordinarily
enjoy.

1°. They are usually so poore that they cannot have time to read a
chapter in the bible or to pray in their families. They come in weary
from their labours, so that they are fitter to sleep than to read or pray:
and their servants are so heavy with early rising and hard working that
they cannot attend to what they heare. The soule is here so tyed to the
body that it hath constant need of its right temperament for its due
operation: a heavy body tired with labour is like a tired horse to a trav-
eller, or a Lute out of tune to a musician, or a knife or toole to cut or
worke with that wants an edge. The aged, weak, and sick do feel what a
weary body is; how unfit for any religious exercise save complaining
and begging mercy of God. I cannot but pitty such when they sleep at
sermon or at prayer, and say as Christ to his sleepy disciples *The Spirit
is willing but the flesh is weak.*[9]

2°. Yea, abundance, bred up in toil and poverty, cannot read, nor
cannot have their children taught to reade. Such an education is as
effectuall as a Popish Canon, to keep the vulgar from reading the holy
Scriptures. Alas what is a Bible to such any more than bare paper
(unlesse they heare another read it). . . .

3°. And those that can read are so poore that they cannot spare
money to buy a Bible nor a smaller book.

4°. And reading much is of so great advantage for knowledge that,
without it, the poore people are the lesse capable of profitting at the

Church by hearing. How little successe have ministers usually with such, by their publike reading or preaching! And how can the Pastor teach all these to understand the catechisme and learne it? The eye taketh in sentiments more effectually than the ears: especially when men can ofter Read than Heare, and can choose a subject and booke that is most suitable to them, and can there review what they had forgotten. They cannot so often heare againe and recall the same sermon which they had heard in publike.

5°. And when poverty and custome have trained up the people in so unhappy a way, they usually grow into a contempt, and thence into a malignant scorne and hatred, of that which [they] want: like the Turkes that banish learning as an enemy to the publike state, that taketh men off from their labour and trades and warfare and service to their great masters. And hence it is that this ignorant rabble are everywhere the greatest enemies against Godly ministers and people. And if they can but get a Literate malignant (Prelate or Priest) out of faction and enmity to encourage them, they will be ready for any mischievous designs. If any would raise an Army to extirpate knowledge and religion, the Tinkers and Sowgawters[10] and crate-carryers and beggars and bargemen and all the rabble that cannot reade, nor ever use, the bible, will be the fowardest to come in to such a militia. And they will joyne with those that cry up the Church, if it may but tend to pull downe the Church and all serious Church-worke and interest. If Papists or forreine enemies or Rebells would raise insurrections, these are fitt to serve them, if they get but advantage by some great Landlords and hypocrite malicious clergymen to seduce them. And poverty, causing ignorance, turneth men to barbarians like the wild Americans and then into bruites and then into devils; unlesse where the publike power prevaileth against them, or God's grace doth notably take hold on here and there one among them. Whereas reading and praying and meditating tendeth to knowledge in the necessary effects of knowledge, and teach men to live if not as Saints yet as Civil men and *emollit mores nec sinit esse feros.*[11] If wisdome had not been necessary Solomon had not so magnified it, nor a Saviour bin sent from heaven to teach it, nor a Scripture and ministry ordered to propagate it.

5. The case of their servants, could they but continue so and containe themselves from marriage, is farre easyer than of the poor Tenants that are their masters. For they know their worke and wages, and are troubled with no cares for paying Rents, or making good markets, or for the losse of corn or cattle, the rotting of sheepe or the unfavourable weather, nor for providing for wife and children and paying

labourers' and servants' wages.

6. But the condition of their Landlords household servants is as farre above these poore Tenants as a Gentleman is above a day labourer. They life in fullness to the satisfying of the flesh and comparatively in idleness. They feed on the variety of flesh and fish that cometh from their masters tables when the poore tenants are glad of a piece of hanged bacon once a week, and some few that can kill a Bull eate now and then a bit of hanged biefe, enough to trie the stomack of an ostrige. . . .

7. It is much easyer with the handicrafts labourer that hath a good trade. A Joyner or a Turner can worke in the dry howse, with tolerable or pleasant work, and knoweth his price and wages. A Weaver or a Shoemaker or a Taylor can worke without the wetting or tiring of his body, and can thinke and talke of the concerns of his soule without impediment to his labour. I have known many that weave in the Long Loome that can set their sermon-notes or a good book before them and read and discourse together for mutual edification while they worke. But so the poore husbandman can seldom do. And though the labour of a Smyth be hard, it is in a dry howse and but by short fittes: and little, in comparison of Threshing and Reaping, but as nothing in comparison of mowing, which constantly puls forth a mans whole strength.. . . .

8. And uppon all this it is observable that though we are most beholden to Husbandry for the maintenance of Prince and people, Rich and poore, and all the lande, yet few are so hardly used as the Husbandmen. And, which I speake with griefe, except here and there one (of the richer sort mostly that are not pincht with the necessity of others) there is far more ignorance of religion among them than among tradesmen and corporation inhabitants and poore men of manuall artifices. And yet they are not usually guilty of the sins of Gluttony, fornication or adultery, idlenes, sloth; nor usually of drunkenness, so much as rich citizens, and great mens' full and idle serving men: for *sine cerere et Baccho friget Venus.*[12] But among merchants, mercers, drapers and other corporation-tradesmen, and among weavers, taylors, and such like labourers, yea among poore naylors, and such like, there is usually found more knowledge and religion than among the poore enslaved husbandmen.

9. I may well say *enslaved:* for none are so servilely dependent (save household servants and ambitious expectantes) as they are on their Landlords. They dare not displease them lest they turn them out of their howses; or increase their rents. I believe that their Great Land-

lords have more command of them than the King hath. If a Landlord be but malignant, an enemy to piety or sobriety or peace, his enslaved tenants are at his beck to serve him, in matters of any publike consequence. . . .

Chap. 3. The Causes of this Common Evill.

1°. Alas, the cases are so notorious that a few words may serve to make them knowne. But no words alone will serve to cure it.

2°. No doubt but the poore sufferers are the chiefe causes of their owne calamity. Did not their sin provoke God to afflict them, he would have saved them from oppression. Alas if conscience be awake within them they may find enough to condemne themselves for, more than any others; and to make them cry to God for pardon, more than to accuse the rich. When Cham abused his father, his curse is, *A Servant of Servants shall thou be.*[13] You may see through all the books of Judges and Kings and Chronicles that when the Israelites sinned against God and did wickedly, he gave [them] up into the hand of such as did oppress them. And when they repented and cried to him, he delivered them.

3°. But this is no excuse to the oppressours. The causes on their part are many and obvious (1) they foolishly so overvalue their Birth and riches, as if these made them more than men; and Pride setteth them so high in their owne conceit that they look downe on the poore with disregard: as a man in a high mountaine that seeth all below him like little things. They scarcely take the poore for Brethren, no, nor for their neighbours; as if their flesh were not corruptible, and their sowles by sin as miserable as the poore's. (2) The Love of money the root of all evill, so blindeth and hardeneth them that they can scarce feele any evill in anything that tendeth to increase their wealth. Let them have never so much, they would have more: *Crescit amor nummi quantum ipsa pecunia crescit.*[14] As Nathan told David in his parable, *The man who had flockes of his owne must take the poore man's lamb.*[15] (3) And the Devil, the Great Tyrant, that ruleth in the children of disobedience, maketh them like himselfe, that is pleased with cruelty. When he hath first hardened them against Love and compassion, he next makes them like angry and malicious men that are restlesse till they do hurt. . . .

4°. And the great cause of oppression is the *sensuality* and *fleshly lusts* of the oppressours. Lust needeth so much that all that they can extort is little enough to feed it. They must be cloathed and fare like Dives sumptuously: with so many dishes and such variety and curiosity, with variety of pleasant liquors, and with musike pompe and so great attendance, in dwellings of so costly furniture, and with the entertainment of so many meerly in pride, for the reputation of greatnes and great housekeeping; that it is no wonder that the wearyed bodies and carefull hearts[16] of their poore tenants do pay deare for all. Ah, miserable fools! that thinke this worse than beastly life to be so desirable as, for it, to enslave reason; to debase human nature; to damne their sowles; and to keepe multitudes of their poore brethren in misery to make provision for their lusts.

5°. And the Atheistical misconceit of their propriety hardeneth them. They thinke they may please themselves with *their owne* as they list. As if they knew not that there is no *Absolute Propriety but God's*. Only He that made and maintaineth all is the *absolute Owner* of all, or anything. No man hath any other propriety than that of a Trusted Servant, or Steward, or a child in minority, who is at his father's will. You have a sub-propriety which, *in foro humane,*[17] may be pleaded against all that would dispossess you. And so a servant hath to that which is committed to his trust. We are no Levellers. He is a thiefe that taketh away that which is yours without your forfeiture or consent. But you shall answer for all, even the uttermost farthing to him that entrusted you.[18] He did not give you your great estates to serve the Devil with them; in serving your fleshly lusts and pampering a greedy appetite, or maintaining odious pride, when you have cause to be humbled in the dust for your manifold sins, and in remembrance of the dust to which, after its rotteness, your body must returne. You look that your stewards and other servants do keepe and give up a just account to you of all your revenews of which they are the receivers, and of all their disbursements for your use. If you care what becomes of your sowles for ever, cast up and keepe the account of your stewardship towards God.[19] For you shall certainly be called to a reckoning ere long. Compare the proportion which you allow the *poore* and other necessary and pious uses, with that which you have allowed for *flesh-pleasing* and *pompe* and *vaine reputation*. Know that all that is thus abused is stolen from God, in your robbing those of it that he obliged you to give it to.

6°. And when worldlings can enjoy no more for themselves, their last self-deceit is to thinke that, whatever it cost their poore tenants, they must leave their *children* as great and dangerous a temptation of riches as they were undone by themselves. They thinke they deale not as Parents with their children unless they crosse all the doctrine of Christ, and make their way to heaven impossible to any but God, and their Salvation to be as a Camel going through the eye of a needle.[20] Doubtlesse, such show that they are Christians but in jeast. And as they give Christ but a name, they must looke for no more from him. It is themselves and not him that they deceive. They have greater things than great worldly estates and temptations to take care for both for their children and themselves. I know that they must provide for them, and that according to their quality and need. But nothing is due to their posterity that is withheld, or extorted by oppression, from the poore, or from any pious or charitable use that God doth call them to lay it out on.

Chap. 4. The Remedies of the poore Husbandman's case proposed to Rich Landlords.

1. I am not, after so long experience, so ignorant of the pravity of corrupted nature as to expect any universall or generall successe of anything that I, or any wiser man, can say. The Great Dog will not be moved by argument or Oratory to give up his bone or carrion, nor to let the little dogs partake with him. But there are some, that really believe the Gospell, that are not sufficiently convinced of their duty and sin, in the present case, whom I may write to with some hope; and there are some men, whose natures are not so desperately debauched and hardened as others to whom we may speake without despaire, who when they heare *Thus saith the Lord* and *thus saith Jesus Xt* will regard it.

2 (Ex. i). Gentlemen (mistake me not) the summe of my request to you is but this *That you will regard the publike welfare of the nation above any few particular cases, and the interest of Christian Religion in the soules of men above all youre worldly interest and fleshly pleasure, and that you will on such accounts, sell youre lands to the poorer sort of youre tenants at such rates as by their labour and frugality they may comfortably live on, so as not to be necessitated by care for their rents and by tiresome excesse of labour, to be strangers to God's word, and to forbeare family religion and to be prayerlesse or sleepe when they should pray, and to live in ignorance for want of good bookes or time to read them, and thinke of what they heare at church; and that poverty constreine them not to educate their children like themselves.* This (is) all that I have now to request of you. . . .

3 (ii). To this end I humbly intreate you, Gentlemen, to retrench youre needlesse and sinfull charges for superfluities, prodigality and fleshly lust. That you may not need so much to feed your sin as will not leave you enough to discharge youre duty to God and to the poore. Cannot you live as healthfully and decently with fewer dishes, and less variety, and less cost and curiosity, and less ostentation, attendance and pompe? Do not youre tables and youre furniture speake unbeliefe and contempt of Christ? While in Luke 16 and throughout the Gospell he so terribly describeth you. Abraham, Isaac and Jacob, and such great man of old, that had hundreds of servants and thousands of cattle and sheepe, yet used not to eate flesh but at a feast, or a sacrifice, or the entertainment of some extraordinary friend. Bread and water and milke and honey and butter and figs were their ordinary food. Ordinary eating of flesh and drinking of wine was called *Royotous.* . . .

4 (iii). And I humbly motion that Gentlemen would not be strangers to their poore tenants; but sometimes go to their howses and see how it goeth with them, and how they live. When I was a child I have heard a poore man praise a neighbour Knight with as much honour as if he had been a Prince, because he would come to a poore man's house and talke familiarly to them, and looke into their pot and cupboard and see how they fared; but a proud disdainfull person none loveth. Did you see their manner of food and labour, and their wants, it would move you more than hearing will do. Strangeness causeth ignorance and neglect.

5 (iv). And when you visit them or speake with them, ask them, *Do you pray in your family? Do you read God's word and good bookes, especially on the Lord's days? Do youre children learne to read? Do you teach them the Catechisme, and how to pray? Do you keepe them from lying and swearing and cursing and railing?*

If they say, *No*, to any of these enquire the reason of it. Do not say this is only the Parson's work. It is *his* and it is *yours*. They will heare you with more regard than most such will heare the Pastor. O what a blessed example were this, for a Lord or Knight to set the Gentry of his Country! and what good might such men's wealth and greatness do, which are commonly used to their owne and others hurt! And what a blessed land would England be, if Lords, Knights, and Gentlemen would duely obey and worship God in their owne families as well as in the Churches and urge their tenants to do the like.

6 (v). Those that have not a Bible or good book in their houses, buy and give them one. I told you in the preface to my *Poore Mans Family Booke* that one or two bookes to every poore tenant is but abating

them so much of their rent, extraordinary, or abating one dish of meat from your tables, what if I said one gaudy lace or toy from the woemens coates or heads? And it need be but once to one house while they live there: for a booke may so long endure.

7 (vi). Enquire whether their children be sent to schoole to learne to read. And if not, or there be none thereabout to teach them, a little money may hire an honest poore man or woaman to set up a reading schoole. At least, pay for those children's learning whose parents cannot pay for them. There dwelleth in London a man that liveth by selling rags and glasse bottles, that, besides finding worke for abundance of the poore, payeth for the teaching of about thirty poore children; though he had not five shillings to set up, and his neerest friends trouble him with the accusations of imprudent excesse of charity. And he saith that God tells him of his acceptance. For the more he giveth the more he thriveth: which made that blessed example of charity, my dear friend Mr. *Th. Gouse*,[21] to write a book for charity entitled *The way to grow rich*. There be men tat have many thousand pounds per annum that dwell neere this poore glass man that do no such work and do not increase their wealth. I will instance but in one man, my deceased friend Mr. Thomas *Foley*,[22] the 3rd son of Mr. Richard Foley, my first Patron; who began but with 500£ stock, given him by his father; and was allwaies liberall to the poore, and managed all his busynes with multitudes, with ease and chearfullnes; and hath setled an Hospitall with a Govenour to teach children to read and write and fit them for trades, and then bind them apprentices; and setled, in land, 500£ a yeare to maintaine it. And God so prospered him that his three sons, now all Parliament men, are judged worth 15000£ a year between them (whom I do hopefully request to use it as charitably as their father did, who lived neither sordidly nor luxuriously nor profusely, as those great men that thinke their pompous grandeur worthy of more than he gave to the poore).

8 (vii). And I humbly advise all Parish Ministers, whose office obligeth them to know and visit the poore, that (besides their owne charity) they will acquaint the rich Landlords with their poore tenants' cases, and move them to compassion. I doubt not but all pious and charitable Gentlemen will take it well, and thank them.

9 (viii). And I humbly intreate all *Lawyers* and *Physicians* that they will spare the poore in their fees and charges. Alas, a shilling is to them more precious than twice its weight of their blood. . . .

10 (ix). One thing more for the poore I intreate of Ministers and Landlords; that they will keep them from Lawsuites by composing

all differences that arise among them, and by persuading them to a just reference and arbitration, and by discountenancing the contentious and revengefull refusers. . . .

11 (x). I have yet one helpe more to motion, that *Rich men will often read what all God's word saith of their duty to the poore.* Surely the passages of this kind are so *many, so urgent* and so *plaine* that, without downright unbeliefe and contempt of Christ, and of God's Law, or without great stupidity, they cannot be so neglected as by most they are, were they but seriously considered: so earnest are the commands, so great the promises, to charity and so terrible the threatenings to the oppressour and unmercifull that they must needs move a considerate believer to thinke money laid out on the poore to be better used than that which is sacrificed to *Bacchus* and *Venus*, as a sacrifice to pride and flesh pleasing, and, as *Clemens Alexandrinus*[23] calls it: to the *Throat-madness* and the *Belly Devil.*

Chap. 5. Some pertinent Texts recited to this use.

Who can prevaile if God's authority cannot? and what can we think will move men if not the Law which they confesse should rule them and will judge them?

How severely did God revenge the oppression of the Israelites on Pharao and the Egyptians by his plagues and the red sea:

Texts quoted are:—

Exodus, i., 11, 13, 14; ii., 23-24; iii., 7-8; xxii., 23-24, 25-26; xxxiii., 11.

Leviticus, xix., 9, 13, 18; xxx., 35-36.

Deut. xv., 7 (−11), 12 (−14).

1 Samuel, xii., 3.

Nehemiah, v., 11-13, 18.

Job. xxix., 12 (13, 15, 16, 17); xxxi., 16 (−22, 24, 25, 38).

Psalms, xii., 5; xli, 1 (−3); lxxii., 4, 12; cxii., 9.

Proverbs, xiv., 21, 31; xxi., 13; xxii., 9, 16, 22, 23; xxviii., 15; xxix., 7, 12, 14; xxxi., 9: xxviii., 27.

Eccles., v., 8.

Isaiah, i., 16 ff., 23, 24; iii., 14, 15; lviii., 6, 7 (Read the whole chapter).

Ezekiel, xvi., 49, 50; xviii., 5 (−9).

Amos, iv., 1 (2).

Isaiah, lx., 17.

Ezekiel, xlv., 9.

Matthew, v., 5, 7, 16, 42; vi., 19, 20, 33, 34; vii., 12, 19; xiii., 44, 45; xviii., 5-7, 14, 8, 9, 10, 32; xix., 21, 22; xx., 26; xxii., 36, 37, 38; xxvi., 11; xxv., 31, 41.

Luke, xii., 20, 21; xvi., 9, 13, 14, 20. (Read all that of Dives and Lazarus); xix., 8. Read the Parable of the Wounded Man, the Prieste, Levite and Samaritan (Luke x. 25-31).

John, xiii., 4, 35, 36; xxi., 15.

Acts, iv., x., 2.

Romans, ii., 6; xii., 5; xiii., 9, 10, 14.

1 Corinthians, vi., 7, 8, 9; ix., 8, 9; xii., 12, 13; xiii.

2 Corinthians, ix., 6, 7.

Galathians, vi., 2, 6, 7. 8.

Ephesians, iv., 32.

Philippians, iv., 17.

Colossians, iii., 14.

1 Thessalonians, iv., 9.

1 Timothy, vi., 17.

Titus, iii., 5.

Hebrews, xiii., 1, 2, 3, 16.

James, i., 27 (Read all James ii., especially 6, 13); iii., 17; iv., 1.

1 Peter, i., 22; iii., 8.

1 John, ii., 15, 16; iii., 14, 27, 23; iv., 7; iii., 7.

Revelation, ii.; iii.; xx.; xxii., 12, 14.

Qu.– *Why need you transcribe so much of the bible? Do you thinke we never read or heard al this before?*

Ans.– I suppose you have. If you practise it, I have my end. If not, I do it to try whether the fullest proofe from the Supreme Authority of God, will prevaile with you. If it will not, what can all my reasonings do? If you can be unmercifull and rigorous exactors from the poore after all this, if Lazarus were sent to you when you are at your pompous entertainments and cherishing your fleshly appetites to tell you what Dives suffereth that you come not to that place of torment you would not be persuaded. But all these words of God your Judge shall be witnesses against you. . . .

Chap. 7. Advice to poore unrelieved Husbandmen.

Because the knowledge of the wickedness of the world perswades me that it is not the most of Rich Landlords that all this will prevail with, yea that there is little hope that they will so much as read it, I will speake to you for yourselves: And if you will not be perswaded to do good to yourselves you are unworthy of clemency or helpe from others.

I. Know what are the Temptations of your sufferings, and carefully resist them (1) Your poverty will tempt you to sinfull discontent and to repining at God's providence, yea and to hard thoughts of God, and to unthankfullnes for all the mercyes that you have had or that yet you have. And all these are sins which are an hundred times worse than poverty.

(2) Your poverty will tempt you to uncharitable thoughts and speeches of your oppressours, and hinder you from loving and forgiving them; and will tempt you to envy the rich; and to overvalue riches, while you too much feele your wantes. Yea, many poore men that cannot get riches, do thinke highlyer of them than those that have them: because the owners are still unsatisfyed, while the afflicted still feel their need.

(3) Your poverty will tempt you to unlawfull wayes of getting, and to thinke that necessity will excuse you, that is, to steale, to overreach others in bargaining or accounts, to use unlawfull trades, to lie, or deale unjustly.

(4) Your poverty will tempt you to omit religious dutyes in your familyes (if not in secret and at the church), and to cast by God's word and prayer and meditation, and to thinke and talke of nothing but the *world,* and to neglect the instruction and godly education of your children, or to do all this heartlessly, heavily and slightly. All this must be considerately prayed and watched against. How oft have I heard some proud fooles tell me that they goe not to church for want of cloaths, as if the Cloaths that they work in may not serve to pray in: some beggars are proud.

II. Understand also what Advantages your poverty giveth you, above the rich and prosperous worldlings; and then you will find that the benefit may weigh downe all your losses. Think of these following.

(1) Is it not a comfort to be so farre conformed to Christ who for our sakes became *poore* that we by his poverty might be made rich. His voluntary poverty, who was Lord of all, was part of his Humiliation as a sacrifice for our sins; and he that hath sanctifyed *death* to us as our passage to eternall life hath sanctifyed our sufferings in the way to death. He that hath predestinated us to glory hath predestinated us to be conformed to Christ in his sufferings.

(2) How great a helpe have you, to escape the too much love of this present world, and to drive you most seriously to seeke a better. If you will love a poore miserable life of trouble better than heaven, you are more unexcuseable than the rich that have a life of pleasure. If you that cannot hope for anything on earth but labour and sorrow, will not joyfully heare the tidings of salvation, and presently labour to make sure of a better habitation, how great is your sin and folly. The poore received the glad tidings of the Gospell in Christ's time on earth, when the rich rejected it. They dreame that they have something surer and better for them than heaven, and choose it to their damnation. But you know that you must have heaven or nothing: for this world is to you but a raging ocean or a bed of thornes.

(3) You little know how great a mercy it is that you have not the constant strong temptations to fleshly pleasures, gluttony and drunkennes and fornication and fleshly lust and bruitish sensuality, as those have that live with the continual baites of those sins before them, that are every day at a full table of flesh and wines. The stronger the temptation, the greater difficulty to overcome it. And God saith, *If you live after the flesh yee shall die, But if by the Spirit you mortifie the deeds of the body yee shall live.*[24] The question is whether you would have the Devil's baites to be more deceitfull, and your salvation made farre more difficult and doubtfull.

(4) And truly it is a great mercy to you that your *calling* and daily labour is so necessary and good that you may call it an acceptable service to God, and expect that he owne and blesse you in it, if you do it with an obedient heavenly mind: whereas the daily life of the voluptuous Rich men in feasting and gaming and play and idlenes is a constant Sin abhorred of God.

III. Thankfully value and moderately use the cheap and course dyet that your condition alloweth you. I have told you before that your dyet is farre more healthfull than Dives's was: and I believe more pleasant to a healthfull appetite. Few of you lye under their gowt and stone and dropsies etc. Your whey and butter-milk possets, is much more healthfull than their sack and claret. And your whey-curds and milke and cabbage and turnips and parsnips and flummery and such like than their venison and costly fowls and fish. A quarter of an acre set with potatoes, and those called Jerusalem Artichokes especially, will find you half a year's wholesom food. When you must have flesh a sheep's head of sixpence or a biefes cheeke will give you better broth and stronger nourishment than most of their costly preparations: . . .

IV. Whatever shift you make, be sure you teach your children to read; and get a Bible and some few good books in your house; and if anyone can read let the rest heare him. If you have not money, beg it of some rich rather than neglect your owne and your children's souls. I have written about 128 books, but I would commend to the poore but a few:—

First, a twopenny book called *How to be certainly Saved.*

(2) *The Call to the Unconverted.*

(3) *Directions for Sound Conversion.*

(4) But if you can get but one: *The Poore man's family book*, which I wrote for them that cannot get many, as conteining all your soule's concernes from the hour of conversion to the hour of death.

V. Be sure to improve the Lords Day. You are then vacant from your labours: be so from your cares. And in long winter nights when men cannot work, you have time to read and pray and catechize your children.

VI. Be not Strangers to your Teachers. Ask them what you doubt of. Desire their necessary helpe and advice about the care of your soules.

VII. Keep peace and love in your families and with your neighbours. Take heed of scandalous living and of divisions, strife and unrighteousness.

VIII. Never borrow money of any man, when you have not sufficient reason to be confident of paying him. If your state be doubtfull, let your creditor know it, and consent to run the hazard, else you rob him while you take his money without his true consent. They are as bad as Highway robbers, that live by borrowing on other men's money, by hideing deceit. It's farre better in your necessity to beg. And debt is a heavy burden.

IX. Adde not to your poverty by indiscretion, idlenes, or gaming or excess.

X. Flatter not yourselves with the thoughts of long life, but spend every day in preparation for death; and in all your business remember whither you are going and where you must dwell for ever. Take not Christ's Redemption and the promises of Heaven for doubtfull things. May[25] the firme beliefe of Heavenly Glory possess your soules, how comfortably may you suffer and live and dye.

Notes

This work was first published in 1926. These extracts are from the revised version published under the title *The Reverend Richard Baxter's Last Treatise* . . . edited by Frederick J. Powicke . . . with an Introduction by . . . George Unwin . . . Manchester: The University Press . . . MCMXXVI.

1. A compound pen-name derived from St Gildas (see p. 72, n. 10), whose History is a 'reproach of kings, princes and priests', and from Salvian of Marseilles (see p. 113, n. 49) whose book *De Gubernatione Dei [Concerning God's Rule]* attributed the downfall of Rome to the corruptions of Roman life.

2. See Luke 16: 19-31; the parable of the 'certain rich man' (Dives) and the beggar, Lazarus, is a recurring motif in Baxter's treatise.

3. 'He who is about to die': Baxter wrote this work when he was dying.

4. The stronger threads of an upright loom (the warp) into which the horizontal threads (the woof) are woven.

5. Counties.

6. A rent based on an annual valuation of land and therefore subject to increases from year to year.

7. Porridge made of flour and oatmeal.

8. Husked wheat boiled in sweetened and spiced milk.

9. Matthew 26:41; Mark 14:38.

10. Possibly 'sow-watchers': pigminders or swineherds.

11. 'Refines behaviour and does not allow them to be wild'.

12. 'Venus freezes without corn and Bacchus': lust decays without food and wine.

13. Genesis 9:25.

14. 'Desire of money increases with wealth'.

15. 2 Samuel 12:1-4:|Nathan's parable of oppression reinforces the many references to Dives and Lazarus (see n. 2).

16. Hearts full of care.

17. 'In a human tribunal'.

18. See Matthew 5:26.

19. See Luke 16:2.

20. See Matthew 19:24-6; Mark 10:23-7.

21. Thomas Gouge (1609-81), a clergyman who resigned his living after the Uniformity Act of 1662; he was celebrated for his almsgiving, and his evangelisation of the Welsh.

22. Thomas Foley (1617-77), a wealthy iron-master who bought an estate near Kidderminster, where he met Baxter.

23. St Clement of Alexandria (150-215).

24. Romans 8:13.

25. If only . . .

Texts cited in the Introduction and Notes and Select Bibliography

The literature on the political, social, religious and intellectual history of the late seventeenth century is vast. The list that follows is intended as a mere sampling of the various scholarly approaches to aspects of the subject raised by the texts in this volume. A comprehensive listing of primary sources would be altogether impracticable, a selective one would be either tendentious or arbitrary.

Texts cited (by cue title)

Bacon 1664: *The History of Athanasius with the Rise, Growth, and Down-fall of the Arian Heresie.* By Nathaniel Bacon Esq. . . . London . . . 1664.

Barbeau 1970: *The Intellectual Design of John Dryden's Heroic Plays* by Anne T. Barbeau. Yale University Press, New Haven and London, 1970.

Blount 1695: *The Miscellaneous Works of Charles Blount, Esq; . . . to which is prefixed the Life of the Author, and an Account and Vindication of is Death. With the contents of the whole Volume.* Printed in the Year 1695 [reprinted in facsimile, Garland Publishing, Inc., New York & London, 1979].

Budick 1970: *Dryden and the Abyss of Light. A Study of Religio Laici and The Hind and the Panther* by Sanford Budick, Yale University Press, New Haven and London, 1970.

Burnet 1680: *Some Passages of the Life and Death of the Right Honourable John Earl of Rochester* . . . By Gilbert Burnet, D.D. London . . . 1680 [reprinted in facsimile by The Scolar Press, Menston, 1972].

Hamilton 1972: 'Two Restoration Prose-writers — Burnet and Halifax', by K.G. Hamilton in *Restoration Literature. Critical Approaches.* Edited by Harold Love. Methuen, London, 1972.

Hill 1969: *A Century of Revolution 1603-1714* by Christopher Hill. Sphere Books edn, London, 1969.

Hill 1984: *The Experience of Defeat. Milton and Some Contemporaries* by Christopher Hill. Faber & Faber, London, 1984.

Hutcheson 1944: *De Religione Laici* by Lord Herbert of Cherbury. Edited and translated by H.R. Hutcheson. Yale University Press, New Haven, 1944.

Jacob 1983: *Henry Stubbe, radical Protestantism and the early Enlightenment* by James R. Jacob. Cambridge University Press, London, 1983.

Keble 1836: *The Works of Richard Hooker*. Edited by John Keble. 3 volumes. Clarendon Press, Oxford, 1836.

Kenyon 1966: *The Stuart Constitution 1603-1688. Documents and Commentary*. Edited and introduced by J.P. Kenyon. Cambridge University Press, London, 1966.

Kelsall 1981: Congreve, *The Way of the World*. Edited by Malcolm Kelsall. Edward Arnold, London, 1981.

Kinsley 1962: *The Poems and Fables of John Dryden*. Edited by James Kinsley. Oxford University Press, London, 1962; all quotations from Dryden's poems are from this edition.

Lamont 1979: *Richard Baxter and the Millenium. Protestant Imperialism and the English Revolution* by William M. Lamont. Croom Helm, Beckenham, 1979.

Lansdowne 1927: *The Petty Papers. Some unpublished writings of Sir William Petty*. Edited from the Bowood Papers by the Marquis of Lansdowne in two volumes. Constable, London, 1927.

Laslett 1949: *Patriarcha and other Political Works of Sir Robert Filmer*. Edited from the original sources with an Introduction by Peter Laslett, Basil Blackwell, Oxford, 1949.

Laslett 1970: John Locke, *Two Treatises of Government. A critical edition with an introduction and apparatus criticus* by Peter Laslett. Second Edition. Cambridge University Press, London, 1970.

Myers 1973: *Dryden* by William Myers. Hutchinson, London, 1973.

Ogg 1967: *England in the Reign of Charles II* by David Ogg. Second Edition, one-volume reprint. Oxford University Press, London, 1967.

Ogg 1969: *England in the Reigns of James II and William III* by David Ogg. One-volume reprint. Oxford University Press, London, 1969.

Peters 1962: *Body, Man and Citizen. Selections from Thomas Hobbes*. Edited with an Introduction by Richard S. Peters. Collier Books, New York, 1962.

Plumb 1969: *The Growth of Political Stability in England 1675-1725* by J.H. Plumb. Penguin Books edn, Harmondsworth, 1969.

Pocock 1977: *The Political Works of James Harrington*. Edited with and Introduction by J.G.A. Pocock. Cambridge University Press, London, 1979.

Robbins 1969: *Two Engish Republican Tracts. Plato Redivivus or, A*

Dialogue concerning Government (c. 1681) by Henry Neville. *An Essay upon the Constitution of the Roman Government (c. 1699)* by Walter Moyle. Edited by Caroline Robbins. Cambridge University Press, London, 1969.

Roper 1965: *Dryden's Poetic Kingdoms* by Alan Roper. Routledge & Kegan Paul, London, 1965.

Said 1984: *The World, the Text, and the Critic* by Edward W. Said. Faber & Faber, London, 1984.

Schwoerer 1981: *The Declaration of Rights, 1689* by Lois G. Schwoerer. The Johns Hopkins University Press, Baltimore and London, 1981.

Scott, Saintsbury 1822-92: *The Works of John Dryden. Illustrated with Notes, Historical, Critical, and Explanatory and A Life of the Author*, by Sir Walter Scott, Bart. Revised and corrected by George Saintsbury. 18 volumes. Paterson, Edinburgh, 1882-92.

Shairani 1911: Henry Stubbe, *An Account of the Rise and Progress of Mahometanism with the Life of Mahomet*. Edited by Hafiz Mahmud Khan Shairani, London, 1911.

Further reading:

Richard I. Aaron, *John Locke*. Third edn. Clarendon Press, Oxford, 1971.

Maurice Ashley, *The Glorious Revolution of 1688*. Hodder & Stoughton, London, 1966.

—— , *James II*. Dent, London, 1977.

Dudley W.R. Bahlman, *The Moral Revolution of 1688*. Archon Books, Hamden, Conn., 1968.

Louis I. Bredvold, *The Intellectual Milieu of John Dryden. Some Aspects of Seventeenth-century Thought*. The University of Michigan Press, Ann Arbor, 1934.

A. Browning, *Thomas, Earl of Danby and Duke of Leeds 1632-1712*. 3 vols. Jackson, Glasgow, 1951.

—— (ed.), *English Historical Documents, 1660-1714*, Eyre & Spottiswoode, London, 1953.

John Colman, *John Locke's Moral Philosophy*. Edinburgh University Press, Edinburgh, 1983.

W.C. Costin and J.S. Watson (eds), *The Law and Working of the Constitution, vol. I, 1660-1783*. Black, London, 1952.

B. Coward, *The Stuart Age*. Longman, London, 1980.

G.R. Cragg, *From Puritanism to the Age of Reason*. Cambridge University Press, London, 1950.

John Dunn. *The Political Thought of John Locke.* Cambridge University Press, London, 1969.

J.N. Figgis, *The Divine Right of Kings*, Harper & Row, New York, 1965.

Boris Ford (ed.), *From Dryden to Johnson. Volume 4 of The Pelican Guide to English Literature* (revised edn). Penguin Books. Harmondsworth, 1963.

Julian H. Franklin, *John Locke and the Theory of Sovereignty: Mixed Monarchy and the Right of Resistance in the Political Thought of the English Revolution.* Cambridge University Press, London, 1978.

J.W. Gough, *Fundamental Law in English Constitutional History.* Oxford University Press, London, 1957.

——— , *John Locke's Political Philosophy: eight studies.* Second edn. Clarendon Press, Oxford, 1973.

K.H.D. Haley, *The First Earl of Shaftesbury.* Clarendon Press, Oxford, 1968.

P. Hayward, *The European Mind, 1660-1715.* Penguin Books, Harmondsworth, 1964.

Geoffrey Holmes (ed.), *Britain after The Glorious Revolution 1689-1714* (Problems in Focus). Macmillan, London, 1969.

Margaret C. Jacob, *The Newtonians and the English Revolution 1689-1720.* Harvester Press, Brighton, 1976.

M.C.V. Jeffreys, *John Locke: prophet of common sense.* Methuen (Library of Educational Thought), London, 1967.

J.R. Jones, *The First Whigs.* Oxford University Press, London, 1961.

——— , *The Revolution of 1688 in England.* Weidenfeld & Nicholson, London, 1972.

———, *Country and Court: England 1658-1714.* Edward Arnold, London, 1978.

——— (ed.), *The Restored Monarchy* (Problems in Focus). Macmillan, London, 1979.

Nicholas Jose, *Ideas of the Restoration in English Literature 1660-71.* Macmillan, London, 1984.

N.H. Keeble, *Richard Baxter, Puritan Man of Letters.* Clarendon Press, Oxford, 1982.

J.P. Kenyon, *Robert Spencer, Earl of Sunderland 1641-1702.* Longman, London, 1968.

——— , *The Popish Plot.* Heinemann, London, 1972.

Bruce King (ed.), *Seventeenth-century English Literature.* Macmillan, London, 1982.

D.R. Lacey, *Dissent and Parliamentary Politics in England, 1661-1689: a study in the perpetuation and tempering of parliamentarianism.*

Rutgers University Press, New Brunswick, N.J., 1969.

C.N. Manton, *Literature and Reality, 1660-1800*. Macmillan, London, 1978.

John Miller, *Popery and Politics in England, 1660-1688*. Cambridge University Press, London, 1973.

——, *The Glorious Revolution* (Seminar Studies in History). Longman, London, 1983.

G. Parry, *John Locke (Political Thinkers 8)*. Allen & Unwin, London, 1978.

W.R. Owen (ed.), *Seventeenth-century England: A Changing Culture* (volume 2. Modern Studies). Ward Lock Educational in association with The Open University, London, 1980.

L.P. Pinkham, *William III and the Respectable Revolution*. Harvard University Press, Cambridge, Mass., 1954.

J.G.A. Pocock, *The Ancient Constitution and Feudal Law*. Cambridge University Press, London, 1957.

David Daiches Raphael, *Hobbes: morals and politics*. George Allen & Unwin, London, 1977.

C. Roberts, *The Growth of Responsible Government in Stuart England*. Cambridge University Press. London, 1962.

Thomas A. Spragens. *The Politics of Motion: the world of Thomas Hobbes*. With a foreword by Antony Flew. Croom Helm, Beckenham, 1977.

G. Taylor, *The Problem of Poverty*, 1660-1834. Longman, London, 1969.

Joan Thirsk, *The Restoration*. Longman, London, 1976.

G.M. Trevelyan, *The English Revolution, 1688-9*. Oxford University Press, London, 1938.

James Tully, *A Discourse on Property. John Locke and his adversaries*. Cambridge University Press, London, 1980.

J.R. Western, *Monarchy and Revolution. The English State in the 1680s*. Blandford Press, London, 1972.

C.C. Weston and J.R. Greenberg. *Subjects and Sovereigns*. Cambridge University Press, London, 1981.

J. Legge Wickham, *English Church Life from the Restoration to the Tractarian Movement*. Longman, London, 1964.

Basil Willey, *The Seventeenth-century Background. Studies in the Thought of the Age in Relation to Poetry and Religion*. Penguin Books in association with Chatto & Windus, Harmondsworth, 1962.

C. Wilson, *England's Apprenticeship, 1603-1763*. Longman, London, 1965.

John W. Yolton, *Locke. An Introduction*. Basil Blackwell, Oxford, 1985.

Index